THE HIDDEN HISTORY OF THE BALFOUR DECLARATION

THE HIDDEN HISTORY OF THE BALFOUR DECLARATION

SAHAR HUNEIDI

OR Books
New York · London

© 2019 Sahar Huneidi

Published by OR Books, New York and London
Visit our website at www.orbooks.com

First printing 2019

All rights reserved. No part of this book may be reproduced or transmitted in any form or by any means, electronic or mechanical, including photocopy, recording, or any information storage retrieval system, without permission in writing from the publisher, except brief passages for review purposes.

Cataloging-in-Publication data is available from the Library of Congress. A catalog record for this book is available from the British Library.

Typeset by Lapiz Digital Services.

ISBN 978-1-682191-45-3 paperback
ISBN 978-1-682191-46-0 e-book

CONTENTS

The Ormsby-Gore Minute	vii
Introduction	1
I. A General Historic Background	11
II. Official British Account of Events Leading Up to the Balfour Declaration as Rendered in the 1922-1923 Inquiries	77
Summary and Conclusion	161
Appendix A: The Balfour Declaration	167
Appendix B: War Cabinet Memorandum, October 1917	169
Bibliography	187
Endnotes	195
Index	231
About the Author	235

1/ I think it very important that the story of the negotiations which led up to the Balfour declaration of Nov 2nd 1917 (before General Allenby's first great advance) should be set out for the S of S and possibly the Cabinet.

The F.O. and Sir Maurice Hankey both have material. The matter was first broached by the late Sir Mark Sykes early in 1916, & he interviewed Dr Gaster & Sir Herbert Samuel on his own initiative as a student of Jewish politics in the Near East. Dr. Weizmann was then unknown. Sykes was furthered by General MacDonagh, D.M.I., as all the most useful & helpful intelligence from Palestine (then still occupied by the Turks) was got through & given with the zeal of Zionist Jews who were from the first pro-British. Sir Ronald Graham took the matter up keenly from the Russian & East European point of view & early in 1917 important representations came from America. The form of the declaration & the preamble was debated more than once by the War Cabinet, & correspondence (printed by Sir M. Hankey as a Cabinet paper) was entered into with leading Jews of different schools of thought.

After the declaration, the utmost use was made of it by Lord Northcliffe's propaganda department, & the value of the declaration received remarkable tribute from General Ludendorff. On the strength of it we got recruited special battalions of foreign Jews in New York for the British army with the leave of the American Govt.

The S/S should have a statement showing whether declaration by other powers up to & including the recent one of the American Senate; & also [summary] of what has been done by the Jews already in Palestine, i.e. 4 millions of money, schools etc. Some of the Zionist organizations election leaflets were really rather effective. The Balfour declaration in its final form was actually drafted by Col Amery & myself. I wrote an article on the question in the "XIXth Century" interesting date about 2 years ago which has gone

W.O. 24.12.22

INTRODUCTION

> *We were persuaded, but remember it was Weizmann who persuaded us. But for Dr. Weizmann there would have been no Balfour Declaration.*[1]
> —Jan Smuts, Prime Minister of the Union of South Africa, 1949

> *I am glad you are keeping your people in order—a la Kerensky!—and not leaving them leaderless.*[2]
> —C.P. Scott, British journalist and newspaper owner, to Chaim Weizmann, President of the World Zionist Organization, 1917

> *The Palestine tragedy, for that is what it is, did not unfold in some obscure era of history . . . . It has been enacted in the twentieth century . . . . It was initiated by deliberate acts of will . . . . The Zionists were the initiators. But they were also, as they still are, the protegés of their Anglo-American sponsors and the emanations of their power, resources, and will.*[3]
> —Walid Khalidi, Palestinian historian, 1971

When the Balfour Declaration, which promised a 'national home' for the Jews in Palestine, was issued by the British Foreign Office in November 1917, it was not clear what the declaration intended or what the policy vaguely outlined in it would eventually lead to. This ambiguity was to cause considerable confusion in the years immediately following its issuance.

The question may be asked, why is it important today to re-examine the Balfour Declaration of 1917, and what remains unsaid about it? Despite the millions of words published on the Balfour Declaration in the last 100 years, many aspects of the British pro-Zionist declaration remain as enigmatic as when it was first announced, despite its disastrous consequences for the inhabitants of Palestine.

In December 2015, *The Independent's* Ian Black wrote that Palestine remains an 'open wound' and quoting Palestinian historian Rashid Khalidi, pointed out that 'The period since the Balfour Declaration has witnessed what amounts to a hundred years of war against the Palestinian people'.[4]

Arthur Balfour was portrayed by many distinguished writers of his day[5] as 'the face of Britain itself at the moment of its greatest power and prestige', . . . 'even today those with no expertise in British political history have heard of the Balfour Declaration of 1917'. He was prime minister and leader of the largest imperial enterprise in the history of the world'.[6]

Despite the esteemed status bestowed on the representative of the greatest power of its day, descriptions of 'Perfidious Albion' were no less common even then. From the Hussein-McMahon correspondence of 1915 to the Sykes-Picot Agreement of 1916 and the Balfour Declaration of 1917, British deceit barely needs further commenting upon, but a few reminders of how this policy took shape will be necessary as this story unfolds.

Unlike most cataclysmic upheavals in history, the Palestine tragedy had a 'specific starting point: the year 1897'. In that year, the World Zionist Organization met in Basel in Switzerland and resolved to establish a Jewish state in Palestine, at a time when the population of Palestine was 95% Arab, and 99% of its land was Arab-owned.[7] However, it was not until 20 years after the formal establishment of Zionism as a political movement in Basel[8] that the real watershed for the Zionist movement occurred when Britain incorporated Zionism into its imperial strategy during the course of World War I.[9] And as Walid Khalidi notes, the instrument that provided the linchpin for this shift was the Balfour Declaration:

> The Balfour Declaration revolutionized Zionist prospects overnight, firmly placing the Zionist seeds within the imperial womb of the paramount power in the Middle East.[10]

When they heard of the Balfour Declaration, Palestine's Arabs were left dumbfounded. They immediately understood its implications; Zionist fortunes were transformed with the sweep of a pen, and their existence in their own country was now under threat.[11] From that day, the occasion of the Balfour Declaration was marked in Palestine as a day of mourning and angry demonstrations, and black flags were hung in the streets and from balconies.

In his 1919 memo on Palestine, British Foreign Secretary Arthur Balfour made it clear that 'we are dealing not with the wishes of an existing community but are consciously seeking to reconstitute a new community and definitely building for a Jewish numerical majority in the future'. What this meant to the Arab inhabitants of Palestine, both in the towns and in villages, was that, given Zionist ideology, their personal and communal property rights would be negated in the interest of the newly arrived Jewish settlers, and their status as a majority in their own country would be reduced to that of a minority.

This was not only a foreign occupation: The whole character of their society and communal life would be taken over by an alien culture and alien values, and their country would be dismembered.[12]

Indeed, the Balfour Declaration was a most extraordinary document, unparalleled in world history. The 69 words contained in it are, in the view of most commentators, a cunning masterpiece of brevity and ambiguity, whose every word was checked and weighed and changed many times over, until the final draft was accepted by a hesitant war cabinet.[13] This, it has to be pointed out, in 1917—before the end of World War I, when Palestine was still under Ottoman rule. Thus, before the British had even set foot in the country (in December 1917), Balfour promised Palestine to world Jewry, to create a Jewish *national home*, in a letter sent to Lord Walter Rothschild, a leader of the British Jewish community (reproduced in Appendix A of this book).

It has often been asserted that the policy of the Balfour Declaration and its inherent ambiguity was beyond the wit of successive British governments to reconcile. That this declaration was a document of 'calculated ambiguity' is highly likely. In his *Analysis of the Balfour Declaration,* JMN Jeffries, a *Daily Mail* correspondent during the early 1920s (who visited Palestine at that time), wrote: 'Drafts for it travelled back and forth, within England or over the Ocean, to be scrutinized by some two score draftsmen . . . who erased [this] phrase or adopted that after much thought. . . . ' He added: 'There is one point upon which there is no doubt. Whatever is to be found in the Balfour Declaration was put into it deliberately. There are no accidents in that text. If there is any vagueness in it this is an intentional vagueness.'[14]

INTRODUCTION

The Balfour Declaration contained two pledges, which were later dubbed by the Royal Commission of Inquiry (the Peel Commission) in 1937 as having been 'incompatible': The British government 'viewed' with favour the establishment of the Jewish national home in Palestine, on condition that the civil and religious rights of 'existing non-Jewish communities' would be safeguarded. Reference by name to the Arab population of Palestine, who then constituted 93 percent of the population, was avoided. This was consistent with the Zionist view of deliberately avoiding the 'Arab problem'.

Today, 100 years later, the Middle East is embroiled in upheavals, and the Palestine problem midwived by the Balfour Declaration remains agonizingly unresolved, with upwards of three—going on four—generations of Palestinians whose lives have been irreparably altered, in many cases gutted, as a result. At the centenary in 2017, the centrality of the Balfour Declaration to the Middle East's maelstrom has once again come to the fore, not only in academic works but also in the media, as the following few examples will show.[15] In a nutshell, the Balfour Declaration is crucial because World War I and the world problems that it spawned never really ended, as author Robert Gertwarth has succinctly explained. And the Balfour Declaration is a legacy of that war.[16] Gertwarth observes: 'The eventful years between 1917 and 1923 are still very much present in the collective memory of people from Eastern, Central, and Southern Europe, as well as those from the Middle East and Ireland'. That is why, within the Middle East, the war itself is a topic of 'marginal interest' compared with the Allies' subsequent 'invention of nations' that the Mandate regime imposed on the peoples of this area and 'the still-ongoing conflict over Palestine'. In the eyes of many Arabs, this all originated with the Balfour Declaration.[17]

As Robert Fisk of *The Independent* wrote in September 2015:

> ... Palestinian refugees, in their hundreds of thousands, ***are*** [emphasis in original] our responsibility. We think, because we made conflicting promises to their grandparents and the Jews a hundred years ago, that this somehow lets us off the hook. But for a Palestinian in the Lebanese refugee camps today, they wake up every morning in dirt-caked shacks amid sewage-washed alleyways. And for them, now, today—they are living the immediate results of the Balfour Declaration. Indeed for them, Lord Balfour signed his 1917 declaration, promising Britain's support for a Jewish homeland in Palestine, only yesterday, last night. The ink is still wet on the paper.[18]

And as the British newspaper, the *Independent* asked: "What's so special about 2017?" It went on to answer:

> First, it will be 50 years since the Israeli military occupation of the West Bank and Gaza Strip, and a reminder that millions of stateless Palestinians continue to live under an apartheid regime alongside hundreds of thousands of settlers. Second, the year is also the centenary of the Balfour Declaration, when the British government promised the Zionist movement its support in the creation of a Jewish homeland in Palestine.[19]

INTRODUCTION

Hence, given its historical centrality and its ongoing relevance to today's Middle East, this book aims to explore aspects of the Balfour Declaration's drafting and later interpretation by the British government. It draws in large part on research that I did for my doctoral thesis at the University of Manchester in the mid-1980s and my subsequent book on the administration of Herbert Samuel, the first British High Commissioner in Palestine (1920-1925).[20] During my research, I encountered a number of highly revealing and little-known documents concerning this history. The present work, based on Colonial Office archives, many previously unknown, is an attempt to provide new insights into these old controversies in light of the documents in question, and to clarify some of the circumstances surrounding the Balfour Declaration, in the hope of adding a new dimension to the debate on this historic document.

In a recent work on the subject, *The Global History of the Balfour Declaration*,[21] historian Maryanne Rhett opens her book by saying,

> Ten[22] drafts of the Declaration, in addition to its final form, appear nowhere together in the historiography and the topic is surprisingly under-discussed in British imperial history. Although the repercussions of the affairs of 1917 and the creation of the Balfour Declaration still resonate in global politics, we have an imperfect understanding of how the document came to be.[23]

The book concludes with the following: 'The work begun in 1917 continues . . . . Today, as then, few who actively work with the Declaration, historians and statesmen alike, can claim with any certainty what the document really sought . . . '[24] Rhett also maintains that 'The Balfour Declaration, although obscured by more recent events, continues to inform international policy both directly and indirectly'.[25]

Despite the overwhelming amount of material on the Balfour Declaration, and a wealth of legal, political, and historical interpretation, to the best of my knowledge, no one has yet looked into *what the British government itself has said* about the origins and motives behind the declaration. Although the Colonial Office discovered in 1923 that the Foreign Office held very little, if any, records on the origins of the Balfour Declaration, an examination of the internal minutes of the Colonial Office from that period shows not only the history of the negotiations that led up to the declaration, but also offers a glimpse of how questions of this nature were influenced by the Colonial Office staff and high-ranking officials. The present study argues that it was the interpretations of the Balfour Declaration emanating from the Middle East Department of the Colonial Office, five years after it was issued, that would influence future developments in the area even more than the declaration itself.

Since this present work was first published in the monograph series of Kuwait University (1998-1999),[26] the thrust of my argument remains unchanged. The present study is a revised version of the Kuwait University publication with a new introduction and updated bibliography. This work therefore focuses on the British government's grappling with its own motives regarding the declaration, *five years after it was issued*, as a result of a parliamentary controversy in 1922, and the discovery that none of the documents that were *known to have existed* in the Foreign Office were found.[27] This gave the head of the Middle East Department of the Colonial Office (responsible for Palestine since 1921), John Evelyn Shuckburgh, the liberty to seek from whomever remembered those events to record *from memory* their recollections of those events in order to salvage any official account on the early origins and negotiations leading up to the Balfour Declaration.

The questions guiding my work therefore revolve around this specific aspect, namely, the revelations made by the Colonial Office about the Balfour Declaration, five years after it was issued.

This book is divided into two chapters. "A General Historic Background" provides a broad general historical context for readers who are not familiar with the diplomatic and regional history, particularly that affecting Palestine. The specialist may wish to skip this chapter and go directly to the second chapter, which is the heart of this work. It explores the official British interpretation of the events that led up to the Balfour Declaration, based on the above-mentioned 1922-23 Colonial Office interpretation of it, throwing light on an unknown aspect, namely, the scarcity of official British records regarding the declaration. Although there is an overwhelmingly extensive literature on the months leading up to the Balfour Declaration (from April to November 1917), British archival sources reveal a shocking and highly surprising near-total lack of documentary evidence on its earlier history. In this context, an important minute by William Ormsby-Gore, the Under-Secretary for the Colonies in 1922, describing from memory the events leading to the declaration, is quoted in full (see p. 81). The second part of the chapter is then largely devoted to a detailed analysis of this important minute. The second chapter also sheds light on the careers of British officials who were instrumental in producing the Balfour Declaration. The roles played by some of them—such as Balfour, Mark Sykes, and Lloyd George—are already well known; that played by others is less so. Men such as Ronald Graham, William Ormsby-Gore, Alfred Milner, Leopold Amery, Maurice Hankey, Jan Smuts, and Military Intelligence men such as George MacDonogh and others were all influential governmental figures who were in favour of the declaration.

The overall aim of the book is not to give a new account of the events leading up to the Balfour Declaration but rather to focus on the official British version and interpretation of this document, as they emerge in available British archives. In so doing, we find that the interpretations of Colonial staff and high-ranking British officials some years after the declaration was issued were instrumental in the policy's ultimate adoption, and would prove even more influential in determining the course of future events than the original declaration itself.

I. A GENERAL HISTORIC BACKGROUND

Appreciating the nuance and complexity of the circumstances in which the Balfour Declaration was drafted, issued, and later explained and interpreted by the British government requires a considerable amount of historical context. This chapter aims to provide that context for the non-specialist reader, albeit with quite a broad brush to cover a vast amount of time and a wide variety of players and interests. It roughly follows chronological order but occasionally skips back and forward in time to focus on particular topics.

FRANCO-BRITISH RIVALRY IN THE LEVANT

French interest in the Ottoman Empire generally and in the Levant in particular dates back centuries. On the eve of World War I, there were no less than 500 French missionary schools in the Ottoman Empire, far outnumbering those of any other nation. The majority of these institutions were concentrated in Syria (at that time including Lebanon and Palestine), counting between 50,000-60,000 students.[1] Moreover, France's connection to Palestine dates back at least as far as the Crusades and even earlier. Ever since, France claimed its monopoly over the transport of pilgrims to the Holy Land, acting as protector not only of religious orders and merchants, but of Roman

Catholic interests in general.[2] By 1860, French influence in Syria and Palestine reached its highest point when missionary orders[3] set up schools and hospitals, as well as charitable institutions, such as orphanages and asylums. This continued well after 1871, when the new anti-clerical secular regime in France persecuted the Jesuits, leading them to expand their activities outside France. Thus, as a result of persecution at home, Jesuit influence grew even greater in the Ottoman Empire. By 1880, these missionary orders proved to be among the most useful tools of French influence abroad. At the same time, British influence was rising, which led one Jesuit to remark that: 'were we not such good Frenchmen, the British flag would presently be flying over all our oriental establishments'.[4]

Towards the final years of the nineteenth century, as Ottoman influence deteriorated, and the French feared growing British influence in the Near East, France concluded that it must increase her influence there to demonstrate to the British that France had not abandoned her traditional interests in the Levant.[5] The French also had to deal with the Germans, whose economic and political influence was growing in Asia Minor, in the form of economic concessions to German companies to build the Anatolia railway.[6]

In 1912, French suspicion of British intentions in the Levant led the British Foreign Secretary to deny such interest to the French ambassador in Cairo. However, this did not mean any 'official' British recognition of French influence in Syria, but rather that the British were still committed to the policy of maintaining the integrity of the Ottoman Empire. France was now openly claiming *La Syrie intégrale* (geographical Syria) as 'the France of the Levant'.[7]

Towards the end of 1913, France was deeply involved in negotiations with the Turkish and German governments for railway concessions in Syria and Lebanon, the success of which would have secured France's economic primacy in the region.[8] Under the capitulation system, foreign powers were allowed to hold certain monopolies in the Ottoman Empire; thus a French company owned and operated the Jaffa-Jerusalem railway. On the eve of the war, France had secured for itself the right to construct new ports at Haifa and Jaffa. The Banque Ottomane represented French interests, and business was conducted in Palestine through the Crédit Lyonnais.[9] However, there were signs of growing British influence, especially in Southern Syria (i.e., Palestine); Gertrude Bell[10] reported in September 1914 that Palestine was 'exceedingly pro-British'.[11]

As will be shown throughout this chapter, Anglo-French rivalry did not by any means come to a sudden end with the creation of the British Mandate in Palestine in 1920. Negotiations between the French and British over borders and other matters continued for the next two years and were not settled until the final ratification of the Mandate for Palestine by the League of Nations in September 1923. Understanding these dynamics is important to understanding the context of the events chronicled in this book.

ORIGINS OF BRITISH ZIONIST POLICY

Britain's interest in Palestine was likewise much older than the strategic considerations that became manifest during the latter part of the nineteenth century and was deeply rooted in her intellectual history and a millenarian concept of the 'restoration of the Jews' to the

Holy Land. By the beginning of the 19th century, the millenarian doctrine, which had been developed by Anglican Messianism and Evangelism and accepted by non-governmental movements whose efforts in this direction played a role in shaping the Palestine policy, was almost completely finalised, so that no new additions to this idea were added during the course of the century. The basic millenarian concept (the foundation of Christian Zionism), can be summarised as follows: An integral element for the fulfilment of the prophecies regarding the Last Day was the return of the Jews to the land of their forefathers, to which they had an 'inalienable right'. The end of their diaspora, their physical and religious restoration, and their ingathering in Palestine and acceptance of the Christian gospel were all thought to be an essential part of the divine plan for human redemption, which would prepare the way for the 'Second Coming' of Christ and the establishment of his Kingdom on earth. The question of whether the conversion of Jews to Christianity must take place before or after their 'repatriation' was not settled.[12]

As early as 1840, after Britain had assisted the Ottoman Sultan in regaining control of Palestine from his rebellious vassal Mohammad 'Ali Pasha, the ruler of Egypt, the British Foreign Secretary at the time, Lord Palmerston, had appointed the first British Vice-Consul in Jerusalem and instructed him to protect the Jews inhabiting Palestine. As Palmerston explained to the British ambassador in Constantinople:

> It would be of manifest importance for the Sultan to encourage the Jews to return to, and settle in Palestine; because the wealth which they would bring with them would

increase the resources of the Sultan's dominions; and the
Jewish people, if returning under the sanction and protection
and at the invitation of the Sultan, would be a check upon
any future evil designs of Mohammad 'Ali or his successor.[13]

Towards the end of the 1870s, the idea of the 'restoration of the Jews' combined with pure imperialist tendencies to produce all kinds of 'secular' projects for colonisation. As the concept of the 'conversion' of Jews to Christianity lost its attractiveness, the vision of the 'return' of the Jews to the land of their fathers lingered and was a common feature of English literature on Palestine during the last quarter of the nineteenth century.[14] During World War I, fascination with this secularised concept of restoration mixed with short-term political considerations and imperial strategies to produce the Balfour Declaration of 1917.[15]

When World War I broke out in 1914,[16] Britain reversed its centuries' old policy of preserving the integrity of the Ottoman Empire, and by 1915-1916, we come closer to the circumstances that led to the dismemberment of the Arabic-speaking provinces of the Ottoman Empire (which included Palestine) and the issuance of the Balfour Declaration.

On 9 November 1914, four days after Britain declared war on Turkey, the then British Prime Minister Herbert Asquith announced that the dismemberment of the Turkish (Ottoman) Empire had now become a war aim, thus overturning the foreign policy of more than a century.[17] After the Asquith announcement, the cabinet discussed the subject, and Liberal MP Lloyd George (who became Prime Minister shortly thereafter), mentioning the 'ultimate destiny in Palestine', assured Herbert Samuel, himself a Jew and a fervent Zionist who was also a Liberal MP and later became the first High Commissioner in Palestine 1920-25, that 'he was very keen to see a Jewish State established in Palestine.'[18]

More than 20 years later, at a lecture delivered on 25 November 1935 on the subject of Great Britain and Palestine, Samuel noted that:

> In November 1914, Turkey joined the Central Powers. It became obvious that, if the war ended in their defeat, the future destiny of the non-Turkish provinces of the Sultan would come up for settlement. They were held precariously. Their populations had been alienated by centuries of misrule. The break-up of the Turkish Empire, long overdue, was now almost inevitable. The future of Palestine would raise a question of the greatest interest. It became plain at once that Zionism had acquired a new actuality—vivid, urgent.... Events that were unexpected gave me a share in the writing of this chapter....[19]

Herbert Samuel went on to inform his audience that he had developed the Zionist position further in a talk with the Secretary of State for Foreign Affairs, Sir Edward Grey, on 9 November 1914. Samuel also reveals that before that date, he had had no connection with the Zionist movement, but now, 'suddenly, the conditions were entirely altered'. He went on to say:

> As the first member of the Jewish community ever to sit in a British Cabinet—(Disraeli [former MP and Prime Minister in the late nineteenth century] had left the

[Jewish] community in boyhood and never rejoined)—I felt that, in the conditions that had arisen, there lay upon me a special obligation.

Samuel informed his listeners that he had then made a study of Zionism and its achievements and knew all that there was to know about Palestine. Soon afterwards, he met the Zionist leader Chaim Weizmann, President of the World Zionist Organization, for the first time and thereupon arrived at the conclusion that when the war ended with an Allied victory, 'the opportunity should be taken to facilitate the establishment of a great autonomous Jewish community there.' Samuel also read out notes of the conversation he had had with Grey on 9 November 1914:

I spoke to Sir Edward Grey to-day about the future of Palestine. In the course of our talk I said that now that Turkey had thrown herself into the European War and that it was probable that their empire would be broken up, the question of the future of Palestine was likely to arise. . . . Perhaps there might be an opportunity for the fulfilment of the ancient aspiration of the Jewish people and the restoration there of a Jewish State.

Samuel went on to say (at the lecture): 'If a Jewish State were established in Palestine, it might become the centre of a new culture. The Jewish brain is rather a remarkable thing, and, under national auspices, the State might become a fountain of enlightenment and a source of a great literature and art and development of science.' Samuel continued that his note (for 9 November) proceeded as follows: 'Grey said that the idea had always had a strong sentimental attraction for him. The historical appeal was very strong. He was quite favourable to the proposal and would be prepared to work for it if the opportunity arose.'[20] It seems that Grey, however, did not envision the creation of a political entity in Palestine, and considered such views from the angle of establishing a Jewish cultural centre. Grey's views were said to have been conveyed by Weizmann, the chief Zionist negotiator, to the Zionist International.[21]

Also, towards the end of 1914, an aide to Lord Herbert Kitchener, Secretary of State for War (1914-16)[22] wrote to Sir Ronald Storrs,[23] an official in the British Foreign Office at the time, for comments on the role of Palestine. Storrs replied:

> A buffer state is most desirable, but can we get one up? There is no visible indigenous elements out of which a Moslem Kingdom of Palestine can be constructed. The Jewish State is in theory an attractive idea; but the Jews, though they constitute a majority in Jerusalem itself are very much in a minority in Palestine generally, and form indeed a bare sixth of the whole population.[24]

This new policy of destroying the integrity of the Ottoman Empire appears to have prompted Herbert Samuel, after having discussed the issue with Lloyd George and Weizmann, to submit to the cabinet, in January 1915, a draft memorandum titled 'The Future of Palestine', in which he advocated British annexation of that country rather than the establishment of an autonomous Jewish State, which he realized was 'impracticable' given 'the conditions that prevailed, five-sixths of the population of Palestine being Arabs.' Instead, to relieve the oppressed Jews of Russia and Eastern Europe, Samuel concluded that annexation to the British Empire, together with 'active encouragement of Jewish colonization and cultural development would be the best solution'. Thus, the memorandum urged British support for Zionist aspirations.[25] Some members of the cabinet (such as Sir Edward Grey, Lord Richard Haldane (who was Lord Chancellor from 1912-1915), Lloyd George, and the Marquess of Crewe) appear to have been sympathetic, while Edwin Montagu (Herbert Samuel's cousin, who was the Secretary of State for India from 1917-1922 and the second Jew to serve in a British Cabinet but unlike Samuel, was a strong opponent and fierce critic of the government's Zionist policy and the Balfour Declaration)[26] and Prime Minister Asquith gave no encouragement to such ideas. It was Asquith who remarked:

> I confess that I am not attracted by the proposed addition to our responsibilities, but it is a curious illustration of Dizzy's [Disraeli's] favourite maxim that 'race is everything' to find this almost lyrical outburst proceeding from the well ordered and methodical brain of H.S.[27]

Asquith also wrote that, at that moment, Grey and himself 'are the only two men who doubt and distrust any such settlement. We both think that in the real interest of our own future, the best thing would be if, at the end of the War, we could say that . . . we have taken and gained nothing'. The Prime Minister told members of his cabinet that when they discussed Ottoman territories, their 'discussion had resembled that of a gang of buccaneers'.[28]

In addition to the war consideration, a rising wave of anti-semitism was sweeping Poland in 1914-15,[29] and this fact could have strengthened the overall Zionist argument for Palestine.[30]

The year 1915 witnessed dramatic developments in favour of the government's pro-Zionist policy. Early that year, according to Leopold Amery, one of the assistant secretaries of the War Cabinet, Zionist leaders under Weizmann's leadership began their 'unrelenting' campaign of lobbying British political leaders and policy makers.[31] It was at the suggestion of Lloyd George that Weizmann renewed his contact with Balfour. It was also during this time that Weizmann informed CP Scott, pro-Zionist editor of the *Manchester Guardian*, that he had succeeded in producing acetone for use in explosives, which was of great military significance.[32]

In March 1915, Sir Edward Grey sent a memorandum to Sir Edward Buchanan, the British Ambassador to Russia, in which he outlined British thoughts on the relationship between Palestine and world Jewry. This memorandum, which the British ambassador was supposed to convey to Sazonoff, the Russian Minister for Foreign Affairs, stated Britain's intention of gaining the support of the majority of the world's Jews for the Allied cause. It expressed the belief that if Jewish colonists in Palestine could compete with the Arab population, then the administration of that country could be placed in Jewish hands.[33]

There were further developments in March 1915, when Herbert Samuel, the talented 'architect' of the Jewish national home, circulated to the British cabinet another revised memorandum from which the word 'annexation' was dropped. Lloyd George and Balfour, already advocates of Zionism, were warmly sympathetic, but Asquith (who was committed to the policy of befriending the Arabs and using them to replace the Turks as friends of Britain in the Near East) remained unconvinced.[34] In his five-page memorandum, Samuel posed five questions and systematically set out to answer them. The memorandum began by carefully asking: 'If the war results in the break-up of the Turkish Empire in Asia, what is to be the future of Palestine?' Samuel gave possible solutions and elaborated on each of them.

a. 'Of the possible alternatives, the one most frequently discussed is annexation by France'.
b. 'A second alternative would be to leave the country to Turkey'.
c. 'A third alternative would be internationalization'.
d. 'Another alternative often suggested is the establishment in Palestine of an autonomous Jewish State'.
e. 'The last alternative is a British protectorate.'

Leaving the country to its Arab inhabitants as one of the suggested possibilities apparently did not occur to Samuel.

Some elaboration is perhaps needed of the opinions expressed in points (d) and (e) of Samuel's memorandum. Samuel dismissed the idea of the immediate establishment of an autonomous Jewish state. He said it was doomed to failure at that point in history, and asserted that:

> ... the dream of a Jewish State, prosperous, progressive, and the home of a brilliant civilization might vanish in a series of squalid conflicts with the Arab population .... To attempt to realize the aspiration of a Jewish State one century too soon might throw back its actual realization for many centuries more. These considerations are fully recognized by the leaders of the Zionist movement.[35]

Towards the end of his memorandum, Samuel concluded that the only feasible solution would be a British protectorate, under which 'facilities would be given to Jewish organizations to purchase land, to found colonies, to establish educational and religious institutions, and to cooperate in the economic development of the country', giving preference to Jewish immigration, 'so that in the course of time the Jewish inhabitants, grown into a majority and settled in the land, may be conceded such degree of self-government as the conditions of that day might justify'.[36]

The enlisting of Jewish support as a war measure is perhaps suggested for the first time in any official record when Samuel stated that 'the course which is advocated would win for England the gratitude of the Jews throughout the world.' Samuel concluded his memorandum by pointing out that although Great Britain did not enter the war with any territorial designs, yet, having made so many sacrifices, it would be disappointing to the country 'if the outcome were to be the securing of great advantages by our Allies and none by ourselves'.[37]

Prime Minister Asquith remained unconvinced. Calling Samuel's memorandum 'dithyrambic',[38] he wrote in his diary on 13 March 1915 that Lloyd George was the 'only partisan' apart from

Samuel.[39] Asquith added in a private conversation that Lloyd George 'does not care a damn for the Jews or their past or their future'. He still could not comprehend the complex motives behind Samuel's and Lloyd George's advocacy of a British protectorate in Palestine. But in the end it was Herbert Kitchener, Secretary of State for War (1914-1916), who stood up against Samuel's proposal. He told the cabinet that Palestine was of little value, strategically or otherwise, and did not even have one 'decent' harbour. Samuel's memorandum, therefore, was not adopted; but Lloyd George continued to disagree with Kitchener over the strategic value of Palestine.[40]

In April 1915, on the instructions of Prime Minister Asquith, a 'Committee on Asiatic Turkey' was formed under the chairmanship of Sir Maurice de Bunsen to advise the cabinet as to what Britain ought to seek in the Middle East.[41] Sir Mark Sykes, who was an adviser to the Foreign Office on Middle Eastern policy during World War I as well as a member of the War Cabinet as expert on the Near East, was appointed to the de Bunsen Committee.[42] All the major departments were represented in this committee; Kitchener's War Office was represented by Charles Caldwell, but, in addition, Kitchener placed Sir Mark Sykes as his 'personal' (as distinct from his departmental) representative, and, through Sykes, Kitchener dominated the Committee's proceedings.[43] From that point onwards, Sykes was put in charge of Near Eastern affairs throughout the war.[44] The Committee, which reported on 30 June 1915, recognized the importance of Palestine in the defence of Egypt and Britain's need for a port on the coast of Southern Syria (i.e., Haifa) serving as a Mediterranean terminus for British railway communications connecting the Mediterranean Sea to the Persian

Gulf (to enable troops to move to and from India rapidly). The Committee warned that Britain could not guarantee today's friends would not be tomorrow's enemies, and worried about the possibility of a future Franco-Russian threat to the Suez Canal and the Persian Gulf.[45] The safeguarding of Britain's imperial communication lines with India was a major theme in the thinking of Mark Sykes, and he seems to have been the main force behind the Committee's advocacy of British control over Palestine.[46]

Some years later in 1923, mention of the de Bunsen Committee was made in a secret Cabinet Paper on Palestine.[47] The Colonial Office wrote that:

> It may be of interest, as bearing on the question of what was in the mind of His Majesty's Government in 1915, to call attention to the report of a Committee appointed in that year to consider the question of British Desiderata in Turkey in Asia, . . . its report seems to have been the first attempt to formulate a policy for the ultimate disposal of conquered Turkish territory. Its recommendations formed the basis of much that took place subsequently.

On Palestine, the abovementioned report argued that it 'must be regarded as a country whose destiny must be the subject of special negotiations, in which both belligerents and neutrals are alike interested.'[48]

In August 1915, a secret memorandum prepared by the Committee of Imperial Defence (C.I.D.) entitled *The Critical Urgency of the Turkish Campaign* set out to formulate a policy on the Arabic-speaking regions of the Ottoman Empire for the next few months. It stated that 'Our present failure to amass really irrestible [sic] numbers against Turkey connotes a stalemate fraught with the possibilities of politico-military disasters'. The memorandum disclosed that the coming month of September would be 'a great turning point in the European war', adding that 'the odds against the Entente may be vastly, perhaps fatally increased, if we cannot at once convince the doubting world that we shall inevitably crush Turkey's resistance within the next two months'. Calling attention to Russia's extremely difficult position (the Russian military was lacking in munitions) the memorandum added that Turkish morale was very high, and that 'only literally overwhelming reinforcements can render mathematically certain a complete solution of the dangers arising for the Entente from the Turkish impasse'. To British decision makers, the future looked very grim indeed.

The memorandum concluded by saying that:

A lightning blow, delivered with the force of a sledgehammer, would crumple up the Turkish resistance, speedily release the bulk of the Entente troops fighting in the Near East, overawe the Balkans, establish our prestige for the carrying out of a crushing offensive, open the granaries of Russia for the Entente, and immeasurably more important, pierce a clear passage through which we could pour in munitions to our gigantic ally who is hourly looking to us for help from the South that never comes.[49]

The events of 1916 were hugely influential in terms of how the British government acquired a more or less well-defined pro-Zionist policy. The year 1916 was a near catastrophe for the Allies. German submarine activity in the Atlantic was so great that nearly half a million tons of merchant shipping were sunk that year alone.[50] In 1915, the Foreign Office received wisdom had been that Jews—whether in America, the Levant, Russia or even Britain—were a 'powerful, collective force antipathetic to the interests of the Entente', and British policy makers did not distinguish between one type of Jew and another, or even between Zionist and non-Zionist Jews. Therefore, by late 1915, there was an implicit consensus amongst the Entente powers, and not just in Britain, that Jews, merely being Jews, were an important consideration in the war effort, and they were collectively on the side of the German enemy.[51]

Thus, early in 1916, the British government took more practical steps to favour the Zionists. In February 1916, Weizmann was appointed to the Admiralty under the supervision of Balfour in connection with the work he was conducting with high explosives and Balfour, remembering his earlier promise, told Weizmann: 'you know, after the war you may get your Jerusalem.'[52]

It was also in February that a scheme of what was later to become a firmly established Zionist policy was quickly emerging. On 23 February 1916, Grey stated that 'Jewish feeling which is now hostile [i.e., to the Allies] and favours a German protectorate over Palestine might be entirely changed if an American protectorate was favoured with the object of restoring Jews to Palestine'.[53]

In December 1916, Lloyd George, by now a strong Zionist sympathizer, replaced Asquith as Prime Minister. With the appointment of Balfour, another pro-Zionist, at the head of the Foreign Office, British commitment to Zionism seemed to have been assured, and 'it was only a matter of time'.[54]

The idea of drawing world Jewry to the Allied cause was a central theme in British policy during those crucial months. Reaching an agreement with the Allies on the Zionist question was largely the responsibility of Mark Sykes, who had just been appointed as assistant secretary to the War Cabinet. Since only two such positions existed,[55] Sykes was put in total charge of Near Eastern affairs, which made him an extremely important figure in the eyes of Zionist leaders.[56] On Sykes' naïve views on the Jewish question, Leslie Shane, Sykes' biographer, gives us a glimpse of his earliest perspective on the subject. Shane maintains that Sykes' Catholicism was what assisted him in understanding the Jewish tragedy, adding that his first steps to Zionism occurred in his 'striking suggestion' of 1904 in favour of Jewish dress: 'Imagine how picturesque and interesting a walk in the City would become, what a blaze of colour Capel Court would be, if the children of Israel retained their ancient and handsome dress'.[57] Another way to view Sykes' many contradictions is that despite his early paranoia about everything Jewish, his Cambridge tutor E.G. Brown complained that young Sykes 'saw Jews everywhere'; he was the one to convey to the Foreign Office his belief that world Zionism would be a useful asset to the Allied cause.[58]

MARK SYKES AND ZIONISM

Because Sykes is the protagonist of this story, it is necessary to elaborate at some length on his pivotal role in defining British policy towards the Arab region immediately following the outbreak of World War I, as a background to the events that will be discussed in this book. In December 1914, the British Foreign Office started negotiating with Sharif Hussein of Hijaz, the last Hashemite Emir of Mecca (and later to become King of the Arabs), through Sir Arthur Henry McMahon, the British High Commissioner of Egypt, with the purpose of persuading Hussein to throw off Turkish supremacy. In return, the British government promised the Emir independence and autonomy in a series of 10 letters exchanged from 14 July 1915 to 10 March 1916 that came to be known as the Hussein-McMahon Correspondence.[59] Hussein wanted to obtain the independence of the whole Arab nation [i.e., the Arabic-speaking provinces of the Ottoman Empire, including Palestine] and restore past Arab glories.[60]

The question of precisely what was or was not promised to Hussein by the British government regarding Arab independence, especially of Palestine, has been, and continues to be, a hotly disputed subject. The fact that the British government never fully published the Hussein-McMahon correspondence, and that it contained internal ambiguities, only intensified the controversy.[61]

In March 1915, the Committee of Imperial Defence (C.I.D.) had decided that one of Britain's principal strategic objectives of World War I was that 'an absolutely safe line of communications must be obtained between the Mediterranean and the Black Sea for the remainder of the war', and that 'Turkey must at once be freed from German influence'.[62]

By May 1915, the de Bunsen Committee had accepted Sykes' view that most of Palestine lay within the British sphere of influence for two main reasons: (1) Britain needed the area between the Mediterranean and Mesopotamia to secure its communications with the Persian Gulf; and (2) Britain could not allow a French presence along the Suez Canal, the Arabian Peninsula, and the Persian Gulf.[63]

In June 1915, in his capacity as member of the de Bunsen Committee, which had considered a number of alternatives to set up an independent state in the Arabian Peninsula, Sykes (a devout Catholic and considered by many a Francophile) set out on a tour in the Near East to ascertain the views of British officials there. At the Residency in Cairo, British officials told Sykes that none of the de Bunsen Committee's proposals seemed entirely satisfactory. Instead, they advocated exclusive British control over Palestine, and that Damascus should be included in this British sphere. Sykes' 'dynamic' personality seems to have quickly convinced these officials that he could represent their views in London.[64] Also while in Cairo, Sykes met Syrian Arab nationalists and brought the surprising news to the Foreign Office that an obscure young Arab from Mosul claimed that his friends could help Britain win the war. Muhammad Sharif al-Faruki, a 24-year-old Ottoman staff officer, maintained that he was a member of the *al-Ahd* secret society in Damascus who had deserted Ottoman forces at Gallipoli in the autumn of 1915 and crossed over to Allied lines, for reasons that remain mysterious even today. This young officer caught the attention of British officials in Cairo during 1916, and acted as a middleman between British officials and Arab leaders, apparently entirely on his own initiative.[65] In

July 1915, Kitchener sent Sykes to Cairo to try and implement the de Bunsen proposals. After six months there, his proposal to establish an Islamic Bureau finally resulted in the Arab Bureau, where TE Lawrence, his intelligence chief Sir Gilbert Clayton (who set up the bureau), and DG Hogarth, the distinguished Oxford scholar, were in residence. It is interesting to note that both Clayton and Hogarth thought very little of Sykes, whom they saw as hopelessly pretentious and intellectually shallow, and whom they believed pretended far more knowledge of the Near East than he actually possessed. On Sykes' death, Hogarth said that he had never worked at anything and that he remained a 'superficial amateur to the end'. Lawrence believed that Sykes was a 'bundle of prejudices and intuitions'.[66] As will be seen in the following pages, Sykes' policy of duplicity and dishonesty drove many British officials on the spot to the limits of their wits. Yet this same policy received high praise from none other than Winston Churchill. In his introduction to Leslie Shane's book, Churchill asserts that '... He [Sykes] acquainted himself with the Levantines and the Palestinians, and even more with the Arabs and the Turks. He went where few if any had ever been before, and mapped out roads and countries which neither the War Office nor the Royal Geographical Society with their combined knowledge could cover or compass'.[67] He went on to say: 'He became an invaluable factor in all that intricate and remarkable policy which split the Arab from the Turk, divided the Moslem world at a most critical juncture, and eventually furnished important forces on the desert flank of Allenby's armies'.[68]

It should be noted that until November 1915, the Allies had still not achieved any great success in the war. A report by the Committee of Imperial Defence the previous month stated that the reason for attaching so much importance to the occupation of Baghdad was that 'primarily . . . it [was] in Mesopotamia that we can inflict the maximum damage upon Turkey at the least cost to ourselves'. The report added that the early capture of Baghdad was considered to be 'most desirable', as it would 'relieve directly the existing situation in Asiatic Turkey, in Persia and in Afghanistan'.[69]

In October 1915, the famous McMahon letter was sent to Sharif Hussein.[70] A chief concern in the Foreign Office was that the question of Arab frontiers had to be settled with French approval, and McMahon's correspondence with Hussein revealed the importance they placed on taking French interests into account.[71] By December 1915, it was decided that the French and the British would divide the Near East into two separate spheres of influence, where Britain would enjoy exclusive rights in one, and France in the other. Thus, the Sykes-Picot Agreement was approved by the British government in February 1916. Sykes and Picot drew the map of the new Near East in which direct French control would include the Syrian littoral up to the north (designated the Blue Area) and that of Britain would include the region of Basra and Baghdad (designated the Red Area). The interior of Syria and northern Mesopotamia was divided into spheres of French influence (Area A), and British influence (Area B). Palestine and the Holy Places were to be internationalised.[72] However, British officials in Cairo were kept totally unaware of this map, and negotiations with Sharif Hussein continued. This suited

Sykes, for it protected his agreement from rejection by Hussein, whom he was to meet a couple of months later.[73]

Because Britain was also interested in Palestine for strategic considerations, Sykes was now thinking of ways to get Palestine out of the French sphere of influence. Under the terms of the Sykes-Picot Agreement, France would have controlled much of Syria, including most of the Galilee with its fertile land. British influence would mainly be in the Acre/Haifa region. The area around Jerusalem was to be internationalised. When the Zionist leader Chaim Weizmann later heard of this, he was appalled, for a joint British-French control of Palestine would have prevented Zionist objectives there.[74]

The French encounter with political Zionism was yet to come, and was, in any case, the result of Sykes' manoeuvres to get the French to meet the Zionist leader Nahum Sokolow.[75] For, during the early meetings between Sykes and a group of young British Zionists, (including Lord Rothschild, Weizmann, Harry Sacher, Nahum Sokolow, and Herbert Samuel) during which a memorandum written by Sokolow was submitted, Sykes encouraged Sokolow to meet with Georges Picot to press Zionist demands. Sykes also explained to Picot what the Zionists sought in Palestine, and impressed upon him that since France and Britain sought to gain the support of world Jewry, it was essential to meet their demands and that it might be possible to find some other government, not France or England, that would be willing to undertake the protection of Palestine.[76] In March 1916, Sykes went with Picot to Petrograd to seal the Sykes-Picot Agreement. Prior to his journey, he met Herbert Samuel and had a conversation with him that seems to have strengthened his interest in Zionism, which up to this point he had had little interest in or knowledge of.[77]

The first meeting between Hussein, Sykes, and Picot took place in Jedda on 19 May 1916, in the presence of Emir Faisal, and Hussein's Foreign Secretary, Fuad al-Khatib. Another meeting took place the following day. It seems that Sykes made a negative impression on Hussein, and in order to overcome this obstacle, al-Khatib made a declaration to the effect that relations between France and the Arab government in Syria would be the same as those between the King and the British in Baghdad. The British representative in Jedda, Colonel Cyril E Wilson, sensing Sykes' opportunist diplomacy, became apprehensive and reported to Cairo that Hussein would never have consented to this had he known what the real situation in Iraq would be. He added that when he knew that Hussein was pressured by Sykes to declare this, he would have 'certainly . . . tried hard to get some principal facts re our position in Iraq stated at the meeting'. Colonel Wilson added that Sykes had 'undoubtedly taken a very heavy responsibility on his shoulders'.[78] And TE Lawrence said that its 'geographical absurdities' would 'laugh it out of court'.[79]

In the course of the next few months, and most critically, according to Jeremy Wilson, during the crucial months between April and July 1917, Sykes maintained his deception. Upon hearing that a French political officer was to join the British army, Hussein became alarmed, and it was decided to send Sykes again to Jedda for talks. In Cairo as well as in the Hijaz, British officials by now suspected that some kind of arrangement had been reached with the

French and expressed deep concern about the way Sykes was handling the whole affair. However, Sykes had no intentions of clearing up any misunderstandings; on the contrary, according to Wilson, 'He remained sublimely confident that the present policy of vagueness and deceit could be continued'.[80]

On 22 April 1917, Sykes and Picot arrived in Cairo, where Sykes had arranged to meet a small number of carefully selected prominent Syrian Arabs. Their aim was to get the Arabs to accept the terms of the Sykes-Picot Agreement, and the two began a series of talks with these representatives. At the meetings, the Arabs were given the impression that after the war, Britain and France would help them create an independent inland state or confederation. However, the author [Wilson] explains, Sykes and Georges Picot took care not to reveal that France and Britain had already divided the proposed autonomous area into distinct spheres of influence. As Sykes put it, they 'maneouvre[d] the delegates, without showing them a map or letting them know that there was an actual geographical or detailed agreement, into asking what we are ready to give them'. Hussein had already heard of the French-British agreement and, alarmed, asked for explanations. The Foreign Office thus decided to send Sykes to Jedda for talks: 'He would reveal certain aspects of the Anglo-French policy, in as much the same way as he had done in Cairo, and would also, if possible, secure the Sherif's agreement to a further meeting in which Picot would be present. Sykes probably found these discussions uncomfortable, and Feisal, an 'acute politician' present at the meeting, already knew about the agreement more than Sykes meant to disclose, and 'his questions were doubtless very penetrating'. TE

Lawrence left no record of the conversation he had had with Feisal, nor is there any account in his notebooks on the discussion of 7 May when Sykes made a second brief visit in Jedda with Hussein. Despite this silence, Wilson reveals 'there is contemporary evidence that he [Lawrence] was extremely alarmed by the way Sykes was handling the discussions with the Arab leaders, and later comments by Sykes suggest that, during this meeting in Wejh, Lawrence disagreed with him openly. In March, Colonel Wilson had urged that the position should be made as clear as possible to the Sharif.[81]

The only agreement to emerge from the May 1917 meeting between Mark Sykes and Georges Picot with Sharif Hussein was a vague understanding that France would act in Syria on the same basis as Britain in Baghdad. Hussein and Picot were 'delighted' with this formula, but only because each had a completely different interpretation of it. Picot, according to the Sykes-Picot terms, thought Britain intended to impose direct rule in Baghdad, and therefore claimed that Hussein had agreed to direct French rule in Syria. Hussein, depending on his correspondence with McMahon, believed that permanent British rule in Baghdad was not intended, and that accordingly, France had relinquished her claim to Syria and Lebanon. 'This absurd formula' according to Jeremy Wilson, 'had been knowingly suggested by Sykes, who doubtless regarded the 'agreement' as a personal triumph. When [Colonel] Wilson discovered the role that Sykes had played, he was disgusted'.[82]

British officials continued to express their unease and apprehension on more than one occasion, and Captain Wilson wrote that a Franco-British settlement 'should not be arranged behind

[Hussein's] back,' and that he [Hussein] was 'well deserving of the trust of the British Government and I feel sure we will greatly regret it in the future if we are not quite open and frank with him now over the whole matter'. Other British officials protested in very strong terms against Sykes' handling of the situation, saying that this policy of deception was causing anxiety in several officers' minds, and that it amounts to 'hoodwinking the Sharif and his people' and 'playing a very false game'. Most deeply distressed by this was Colonel TE Lawrence, who was about to lead the Arab Revolt out of Hijaz and into Syria. By now, he knew that because of Sykes' diplomacy, British officers were expected to keep the Arabs fighting alongside the British at whatever cost, but that Britain would not keep her word after the war was over. Sykes' 'disingenuous attitude' made British officers, according to British historian Jeremy Wilson, deeply aware of their own moral responsibility and they believed that Sykes' policy of deception was morally indefensible and would almost certainly be counterproductive.[83] Lloyd George said of the Sykes-Picot Agreement that it was a 'foolish document' blemished by the imperfect and unscientific manner in which the boundaries of every area were drawn.

According to Wilson, it has been argued that Sykes' ostensible extreme self-confidence disguised a different nature: apart from being politically short-sighted, he was illogical, disorganised and lacked the ability to perform 'any systematic examination of detail.' Even worse, he advocated contradictory policies on successive days with great enthusiasm without even realising that such changes involved rethinking his entire policy. When it was pointed out to him that his policy would raise difficulties in the future, he once stated that he 'was not looking so far ahead' and that 'to do a good job, one must seek the immediate benefit',[84] adding that 'As for dividing territories we will always be able to make arrangements when the war is over'. Lieutenant Millet's opinion of Sykes was also damning: 'No subtlety, crude common sense, simplistic politics, scant knowledge of the people and places involved, great self-satisfaction'.[85] Interestingly, Sykes' biographer, Leslie Shane, reveals that the Foreign Office correspondence maintains that 'It may be remarked here that the late Sir Mark Sykes himself was fully conscious of the shortcoming of the Arrangement . . . ' and that 'In his view the Arrangement was one of imperative expediency between Great Britain, France and Russia, and the linking of his name with it he considered an implication of authorship of its conditions which he desired to be spared'.[86]

By October 1916, a certain James Malcolm, an Armenian-born engineer educated at Oxford, entered the picture.[87] Malcolm approached Sykes and revived his interest in Zionism, stressing the fact that Louis Brandeis (a Supreme Court Justice who was a prominent American Zionist) had considerable influence on President Woodrow Wilson and suggesting to Sykes that winning the American Zionists to the British side by offering Palestine (to the Jews) would pave the way for America's entry into the war, which was Britain's foremost objective, but in which the British had thus far been largely unsuccessful.[88] It is not known whether Malcolm was designated by the Zionist Organization for that mission, but he did serve as a go-between between Sykes and the Zionist leaders. In the face of this success, the Zionists took immediate action. Their first request was to be granted permission to use British communication facilities to contact Zionists throughout the world. The request was granted by the cabinet, 'thus unwittingly establishing a precedent of cooperation with the Zionists and making it impossible to reverse this policy', since the communication facilities were used to proclaim British support for Zionism throughout world Jewry.[89]

Towards the end of January 1917, largely on Weizmann's initiative and with the help of friends such as Norman Bentwich, Harry Sacher, Rabbi Moses Gaster (Chief Rabbi of the Sephardic Jewish community in England), and Asher Ginzberg (known as *Ahad Ha'am*, which in Hebrew means 'one of the people'), a memorandum was submitted to Mark Sykes,[90] entitled: *Outline of Programme for Aspirations of the Zionist Movement.* According to Weizmann, this document was 'the first approach to the integration of Zionism with the complex of realities'.[91] Looking at it retrospectively, Weizmann asserted that it 'does seem to have anticipated the shape of things to come'.[92] According to the account of Vera Weizmann, the new memorandum mainly emphasised two points. First, it asked for the recognition of the Jewish nation; and second, for the right of this nation to settle in Palestine with full civic, national, and political rights.[93] However, it is significant that when Sykes met Rabbi Gaster early in 1917, the understanding he got from him was that Palestine should be organized on the lines of the Ottoman *millet* system.[94] Gaster seems to have been quite happy for the Jews to be recognized as a 'nation' within such a system and granted the same internal autonomy as other millets or 'nations'. Moreover, Dr. Gaster later wrote in his diary on 30 January 1917 that Sykes was very pleased with the idea.[95]

As Sykes became more committed to the Zionist cause, it was becoming increasingly evident to him that the secret Sykes-Picot Agreement of 1916 that he had been instrumental in arranging was an obstacle to Zionist aspirations. Moreover, subsequent events gave ample proof that the British government no longer wished to commit itself to the terms of that Agreement, which proposed to place Palestine under a Franco-British condominium. It is interesting to note in this respect that Georges Picot of the French Foreign Office was himself attached to Allenby's staff as the French Political Representative when British troops entered Palestine. Sir Archibald Wavell, Allenby's commander-in-chief in the Near East, described what went on between Allenby and Picot on the day of the official entry into Jerusalem: 'And to-morrow, my dear General, we will take steps to set up an administration in this city,' said Picot. Wavell noted that Allenby's chin 'went up and out a little further than usual', as he replied that 'Jerusalem was and would remain under martial law, for which he alone was responsible'.[96]

Between August and December 1917, a new factor had entered Sykes' mind. America had just entered the war, and in January 1918, US President Woodrow Wilson had declared his famous 14 points, making it clear that America would not accept a scramble for new colonies when the war ended. After the fall of the Czarist government in Russia in March 1917, the new provisional government under Kerensky adopted a similar policy. Liberal-minded English politicians accepted the view that if the war ended in defeat for the Central

Powers, Britain would have to renounce her former colonies. It was now evident to Sykes that the still-secret Sykes-Picot Agreement was in direct contradiction to this policy, and it was at this point that Sykes began to consider Zionism as an alternative approach to the question of how to achieve British goals in the region.[97] Thus, as the Sykes-Picot Agreement was dying away and losing its viability, Sykes played a major part in the steps that led to the promulgation of the Balfour Declaration of November 1917.

The fall of Jerusalem to the Allies in December 1917 opened a new phase of conflict and tension in Franco-British relations over the future settlement of the Near East. The French were well aware that their insignificant contribution to the Palestine campaign placed them in an awkward position, however great their claim was. The rising anti-imperialist feeling further undermined their claim to the region. Moreover, the French presence in a military-controlled Palestine was merely symbolic, and British officials had little sympathy with the terms of the Sykes-Picot Agreement. It was then that Lloyd George decided that direct British control in Palestine was preferable to international control.[98]

Subsequently, in July 1918, Balfour said in a meeting of the Eastern Committee that 'our object apparently now was to destroy the Sykes-Picot Agreement'. Later, in August of the same year, he told the War Cabinet that the Sykes-Picot Agreement, though 'still remaining as a diplomatic instrument, was historically out of date'.[99] Thus, 'largely through the efforts of one of its signatories', nothing came out of the Sykes-Picot Agreement, and from that point onwards Sykes gave his whole-hearted support to

Zionism. Chaim Weizmann described him as 'one of our greatest finds'.[100]

Did Sykes decide to lend his support to Zionism in order to get rid of the Sykes-Picot Agreement? Or was it the opposite? It is difficult to answer this question, but tempting to assume, at least for the moment, that by promising Palestine to the Jews on 'religious' grounds, Sykes found a way out of the increasingly embarrassing agreement of 1916 that bore his name.

A final observation before we move on to the next point concerns the dearth of material on this subject. One would have expected Leslie Shane's book, *Mark Sykes: His Life and Letters,* published in 1923 a few years after Sykes' death, to provide some answers. However, there is almost nothing in the book from Sykes' papers on either the Sykes-Picot Agreement or the Balfour Declaration, for which Sykes was the main protagonist. In fact, there is only one comment on the Balfour Declaration: Until November 1917, he [Sykes] was arranging the preliminaries of the Balfour Declaration. Sokolow wrote 'In the midst of this busy world . . . Zionism maintained its prominent position. Everything had to pass through Sykes' hands'. And on the Sykes-Picot Agreement, this is discussed only in 10 pages in which Shane quotes the official version [which has been provided by the Foreign Office to the author], officially known as 'The Arrangement[101] between Great Britain, France and Russia, Regarding Syria, Mesopotamia and Eastern Asia Minor, commonly known as the Sykes-Picot Agreement, May 1916'. Quoting from this FO correspondence, Shane reveals: 'The Sykes-Picot Agreement may be said to have been made necessary by the long and persistent French claim to Syria. France had taken a sentimental interest in the country from the days of the crusades and the Frank Kingdoms. The Syrian campaign of Napoleon confirmed and added to this interest. From the earliest times France had claimed to be the protector of all Latin Christians in the Ottoman Empire in general and in Syria in particular. Since 1860 France had made the Maronites of Lebanon her particular care. French schools had become numerous in Syria; French capital there sought and found investment; the French language and French culture, it was claimed, had there struck deep roots'.[102]

THE ROAD TO THE BALFOUR DECLARATION

During 1917, the military situation continued to worsen on all fronts for the Allies. In February, Britain faced a food shortage so severe that starvation threatened. A War Cabinet memorandum, based on information from the Ministry of Food, stated on 3 February 1917 that 'the present stock of wheat in the UK is 7,673,001 quarters, or 12.25 weeks' consumption. Of this stock, 6 weeks' supply represents the irreducible minimum required to avoid local famine in view of the difficulties of distribution'. The memorandum went on to state that to import this quantity for current British levels of consumption would require one voyage each from 307 vessels of 25,000 quarters capacity each. 'If these vessels,' the memorandum added, 'were sent to North America, the nearest supply, the round voyage would consume approximately two months . . . '[103]

The situation looked very bleak, and to make matters worse, the Russian Revolution broke out in March of that year, after which Russia ceased to be an effective ally. A British offensive in Palestine (in Gaza) and in Mesopotamia failed. The French and Italian armies sustained heavy losses.[104] Leopold Amery noted that:

> All these setbacks sank into insignificance compared with the appalling loss of shipping resulting from the new German policy of unlimited submarine warfare. Every month the figures rose higher. Over half a million tons of British and neutral shipping were sunk in February 1917, and over 600,000 tons in March, not far off a million in April. At one moment, of every 100 long-distance ships which left these shores, twenty-five failed to return. At that rate we could never have lasted out the year.[105]

Thus, disasters on the Western front made the Eastern front especially crucial.[106] Furthermore, in April 1917, the Imperial War Cabinet Committee on Territorial Desiderata argued that if Palestine and Mesopotamia were under hostile control, they would pose a threat to Britain's Eastward lifeline. The Committee recommended modification of the Sykes-Picot Agreement in order to give Britain outright control over those two lands.[107] Under Lloyd George's instructions, Sir Maurice Hankey, the first Secretary to the recently established War Cabinet, submitted a memorandum on 18 April 1917 reviewing the war situation. He wrote that 'military and political events of tremendous import have occurred with the result that the situation has completely changed'. The Germans had intensified their submarine warfare, 'unhampered by any regard whatsoever to international law or humanitarian considerations'. There was also the entry of the US into the war, and the Russian Revolution to be contended with. Dismissing the likelihood of any military decision, Hankey concluded that 'it would be unwise to expect a decisive victory in 1917'.[108]

This being the situation, the British government took immediate steps towards launching its great offensive in the East. It sought to secure its aims in Palestine through a combination of military, diplomatic, and political pressure.[109] On 25 April 1917, Weizmann met Herbert Samuel. According to the account of Vera Weizmann, Samuel told the Zionist leader that the Sykes-Picot Agreement was unacceptable from the British point of view. He advised Weizmann to see the Foreign Office, and promised to go with him to meet Lloyd George.[110] All through this critical period in the few months preceding the Balfour Declaration, Weizmann received considerable help from Herbert Samuel.[111]

It was also in April of 1917 (when the Sykes-Picot Agreement was still a secret document) that Weizmann was 'urged by British official quarters to go to Egypt, whence he was to go to Palestine with the object of raising world Jewish opinion in favour of some kind of nebulous scheme the full terms of which he himself did not know'.[112] However, despite Foreign Office encouragement, Vera Weizmann asserts that his visit to Palestine did not occur, and instead, 'an interlude which Chaim called "Opera Bouffe *intermezzo*"[113] divided the year at its middle'.[114]

As will be shown, from September 1917, Alfred Milner, a long-time colonial administrator (in Egypt and South Africa) and leading imperialist who was appointed to the War Cabinet as Minister of War in the last seven months of the war, together with Amery took charge of the declaration. Milner and his group of influential men—including Philip Kerr, of the Prime Minister's secretariat and editor of the magazine *The Round Table*—advocated a pro-Zionist policy in the light of Palestine's perceived importance to British imperial-strategic interests.

Sykes, the 'architect of the government's Zionist policy' (as he was described by Mayir Vereté)[115], was supported by William Ormsby-Gore; together they succeeded in converting the War Cabinet Secretariat to the Zionist cause. Balfour, already convinced of the Zionist cause by that time, was pushed forward by such men within his own department as Ronald Graham and Robert Cecil. Jan Smuts[116] was deeply pro-Zionist.[117] Lloyd George himself had for a long time planned to carry out a Zionist programme in Palestine.[118] Those in government who opposed the Zionist programme and at one stage almost brought it to an end—including Edwin Montagu, Secretary of State for India (and anti-Zionist Anglo-Jew) and Lord George Nathaniel Curzon, Foreign Secretary from 1919-1924 and thus member of the War Cabinet—stood little chance in the face of such whole-hearted supporters of Zionism.

Zionists were asked to submit a draft declaration, the first of which was drafted by Harry Sacher on 18 July upon Weizmann's request, and along lines drawn by Balfour and Sykes, but this first draft was too extreme to be accepted by the British government.[119] Thus the months between July and November 1917 witnessed numerous drafts written by Zionists, going back and forth between them and the British governments: these were refused, drafted and redrafted, hopes were raised and dashed, there were War Office objections and threats of postponement, anti-Zionist Jews up in arms, frustrations and threats of resignation by Weizmann, all this alarmed Zionists; it was a long protracted process. Finally, by October 1917, there were three drafts: authored by Rothschild, Balfour, and Milner. Minutes reveal that Montagu objected vehemently to any description of Palestine as the home of the Jewish people. By September, President Wilson's views were sought, and Colonel House's advice to Wilson was that 'there are many dangers lurking in it, and if I were the British, I would be chary about going too definitely into that business'.[120] Wilson advised the British to postpone the Balfour Declaration indefinitely. The declaration seemed to hang by a thread.[121] Until October 1917, Balfour continued to delay and hesitate and did not press for passage. In fact, the British were until 1917 indecisive as to the course they should follow in Palestine. But if the British did not yet have a clear policy, Reinharz asserts, Weizmann did.[122] Weizmann thought that the most dangerous enemies of Zionism were not the government officials he was negotiating with; it was the opposition of anti-Zionist Jews that worried him most.[123] In his last effort to stop the Zionist declaration, Edwin Montagu concluded by saying that the declaration 'would be felt as a cruel blow by the many English Jews who love England'.[124] In the months before Montagu assumed his new role in India, he found himself entangled in one of the most vicious conflicts of his career. Because of this, he became known as the 'renegade Jew who almost single-handedly defeated the Balfour Declaration'. In this bitter conflict, however, Montagu was not alone, and in fact was supported by the majority of the leadership of the Jewish community in England, who were all critics of the idea of a 'Jewish people' in need of a 'homeland' in

Palestine.[125] By the middle of September 1917, Weizmann referred to Montagu and anti-Zionist Jews as the 'dark forces' in English Jewry, and that the declaration was still in limbo due to the opposition of anti-Zionist Jews.[126] Months after Montagu's appointment as Secretary of State for India, Rothschild wrote to Weizmann: 'I said to you in London, as soon as I saw the announcement in the paper of Montagu's appointment, that I was afraid we were done'. At this point, it seemed that the future of Zionism, as well as Weizmann's own future, were at great risk.[127]

In his article 'The Balfour Declaration and Its Maker', Jehuda Reinharz makes the case for Weizmann's pivotal role in the Balfour Declaration. He demonstrates that from 1914-1917, with the exception of a small group of young men and women in Manchester and London—amongst whom was Vladimir Jabotinsky, who years later founded the far right revisionist movement and Zionist paramilitary groups, including the Irgun—Weizmann virtually functioned alone, and 'had little, if any, individual or institutional support'.[128]

Weizmann always knew 'which arguments to use and with whom and he was able to keep the political process on track by appealing to the prime minister when the policy was threatened to be derailed. Even as late as 23 October, when Weizmann heard of yet another postponement by the War Cabinet to announce the Zionist declaration, he was alarmed: 'I shall never in my life forget that day', he wrote to Ahad Ha'am. Reinharz observes that from Ahad Ha'am's letter to Sokolow of 11 July 1917, 'it can be inferred' that the general directions for the formulation of the Zionist draft declaration came from Balfour himself.[129]

Two weeks before the declaration, Edwin Montagu[130] had sailed to India, and it was left to Curzon alone to stand up in opposition.[131]

Nor was securing the declaration the end of Zionist worries about its fate. In 1921, Rothschild cabled from the British Embassy in Washington to Balfour saying: 'Situation very critical Balfour declaration menaced and Zionist cause gravely jeopardized strongly support Weizmann's appeal to you'.[132]

On 2 November, 1917, one month before General Allenby's 'historic' advance in Palestine, the Foreign Office sent a message, signed by AJ Balfour, Foreign Secretary of the British government, to Lord Rothschild, at his home at 148 Piccadilly. The fact that it was sent to his home address is often commented upon, as he didn't have any official standing and normally officials do not get such correspondences to their home addresses. The implication is that the British government didn't know to whom to address this letter and therefore simply chose a distinguished member of the Jewish people and sent the letter in no official capacity to his home address, because they didn't know where else to send it.[133] The letter, which comprises the actual Balfour Declaration read:

Dear Lord Rothschild,

> I have much pleasure in conveying to you, on behalf of his Majesty's Government, the following declaration of sympathy with Jewish Zionist aspirations which has been submitted to, and approved by the Cabinet.
>
> 'His Majesty's Government view with favour the establishment in Palestine of a national home for the Jewish people, and will use their best endeavours to facilitate

the achievement of this object, it being clearly understood that nothing shall be done which may prejudice the civil and religious rights of existing non-Jewish communities in Palestine, or the rights and political status enjoyed by Jews in any other country.'

I should be grateful if you would bring this declaration to the knowledge of the Zionist Federation.[134]

In Britain, the letter reached the general public on 9 November, when it was reproduced in *The Times* as well as in the *Jewish Chronicle* and other national papers.[135] To inform world Jewry, millions of leaflets were dropped from the air on Austrian and German towns, and over areas with high Jewish populations—namely, in the Jewish belt from Poland to the Black Sea.[136]

In Palestine, the letter was not officially read until three years later. When Palestine came under British military control towards the end of 1917, the Military Administration, well aware of the depth of Arab hostility towards Zionist designs in Palestine, withheld its publication for fear of an uprising. It was not until May 1920, during the final days of the British Military Administration in Palestine (known as Occupied Enemy Territory Administration—OETA South) that the text of the declaration was officially read out in Nablus by Sir Louis Bols, third and last of the Chief Military Administrators.[137]

Why did General Edmund Allenby, Commander of the British Egyptian Expeditionary Force, which conquered Palestine from the Turks in late 1917-1918, remain silent on the declaration, censoring all mention of it as he launched his great offensive? The best answer to this question can be derived from Allenby's biographer, General Wavell, who noted that:

> ... with the entry into Palestine and capture of Jerusalem political as well as military problems began to occupy Allenby. Palestine presented some very thorny and difficult questions. The awkwardness of reconciling our pledges to the Arabs, our undertakings to our Allies (the Sykes-Picot Agreement), and the Balfour Declaration to the Zionists was already becoming evident to those who knew of them.
> ... He refused to allow the Balfour Declaration to be published in Palestine.

Wavell also noted that the declaration had been made on the very day the third battle of Gaza[138] was in full swing, adding that 'few realized its significance or danger at the time'.[139]

Other officials on the spot held similar views. Sir Gilbert Clayton, chief political officer to Allenby, and later Chief Secretary in Palestine (1922-25), wrote to Sykes one month after the issuance of the Balfour Declaration, suggesting that it might have been a mistake: 'I am not fully aware of the weight which Zionists carry, especially in America and Russia, and of the consequent necessity of giving them everything for which they may ask'.[140]

A few years later, JMN Jeffries, the *Daily Mail* correspondent who was sent to Palestine to report on the situation there, wrote on 10 January 1923, quoting from a Zionist report, that: 'Naturally anxious to avoid any friction which might hinder the freedom of further military operations, they preferred to abstain from any mention of the fact that the British Government had promised to support Zionist aspirations'. Jeffries here poses a question: 'Now what does that mean, put into plain English? It means that the British Government has issued a Declaration so high-handed, unwarranted and dangerous that it was an impediment to the progress of the British Army, it had to be suppressed', and continued: 'has any British Government before been censored by its own forces in the field, as if its pronouncements had been written by the enemy?. . . . It is a strange Magna Charta [sic] which cannot be published in Runnymede.'[141]

Balfour's motives for supporting the pro-Zionist declaration remain unclear.[142] The influx of Jews from Russia and Romania to Britain during the early 1880s caused the British government to introduce the Aliens Bill of 1904 and the Aliens Act of 1905 to control unrestricted immigration. The 1904 Aliens Bill was based on the recommendations of a Royal Commission,[143] appointed in March 1902. The Bill recommended, *inter alia,* that an alien arriving in Britain might be required to furnish a certificate with respect to their character and antecedents, that 'undesirables' might be refused permission of entry, that power should be given to the Secretary of State to exclude criminals, and that the residence of aliens in a 'prohibited area' might either be prohibited or regulated.[144]

The Bill was heavily attacked by the leaders of Anglo-Jewry. It was also the first instance in which Winston Churchill, a Conservative MP (who years later became Prime Minister), participated in a public debate opposing the Bill, on the grounds that it was contrary to Britain's traditions to shut its doors against unfortunates who had fled there. Eventually the Bill was modified, and replaced by the

Aliens Act of 1905 under Prime Minister AJ Balfour. However, this, too, was received by the Jews of England with deep resentment.[145] Although the Aliens Act of 1905 was considered by its opponents as an improvement upon its predecessor, it was attacked on numerous grounds, such as that it did not make any exception in the case of victims of religious persecution, that persons refused permission to land had no right of appeal to the ordinary courts of law, and that the Act enabled the expulsion of persons on 'trivial' grounds. It was also criticised for placing the cost of returning those aliens who subsequently had to be expelled on shipping companies, which was bound to affect the traffic in immigration.[146]

But Balfour's name had been inextricably linked to the unpopular Act. At the time, Balfour was bitterly attacked by the *Jewish Chronicle*, as well as in the Seventh Zionist Congress, and was charged with 'open anti-semitism against the whole Jewish people'.[147] Twelve years later, the same Balfour was to endorse the Zionist cause with his 'Balfour Declaration'. It has been suggested that he may have been driven by a desire to 'correct' his previous deeds and to annul the radioactive label of 'anti-Semite' that had attached to him. Though it would be useful to gain insight into this issue, our sources do not reveal more.

THE AFTERMATH OF THE BALFOUR DECLARATION

As already mentioned, following General Allenby's entry into Palestine in December 1917, and as the war ended and Britain had conquered Palestine, a British military administration was set up in Palestine, known as Occupied Enemy Territory Administration (OETA), under Allenby's command, which was later extended to the whole country and lasted from 1918 till July 1920. Seeing the volatility of announcing the Balfour Declaration at a critical military moment, the military authorities banned all mention of it for fear of an uprising.

In January 1918, and in the immediate aftermath of the Balfour Declaration, Sykes tried to influence Arab leaders to moderate their views towards Zionism and invited Weizmann to meetings in Damascus and Haifa with Arab leaders from Palestine, Syria, and Beirut.[148] While British military operations were still in full progress, and while the northern half of Palestine was still in Turkish hands, Mark Sykes, at the Foreign Office, informed Reginald Wingate, the High Commissioner of Egypt, that a Zionist Commission had been created and would soon be despatched to Palestine. It was to be headed by Chaim Weizmann under the charge of William Ormsby-Gore, who was attached to the Commission as Political Officer. Its object was to pave the way for the carrying out of the Balfour Declaration.[149] Ormsby-Gore had served in the Arab Bureau in Cairo in 1916-1917 and held that 'Mark Sykes was the chief motive force in London behind the British Government's Near East policy in the war . . . .'[150]

After the war had ended in the summer of 1918, Syrian Arab nationalists resident in Cairo strongly protested the division of Arab territory and demanded a clarification of recent pronouncements in favour of self-determination made in speeches by British Prime Minister Lloyd George and US President Wilson. Politicians in London tried to reconcile their previous contradictory promises, and the matter was passed to Sykes, who sent a 'carefully worded' reply. The Sykes-Picot Agreement was now, for all practical purposes, a dead document.

Towards the end of June, Sykes and Picot met in order to review the whole situation in light of recent developments. Sykes tried to impress upon Picot that the agreement should be modified as it contradicted the principle of self-determination, but Picot was adamant that it could not be abolished. The Foreign Office decided that Allenby should be consulted as to the question of a French administration in Syria, but it was finally decided that Syria should be handed over to the French.[151]

As noted, tension was rising throughout the region. In Palestine, the Military Administration upheld the announcement of the Balfour Declaration, for fear of an uprising. However, the aggressive policy of the Zionist Commission, which demanded immediate measures to be taken by the administration in favour of establishing a 'national home' for the Jews, brought it into direct conflict with the Military Administration.[152] Sykes' policy of ambiguity and deceit over the last two years was now bearing a bitter harvest. Even Sykes himself, who visited Palestine in September 1918, was showing signs of growing anxiety over the situation. In dismay, he telegraphed Ormsby-Gore in London, saying 'Non-Jews want to know whether Zionist objective is an independent Jewish State'. At the Foreign Office, Arnold Toynbee, who was in the Political Intelligence Department, commented on this telegram on the 2nd of December:

> . . . surely our foundation should be a *Palestinian* State with *Palestinian citizenship* for all inhabitants, whether Jewish or non-Jewish. This alone seems consistent with

Mr. Balfour's letter. Hebrew might be made an official language, but the Jewish element should not be allowed to form a state within the state, enjoying greater privileges than the rest of the population'.[153]

From the scanty material that is available, there is evidence to suggest that Sykes did indeed change his views on Zionism towards the end of his life. His biographer Leslie Shane wrote a few years later, that Sykes, 'From being the evangelist of Zionism during the war he had returned to Paris with feelings shocked by the intense bitterness which had been provoked in the Holy Land. Matters had reached a stage beyond his conception of what Zionism would be. His last journey to Palestine had raised many doubts, which were not set at rest by a visit to Rome'. Shane adds: 'To Cardinal Gasquet[154] he admitted the change of his views on Zionism, and that he was determined to qualify, guide and, if possible, save the dangerous situation which was rapidly arising'. Shane concludes that 'If death had not been upon him it would not have been too late'.[155]

One year later, towards the end of January 1919, after a disappointing trip to Syria in which he tried unsuccessfully to bring Arab leaders to meet Picot, Sykes arrived at the Paris Peace Conference an exhausted and defeated man. Discredited by his wartime policy, none of the attendees would listen him. He contracted influenza on 11 February and then died five days later at age 39. Lloyd George noted that Sykes had no 'reserves of energy' and was exhausted and anxious, and that that was the cause of his death. Lloyd George later blamed himself for Sykes' death and was quoted as saying:

He was responsible for the agreement which is causing us all the trouble with the French ... Sykes saw the difficulties in which he had placed us, and was very worried in consequence. I said something to him about the agreement, and at once saw how I had cut him. I am sorry. I wish I had said nothing. I blame myself ... [156]

THE PARIS PEACE CONFERENCE OF 1919 AND THE KING-CRANE COMMISSION

At the end of World War I, after the armistices were signed in 1918, the Paris Peace Conference was held in 1919 for the victorious Allied Powers to set peace terms for the defeated Central Powers. During the conference, the American, British, French and Italian governments agreed to send an international commission called the King-Crane Commission to ascertain the wishes of the Near East peoples. After British, French, and Italian refusal to participate, the American team, composed of Henry Churchill King, the Christian higher education reformer and President of Oberlin College, and Charles Crane, a wealthy American businessman, foreign policy entrepreneur, and Democratic Party supporter, proceeded to the Near East as an exclusively American Commission on behalf of President Wilson. The commission toured Syria and Palestine from June to August 1919 and met with representative delegations everywhere they went, after which they submitted their report to the League of Nations on 28 August 1919.

Though a comprehensive treatment of the subject is beyond the scope of this book, the conclusions and recommendations of the

King-Crane Commission, which were submitted to the Paris Peace Conference on 28 August 1919, were ignored. Instead, in April 1920, Britain and France agreed in San Remo that Britain would receive the Palestine Mandate, therefore implementing the Balfour Declaration, which was later endorsed by the League of Nations in July 1922. The consequences of this wartime strategy still haunt the Middle East today.[157]

Nevertheless, these recommendations are sufficiently important to require some consideration here. The report recommended 'Serious modification of the extreme Zionist Program for Palestine of unlimited immigration of Jews, looking finally to making Palestine distinctly a Jewish State'. It also reported that 'definite encouragement had been given to the Zionists by the Allies in Mr. Balfour's often quoted statement', adding that 'it can hardly be doubted that the extreme Zionist Program must be greatly modified'. They concluded that, '. . . a national home for the Jewish people is not equivalent to making Palestine into a Jewish State; nor can the erection of such a Jewish State be accomplished without the gravest trespass upon the civil and religious rights of existing non-Jewish communities in Palestine'.[158] Furthermore, the Commission noted, their repeated conference with Jewish representatives indicated that 'the Zionists looked forward to a practically complete dispossession of the present non-Jewish inhabitants of Palestine by various forms of purchase'. The report concluded that 'the non-Jewish population of Palestine—nearly nine tenths of the whole—are emphatically against the entire Zionist program. . . . To subject a people so minded to unlimited

Jewish immigration, and to steady financial and social pressure to surrender the land, would be a gross violation of the principle just quoted, and of the people's rights'. The Commission thus pleaded with the Peace Conference:

> ... not to shut its eyes to the fact that anti-Zionist feeling in Palestine and Syria is intense and not lightly to be flouted. No British officer, consulted by the Commissioners, believed that the Zionist program could be carried out except by force of arms ... That of itself is evidence of a strong sense of the injustice of the Zionist program, on the part of the non-Jewish populations of Palestine and Syria.[159]

The Commission also challenged the 'initial claim' submitted by Zionist representatives that Jews have a 'right to Palestine based on an occupation of two thousand years ago' as a claim that 'can hardly be seriously considered'. In view of the above considerations, and 'with a deep sense of sympathy for the Jewish cause', the Commissioners recommended that 'only a greatly reduced Zionist program be attempted by the Peace Conference, and even that, only very gradually initiated ... and that the project for making Palestine distinctly a Jewish commonwealth should be given up.' The King-Crane Commission saw 'no reason why Palestine could not be included in a united Syrian State'[160] and recommended placing the whole country [i.e., Syria and Palestine] under one single mandate. The Commission also proposed a constitutional monarchy with Faisal as ruler. In spite of these findings, or more likely because of them, the British government refused to publish the report and it remained secret until 1922, when parts of it were published.[161]

The significance of the King-Crane Commission is that it was the only international body to ascertain the wishes of the local inhabitants when the future of the Near East was being discussed at the Peace Conference. However, nothing came of the King-Crane Commission, its only significance being eventually that of a historical document for the use of future researchers.

In fact, the fate of Palestine seems to have been decided before the King-Crane Commission embarked on its trip to the Near East. About two weeks earlier, on 11 August 1919, Balfour had stated that the four Great Powers were committed to Zionism, and that 'Zionism, be it right or wrong, good or bad, is rooted in age-long traditions, in present needs, in future hopes, of far profounder import than the desires and prejudices of the 700,000 Arabs who now inhabit that ancient land'.[162] Indeed, Balfour had other plans concerning the future of Palestine. In a secret memorandum to the British cabinet, *Respecting Syria, Palestine and Mesopotamia,* he made it flagrantly clear that consulting the wishes of the inhabitants was definitely not on his agenda in 1919:

> Take Syria first. Do we mean, in the case of Syria, to consult principally the wishes of the inhabitants? We mean nothing of the kind . . . So whatever the inhabitants may wish, it is France they will certainly have. They may freely choose; but it is Hobson's choice after all . . . The contradiction between the letter of the Covenant and the policy of the Allies is even more flagrant in the case of the 'independent

nation' of Palestine . . . For in Palestine we do not propose even to go through the form for consulting the wishes of the present inhabitants of the country.[163]

With the backdrop of President Wilson's principle on self-determination, it was decided by Balfour and Brandeis, that 'numerical self-determination' was to be 'excluded'[164] It was furthermore, through political control that the numerical Arab majority could be challenged 'in the shortest possible time'.[165] Self-determination was to become operative in Palestine only after the Jews had become the majority.[166]

Beyond the issue of the specific political arrangement in Palestine remained the unresolved question of Franco-British rivalry for influence in the region. In March 1919, when Britain finally decided to hand over the mandate over Syria to the French, France had yet to acknowledge British influence in Palestine. Still continuing to call for an 'integral Syria', French agents, exploiting anti-Zionist feeling in Palestine, organised an anti-British anti-Zionist propaganda campaign which proved effective. At this point, the Zionists had not yet come to any agreement with the French, and needless to say, the idea of an 'integral Syria' under French control would have blocked the Zionist plans, for the French did not have it on their agenda to set up a 'national home' for the Jews in Palestine (the Sykes-Picot Agreement would have overruled this possibility too). Nevertheless, in the end, the French were prepared to overlook the Sykes-Picot Agreement in return for British recognition of French supremacy in Syria.[167]

THE SHORT-LIVED UNITED SYRIA AND THE ESTABLISHMENT OF THE BRITISH CIVIL ADMINISTRATION IN PALESTINE

In March 1920, Faisal, Sharif Hussein's son, was proclaimed by the Syrian Congress King of a united Syria, including Palestine. However, his kingdom was short-lived, and it was only three months later that the French forces were allowed by the British to occupy Syria and oust King Faisal.

In Palestine, to replace military rule, the British established a Civil Administration in July 1920 that was entrusted with carrying out the Balfour Declaration's promise of a 'Jewish national home.' In appointing Herbert Samuel—who had helped the Zionists secure the Balfour Declaration and had represented them at the Paris Peace Conference in July 1919 alongside the Zionist leader Chaim Weizmann[168]—Prime Minister Lloyd George 'deliberately' had chosen as high commissioner a Zionist sympathizer who 'would try to make a success of the Zionist programme'. The end of the military administration and the choice of Herbert Samuel to head the civil administration in Palestine in 1920 was a Zionist triumph, for Samuel's extreme Zionist interpretations of the Balfour Declaration tipped the scale towards the Zionists, at a time when the Balfour Declaration itself was considered an experiment, the results of which were to be determined with the passage of time.

In this respect, it is interesting to mention that Lord Milner, one of the strongest advocates of the Balfour Declaration, gave a Palestinian Arab delegation that met him in April 1922 confidential assurances to the effect that the national home policy was no more than an experiment:

> If practical experience will show it to be impossible, there will be no escape from altering the policy. I consider the entry of Jews into Palestine an experiment, and if they do not succeed and failure follows I shall recognize that a mistake has been made.[169]

Major General Bols, the last of the three British military administrators in Palestine, reported how the news of Samuel's appointment as first High Commissioner in Palestine was received: 'Consternation, despondency, and exasperation express the feelings of the Moslem Christian population ... They are convinced that he will be a partisan Zionist and that he represents a Jewish and not a British government'.[170] By contrast, the British army, which had remained in Palestine as a security force after the establishment of the Civil Administration in July 1920, was openly anti-Zionist. In fact, the extent of the military administration's hostility to the Zionist programme in Palestine and the growing irritation of the military administration to the Zionist Commission prompted the exiting Bols to complain that the tone of Zionist letters were 'peremptory and dictatorial, and such as no Administration could be expected to tolerate'.[171] On the last day of the military administration, Bols, about to leave, half-jokingly made Herbert Samuel sign a receipt.[172]

Herbert Samuel, the newly appointed High Commissioner in Palestine, realised that recognising Faisal as king of a united Syria 'would tend to take life out of Zionist movement' and was instrumental in the British decision to oust him.[173]

In the end, the French were prepared to overlook the Sykes-Picot Agreement in return for a British recognition of French supremacy in Syria.[174]

DRAFTING OF THE BRITISH MANDATE FOR PALESTINE

Throughout its two-and-a-half years of existence, the OETA was guided by two main objectives: the preservation of the status quo, and the prohibition of any agreement for the transfer of immovable property until the land registries were re-established. Allenby saw to it that fulfillment of promises in the Balfour Declaration could only be fully addressed after the conclusion of peace with Turkey, and he therefore sought to apply 'rigorously' the principles of military law in regard to occupied enemy territory, the main objective being the maintenance of order and the treatment of all sections of the community with complete impartiality. This ran counter to Zionist aims, and their leaders quickly perceived the military administration as an obstacle to their extreme programme and sought its replacement by a more friendly administration. As it was becoming increasingly evident to Western leaders that a peace deal with Turkey would not be signed in the near future, the Allies decided at the San Remo Conference in April 1920 that in the Arabic-speaking part of the Ottoman Empire, they would 'implement the provisions of such a treaty as they envisage', although this action, it can be argued, was highly illegal.[175]

It was thus decided in San Remo that a civil administration would replace the military one, and Lloyd George chose Herbert Samuel, a Zionist Jew, to head the new civil administration, although other options had been considered. However, both Allenby and Bols questioned the wisdom of appointing a Zionist Jew to head the first civil administration, causing Lord Curzon to ask Samuel (on 12 May 1920) to reconsider accepting the post. The legal and political ambiguities created by the Balfour Declaration and attempts to embody its substance in the Mandate for Palestine left a good deal of room for political interpretation. Thus, until the Mandate came into force in September 1923, there were disputes as to how, and if, pledges in the Balfour Declaration could be accommodated with other commitments made by the British government to the Arab people of Palestine. The early 1920s, therefore witnessed a political struggle between, on the one hand, the Zionists and their supporters who sought to incorporate the most extreme interpretation of the Balfour Declaration, and the Palestine Arab political leadership and their British supporters, on the other, who sought to prevent the Declaration being included in the Mandate at all.[176] In this context, the minute of December 1922 by William Ormsby-Gore (who was to become Colonial Secretary 1936-38) can be seen in this light to have contributed in no small measure in winning to the Zionist cause the most extreme interpretation of the Declaration. In 1937, it was none other than Ormsby-Gore, Lord Harlech, representing the British government at a meeting of the LON Permanent Mandates Commission, who stated that partition 'transformed the Balfour Declaration from a declaration regarding the beginning of a policy into a policy of which they could see the end, namely the establishment of an independent sovereign Jewish State', and that, Ormsby-Gore added: 'certainly, was the conception in Lord Balfour's mind.'[177]

It is important to bear in mind that when the Mandate draft was circulated to the Foreign Office for comment in March 1920, Lord Curzon, the Foreign Secretary, commented that the phrase 'development of self governing Commonwealth' was 'surely most dangerous'. And that it was a 'euphemism for a Jewish State, the very thing they accepted and we disallow', subsequently adding in another minute, 'I at any rate cannot accept it'. When the term 'self-governing institutions' was adopted in the draft Mandate to replace 'self-governing Commonwealth', Curzon wrote on 20 March 1920:

> It all turns on what we mean. The Zionists are after a Jewish State with the Arabs as hewers of wood and drawers of water. So are many British sympathisers with the Zionists ... That is not my view. I want the Arabs to have a chance and I don't want a Hebrew State.[178]

Curzon admitted that he had not been consulted as to the Mandate at an earlier stage, and that he greatly disliked the idea that the draft was continually shown to the Zionists,[179] adding, 'It is quite clear that this mandate has been drawn up by someone reeling under the fumes of Zionism. If we are to submit to that intoxicant, this draft is all right. Perhaps there is no alternative'.[180]

The following short exchanges will give a glimpse not only to the nature and extent of such complications, but also to the scale of pressure that Zionist leaders, Weizmann in particular, still had to exercise in this diplomatic context. In 1920, when the draft Mandate for Palestine was still under discussion between the British and French governments, the French raised territorial claims in the north (based as they were on the Sykes-Picot Agreement), which Zionists pointed out would deprive the national home of water resources, a possibility that brought Zionists to a heightened state of alarm.[181]

On 24 September, 1920, Weizmann sent the following letter to Lord Balfour:

> My dear Balfour, I venture to trouble you with a request to be so kind and grant me a short interview. The question of the Mandate for Palestine and also the negotiations about the frontiers are in a rather precarious state at present and unless a decisive change is brought about there is a serious danger that the National Home may be crippled economically almost beyond redemption. If it is at all possible for you to give me a few minutes I would be extremely grateful, as I feel very perturbed about the position. . . . .[182]

Balfour obliged. A few days later, he wrote to the Permanent Under-Secretary at the Foreign Office, Sir Charles Hardinge[183] on 29 September 1920, saying that he believed Curzon was still on holiday, and that 'I am unwilling to bother him, so I turn to you'. Balfour enclosed Weizmann's above-mentioned letter, and went on to say:

> . . . Our Jewish friends, who are not always easy to deal with, sometimes get dreadfully perturbed over matters of comparatively small moment. But the question of frontiers is really vital, because it affects the economic possibilities of developing Palestine, and on these economic possibilities depend the success or failure of Zionism. That

experiment is, in any case a bold and rather hazardous one, though in my opinion, well worth attempting. . . .

He then added a handwritten note at the end of the letter: 'Can you give me any indication of what is going on?'[184]

The above examples just give a glimpse of the precarious nature of the Palestine Mandate in those early years. Successive British governments varied in their enthusiasm for the Zionist project, and indeed, until September 1923, when the Palestine Mandate was finally conferred on Britain, there was no *fait accompli* as to Palestine's future, and a different outcome was unquestionably conceivable. Britain's policy in Palestine had never seemed less firm than during the first half of 1923, when the government appeared preoccupied with delving into its very foundations.[185]

THE MIDDLE EAST DEPARTMENT IN LONDON

During 1915-16, Sykes, like many other observers, had recognized the lack of coordination in British policy towards the Near East. Decisions were taken in London, Cairo, Aden, Basra, and New Delhi with little direct contact between the concerned civil servants and policy makers. Much work was duplicated, while the big questions that could not be dealt with from one place were ignored.[186] From April to June 1917, Sykes was in Egypt. On 15 April 1917, he wrote from Rome the following revealing observations: 'The complexities of my work are to me appalling—just look—

Anglo-India v. Anglo-Egypt
Latins v. Greeks

Army v. civilians
French v. British
French v. Italians
Christians v. Moslems
Jews v. Christians
Arabs v. Arabs
Syrians v. Hejaz'.
Plus, the War Cabinet and the F.O.[187]

A few years later, the Middle East Department of the Colonial Office was created in February 1921 at the initiative of Winston Churchill, who had just become Colonial Secretary, to take over responsibility for the Arabic-speaking areas that came under British rule at the end of World War I. As such responsibility had previously been divided between the Foreign Office (Palestine, Egypt, the Hijaz, and Aden) and the India Office (Mesopotamia and Arabia), a single department in the Colonial Office represented a considerable advance from an administrative standpoint. Churchill saw, as had Sykes before him, that Britain's Middle East policy was rendered incoherent by the different government departments running their own separate territories and operations. It was thus decided at the instigation of Churchill on 31 December 1920 to set up a special Middle East Department within the Colonial Office to be in charge of the mandated territories.[188] For Palestine, however, transfer from the aegis of the Foreign Office to the Colonial Office had political ramifications: Whereas the Foreign Secretary, Lord Curzon, was the sole member of Lloyd George's cabinet who had extremely strong reservations about the Jewish national home policy and had fought strenuously to apply the most restrictive interpretation of the term,[189] Churchill was an unwavering supporter of Zionism. Despite Curzon's misgivings, the Balfour Declaration had been endorsed at the San Remo conference of April 1920 and figured in the August 1920 Treaty of Sèvres formally entrusting to Britain the Mandate for Palestine—which awaited ratification by the League of Nations. The Declaration was further incorporated into the writ of the Mandate, successive drafts of which were still, at the time of the department's creation, undergoing revision.

With regard to Palestine, the Middle East Department's task was to oversee and carry out Britain's policy there, acting as the link between the policymakers in London and the Civil Administration in Palestine.

In contrast to the civil administration in Palestine, where the three most important positions were held by avowed Zionists,[190] the Middle East Department was staffed by traditional career civil servants drawn from various government offices. To head the new department, Churchill brought Sir John Evelyn Shuckburgh from the India Office, where he had served for 24 years. Hubert Young, an Arabist and Middle East expert from the Foreign Office's Eastern Department who had served with TE Lawrence, was officially joint assistant secretary but in effect the 'second in command', and Lawrence himself joined the department as political advisor. Others came from the Treasury, the War Office, the Mesopotamian section of the India Office, and the Foreign Office.[191] Of the senior staff, only Colonel Richard Meinertzhagen, the military advisor, was a declared Zionist.[192] As for Shuckburgh, he was no Zionist but from the beginning was driven by the conviction that Britain was duty-bound to uphold the Balfour policy, whilst insisting that this would not lead to a Jewish state.

More evidence of what was in store for Palestine can be derived from an intriguing conversation that is said to have taken place in Mr. Balfour's house, two years later, on 22 July 1921. Present were Lloyd George, Arthur Balfour, Winston Churchill, Maurice Hankey, Edward Russell and Chaim Weizmann. Weizmann is said to have asked Churchill: 'If you do the same thing in Palestine [i.e. introduce self-government] it means giving up Palestine, and that is what I want to know.' To this Lloyd George remarked: 'You mustn't give representative government to Palestine'; whereas Churchill answered that he 'might have to bring it before the Cabinet'. Churchill added that enormous difficulties had arisen owing to the Balfour Declaration, 'which was opposed by the Arabs, nine tenths of the British officials on the spot, and some Jews in Palestine'.[193]

THE 1921 JAFFA RIOTS AND THE FIRST ARAB DELEGATION TO LONDON

Despite the Lloyd George government's firm embrace of the Balfour Declaration as official policy, the first years of British rule in Palestine were marked by a degree of uncertainty. The intense Jaffa riots of May 1921, after a year of calm, shocked the civil authorities and showed the extent to which the Arabs were unreconciled to the "Jewish national home" called for in the Balfour Declaration. In the wake of the riots and encouraged by an important speech by Samuel on 3 June 1921 asserting that the Balfour Declaration did not mean that Palestine would be taken away from Palestine's Arabs and 'given to strangers', an Arab Delegation proceeded to London in the hope of bringing about a change of policy. They spent months there trying fruitlessly to change the views of the Colonial Office while Shuckburgh directed that they should not be given any hope for change. Even before the delegation arrived, Shuckburgh had spelled out, in a memorandum dated August 1921, the line that was to be taken. The Arabs 'must accept as the basis of all discussion' that it was the 'fixed intention' of the British government to fulfill its pledges in the matter of the establishment of a national home for the Jews.[194] In an exhaustive draft statement dated 7 November 1921, Shuckburgh asserted that since the Arabs failed to realize that abandonment of the Balfour Declaration was 'out of the question' any discussion with them in London was 'a mere waste of time.' He noted that the government was 'deeply pledged to the Zionists and have always made it clear to the Arabs that there is no prospect of our wavering on this point'.[195] Likewise Churchill told the Arab delegation in the summer of 1921:[196]

> The British government mean to carry out the Balfour Declaration. I have told you so again and again. I have told you so at Jerusalem. I told you so at the House of Commons the other day. I tell you so now. They mean to carry out the Balfour Declaration. They do.[197]

RISING DOMESTIC OPPOSITION AND THE WHITE PAPER OF 1922

The British press, initially favorable to the Jewish national home policy, had by the early 1920s become increasingly skeptical if not hostile, and a movement opposed to the Balfour Declaration was gaining ground within parliament. For example, in 1922, *The Times* (London) published a series of articles attacking Britain's involvement in Palestine, mainly from the taxpayer's viewpoint, and concluded that although it was an 'interesting experiment', the question was whether Britain could afford it.[198]

Faced with the first outbreaks of violence in 1919 and 1921 against Zionist policy and rising domestic opposition, the British government was cornered into explaining what the Balfour Declaration meant. Moreover, the inherent ambiguities allowed British officials throughout the first half of the 1920s to interpret the commitments given in the Declaration in different ways. Herbert Samuel made the first public attempt to interpret the Declaration in a speech on 3 June 1921 in which he claimed that there was an 'unhappy misunderstanding' about the Declaration, and that it did not mean that the country would be taken away from its Arab owners, and given to Jews.

The 1922 Statement of Policy, issued on 3 June and known as Churchill's White Paper, was the first official and written attempt by any British government to interpret the Balfour Declaration. Samuel had been instrumental in drawing up the policy. This was certainly an additional powerful tool in the hands of the Zionists, who effectively used this text as an argument to further their most extreme interpretation of the Balfour Declaration. However, the White Paper asserted that the British government 'did not contemplate the subordination or disappearance of the Arab population, language or culture', but it went a step further than the Declaration by asserting that Jews were in Palestine 'as of right and not on sufferance'. Thus, the White Paper confirmed the inherent ambiguity and ambivalence of the Balfour Declaration, as it did not resolve the question of how the Jews could be in Palestine by right without infringing on the rights of the local inhabitants. The 1922 White Paper clarified that 'Phrases have been used such as that Palestine is to become "as Jewish as England is English." His Majesty's Government regard any such expectation as impracticable and have no such aim in view. They would draw attention to the fact that the terms of the Declaration referred to do not contemplate that Palestine as a whole should be converted into a Jewish National Home, but that such a Home should be founded "in Palestine."'[199]

Equally important, this statement of policy served as a palliative to the British parliament itself, and it was meant to pave the way, on the international level, for the ratification of the Mandate by the League of Nations. For it was only after the consent of the British parliament that the League of Nations could ratify the British Mandate in Palestine. This statement of policy, moreover, guided the British government until 1929, when Palestine witnessed another eruption of violence against Jewish immigration.[200] Since 1917, at the same time as Zionists were demanding a Jewish state, they asserted that a Jewish state 'was never part of the Zionist programme'. Influenced by such statements, the War Cabinet of 1917 was officially advised by Mark Sykes that in asking for a 'national home', the Zionists were not seeking a 'Jewish republic'. Christopher Sykes comments that 'they were in fact seeking just that, is clear to-day', adding, 'The unpleasant truth must be faced that the Zionists in London in 1917 were undoubtedly guilty of double-dealing. For every utterance of a Sokolov or a Leon Simon that the Zionists had no ambitions for a State, there were contrary assertions, usually addressed to Jews'.[201] In trying to find reasons for these extraordinary Zionist contradictions, Sykes states that 'It was that they were engaged on a venture without precedent in recorded history, and in consequence neither they nor their friends could have any idea at all what immediate (as opposed to ultimate) goal they were making for'.[202]

In June 1922, a motion was introduced in the House of Lords declaring that the Mandate for Palestine, which incorporated the Balfour Declaration, was 'unacceptable'. Although 60 peers voted for the motion, and 25 against, it was a non-binding motion, and Churchill, Colonial Secretary at the time, succeeded in reversing its effect when he convinced the House of Commons that he had cut the cost of maintaining Palestine from £8 million in 1920 to £4 million in 1921, and to an estimated £2 million in 1922.[203] With Commons voting in favour of the policy, the way was open for the League of Nations to formally approve Britain's Mandate for Palestine on 24 July that same year, 1922.

Although the House of Lords motion was unsuccessful, it had one important effect, for it focused attention on the Jewish question, and the Colonial Office was asked to explain the government's policy and intentions regarding Zionism and the policy to be adopted in Palestine.

When, against this background, a Conservative government came to power at the end of 1922, there seemed a real possibility that the pro-Zionist policy could be reversed, and a spate of government inquiries into that policy continued well into 1923. Adding to this pressure, a second Arab Delegation arrived in London on 24 December 1922. They made it their mission to meet representatives of many major newspapers and distribute copies of the Hussein-McMahon correspondence, hoping to raise questions about the course of British policy in Palestine. The publication in the British press in early 1923 of parts of the second correspondence, provided by the second Arab Delegation, revived precisely the kind of scrutiny the Middle East Department had tried so assiduously to avoid.

Not long after the new government took office, Shuckburgh, anticipating new inquiries, took it upon himself to look into the origins of the Balfour Declaration. Subsequently and adding fuel to the fire, the Duke of Devonshire demanded the cabinet undertake a more far-reaching and explicit inquiry focusing on three important questions:

1. 'Is there anything in the British Government's pledges to the Arabs that precludes effect being given to the Balfour Declaration in favour of setting up a National Home for the Jews in Palestine?'

2. 'If the answer is in the negative, are we to continue the policy of the late Government in giving effect to the Balfour Declaration on the lines laid down in the White Paper of June 1922?'
3. 'If not, what alternative policy are we to adopt?'[204]

These questions and the flurry of communication they produced is the focus of Chapter Two.

II. OFFICIAL BRITISH ACCOUNT OF EVENTS LEADING UP TO THE BALFOUR DECLARATION AS RENDERED IN THE 1922-1923 INQUIRIES

THORNY QUESTIONS AND A DEARTH OF OFFICIAL RECORDS TO ANSWER THEM

During this time—from the fall of the Liberal government of Lloyd George (who was deeply committed to the pro-Zionist policy) in October 1922, the overwhelming electoral victory of the Conservatives the following month and the subsequent formation of a new Conservative government, through July of the following year, when the future of Britain's involvement on Palestine was finally decided by a high-powered Cabinet committee—the Middle East Department, and particularly Shuckburgh, directed a steady stream of communiqués at the new Colonial Secretary, the Duke of Devonshire. Unlike his predecessor, Churchill, the Duke of Devonshire lacked firm convictions on the subject of Palestine. Two messages in particular were driven home repeatedly: (1) that if Britain failed to honor its pledge, 'We certainly should stand convicted of an act of perfidy from which it is hardly too much to say that our name would never recover', and (2) that the 'real alternative' facing the government was between 'complete evacuation or continuing to honor the Zionist pledge'.

The internal minutes and memoranda[1] reveal that as the Colonial Office set out to answer these questions, it faced some thorny issues that it would have preferred not to discuss at all, such as the McMahon pledge to Sharif Hussein in 1915 and the Allenby Proclamation of 1918 (known also as the Anglo-French Declaration of November 1918). Nevertheless, after some investigation, the Colonial Office eventually concluded that there was 'nothing' in those previous pledges to prevent the 'national home' policy from being executed, since 'nothing' had been promised to the Arabs; and that the policy of the Balfour Declaration—whether justified or not, whether 'wise or unwise'—was to continue despite many warnings of the danger of this policy and its consequences and regardless of the wishes of the vast majority of the population of Palestine. In December 1922, Shuckburgh submitted a memorandum to this effect, entitled *Palestine: The Zionist Policy,* in which he wrote:

> In spite of the protests of the Arabs, who form much the largest part of the population of Palestine, and of repeated criticisms in the Parliament and the press, His Majesty's Government have consistently adhered to the position that they are bound to give effect to the Balfour Declaration and intend to do so . . . whatever may or may not have been our motives, it must always be remembered that the Declaration was made at a time of extreme peril to the cause of the Allies. Our offensive of the previous summer and autumn had failed to achieve any decisive result. Russia had dropped out of the alliance, and the Germans were busy transferring army corps from the Eastern to the Western front in preparation for the grand attack which in the Spring of 1918 was to sweep the British and French

armies into the sea. How narrowly the German attack failed in its object is a matter of history. The point is that, having cried out to the Jews in our moment of agony (that is how they would put it), we cannot throw them when the peril is past ... A Jewish National Home will be founded in Palestine. The Jewish people will be in Palestine as of right and not on sufferance ... [2]

The story and details of the crucial months (April to November) that preceded the final announcement of the Balfour Declaration are the subject of a very substantial literature.[3] It is curious that, although the published material is overwhelming, the actual *official* records in British archives reveal an almost total lack of documented evidence. As the Colonial Office (responsible for Palestine since March 1921) sought to review the entire problem in 1922-23, it 'discovered' that 'very little is recorded', and Ormsby-Gore had to be asked to add what he remembered to the very 'scanty material available'. When Balfour was consulted, the official story asserts that he was unable to help. He had a bad memory, and regretted the death of Mark Sykes, whom, he said, 'had the whole thing at his finger's ends'. From the little material available to him, Shuckburgh was not able to find out what were the 'precise reasons' that led His Majesty's Government to issue such a Declaration. Furthermore, he discovered that the correspondence previous to the declaration was not available in the Colonial Office, although Foreign Office papers were understood to have been lengthy and to have covered a considerable period.[4] This being the case, it is hardly surprising that the Balfour Declaration, in its origins and in its motives, even regarding the identities of those who had a hand in drafting it, remains a controversial issue more than 100 years since its publication.[5]

This belief is further reinforced when we learn that the Colonial Office was not able to find any material of importance relating to this question in the records of the Foreign Office either. Shuckburgh wrote to Ormsby-Gore on 21 December 1922, telling him that the contents of the Foreign Office papers had been found to be disappointing.[6]

The following section attempts to shed fresh light on little-known aspects of the Balfour Declaration from the documents in question.

RECONSTRUCTION FROM MEMORY: HOW THE BALFOUR DECLARATION CAME TO BE

Towards the end of 1922, after Sir John Evelyn Shuckburgh found that very little existed in government files to show conclusively why the government came to its decision regarding the Balfour Declaration, he sought information from all relevant sources available to him in order to reconstruct the history of the negotiations.

On 10 January 1923, Shuckburgh sent a note to William Ormsby-Gore, Under-Secretary of State for the Colonies (Colonial Office), informing him that the records obtained from the Cabinet Secretariat threw no light on the earlier history of the negotiations. He admitted that he feared his own memorandum was 'very inadequate', because the 'material available has not been sufficient to enable [me] to compile a complete and connected narrative'.[7] Nevertheless, Shuckburgh submitted the memorandum 'for what it may be worth as a humble experiment', as he put it, 'in the art of making bricks without straw.'[8]

OFFICIAL BRITISH ACCOUNT OF EVENTS

On the same day, Ormsby-Gore, who had been previously asked to write a memorandum from memory on what he remembered, suggested that both his own handwritten minute from the 24 December 1922 and Shuckburgh's memorandum might be worth printing for distribution to the government. Ormsby-Gore also referred to a War Cabinet Paper[9] (see Appendix B) which, he stated, 'gives a great deal of the information on which the Cabinet came to its decision', adding that he could state as a fact 'that General MacDunagh [sic] as head of the Military Intelligence was one of the chief advocates of the declaration.' Shuckburgh was also certain of MacDonogh's involvement. In the same minute to Ormsby-Gore, he said that he had a 'strong personal recollection that General MacDonogh used to urge the claims of Zionism in the days of the old "Eastern Committee" and its predecessors', but added that, after having searched the records of the Committee, he had been unable to find anything in them to prove his point. Moreover, Shuckburgh added, MacDonogh's name 'did not appear at all in Foreign Office files'.[10]

After hearing these arguments, Devonshire, the Secretary of State for the Colonies, was convinced. 'I think', he wrote on 10 January 1923, that 'the time has come when the attention of the Cabinet should be directed to this aspect of the Palestine question and the best way of doing so will be to circulate the memorandum [of Shuckburgh] and Mr. Ormsby-Gore's minute.'

Here is the full text of this important minute by Ormsby-Gore:

> I think it is very important that the story of the negotiations which led up to the Balfour Declaration of Nov. 2nd 1917 (before General Allenby's first great advance) should be

set out for the Secretary of State and possibly the Cabinet. The F.O. [Foreign Office] and Sir Maurice Hankey both have material. The matter was first broached by the late Sir Mark Sykes early in 1916, and he interviewed Dr. Gaster and Sir Herbert Samuel on his own initiative as a student of Jewish politics in the Near East. Dr. Weizmann was then unknown. Sykes was furthered by General MacDunagh [sic], DMI [Director of Military Intelligence] as all the most useful and helpful intelligence from Palestine (then still occupied by the Turks) was got through and given with zeal by Zionist Jews who were from the first pro-British. Sir Ronald Graham took the matter up keenly from the Russian and East European point of view and early in 1917 important representations came from America. The form of the Declaration and the policy was debated more than once by the War Cabinet, and confidential correspondence (printed by Sir Maurice Hankey as a Cabinet paper) was entered into with leading Jews of different schools of thought. After the declaration, the utmost use was made of it by Lord Northcliffe's propaganda department, and the value of the declaration received remarkable tribute from General Ludendorff. On the strength of it we recruited special battalions of foreign Jews in New York for the British army with the leave of the American government.

The S of S [Secretary of State] should have a statement showing similar declarations by other powers up to and including the recent one of the American Senate, and also a summary of what has been done by the Jews already in Palestine, i.e. 4 millions of money, schools etc. Some of the Zionist organizations [sic] election leaflets were really rather effective. The Balfour Declaration in its final form was actually drafted by Col. Amery and myself. I wrote an article on the question in *The XIXth Century* [a publication at the time] about 2 years ago which has some interesting data.[11]

The second part of the Cabinet Paper that Ormsby-Gore mentions (that was printed by Sir Maurice Hankey) is, in fact, Shuckburgh's four-page memorandum, entitled 'History of the negotiations leading up to the Balfour Declaration'. It covered a period of about six months from April to November 1917 and was compiled from papers obtained from the Foreign Office and the Cabinet Secretariat, since the Middle East Department held no records regarding these negotiations, which had occurred in 1917, long before the Colonial Office had any concern with Palestine. Shuckburgh's memorandum confirms that 'Such papers as it had been possible to obtain are very meagre and do not afford material for anything like a complete statement of the case', adding that 'the following explanation is given in an unofficial note furnished by the Foreign Office for the purposes of this memorandum':

Upon the origins of the Declaration little exists in the way of official records; indeed; little is known of how the policy represented by the Declaration was first given form. Four, or perhaps five men were chiefly concerned in the labour—the Earl of Balfour, the late Sir Mark Sykes, and Messrs. Weizmann and Sokolow, with perhaps Lord Rothschild as a figure in the background. Negotiations seem to have been mainly oral and by means of private notes and memoranda of which only the scantiest records are available, even if more exists.[12]

The Foreign Office's 'unofficial' note added that the official papers of Sir Mark Sykes had been 'unfortunately dispersed', and that 'little referring to the Balfour Declaration has been found among such papers as have been preserved'. The staff of the Middle East Department examined the Foreign Office papers, and, although finding nothing in them relating to the year 1916, were able to reconstruct the following account about the origins of the Balfour Declaration. The earliest document in this narrative was a letter dated 24 April 1917, in which a certain Mr. Hamilton suggested that a Zionist mission should be sent to Russia for propaganda purposes. In the same month, Balfour visited the US on an official mission. A Foreign Office note observed that during Balfour's visit to the US, the policy of the Balfour Declaration as a war measure seemed to have taken 'more definite shape'.

In the following months, Foreign Office papers show that various conversations took place with Dr. Weizmann and other Zionists, and that there was much telegraphic correspondence on the subject with Sir Mark Sykes, who was then in Cairo. He proposed that Weizmann should proceed to Egypt, and that Sokolow and Goldberg[13] should go to Russia for the purpose of attending a Zionist Conference in Petrograd.

On 13 June 1917, an important minute by Sir Ronald Graham[14] was put before the Secretary of State, recording a conversation with

Weizmann in which the latter told Graham there was no doubt now that Germany was about to announce a declaration sympathetic to German Zionists, 'aimed at utilizing them for the purposes of a peace agitation'. Weizmann agreed that German policy was 'calculated to drive a wedge into the Zionist organization, to influence Jewish opinion especially in America and Russia and to utilize it in the interests of German propaganda against the Entente'. Weizmann urged very strongly that it was now desirable for the British government to give an open expression of sympathy with Zionist aims, adding that 'this would only be a confirmation of the opinion which certain of the most eminent members of his Majesty's government had expressed to him and to his colleagues and which had formed the basis of his negotiations throughout the last three years'. Here, the Colonial Office memorandum draws attention to these last words as being significant, for they indicate that 'some form of negotiations' between the Zionists and the British government had been going on since the outbreak of the war. The memorandum then concluded that 'as the official records are silent, it can only be assumed that such discussions as had taken place were of an informal and private character',[15] and that they were mainly conducted by Sir Mark Sykes. Graham, writing this minute to the Secretary of State, agreed that the moment for issuing such a declaration had indeed arrived.

On the basis of all the above, Balfour asked Weizmann to submit a formula for such an assurance, and the Colonial Office memorandum reveals that 'no doubt Dr. Weizmann complied with this request, but the Foreign Office papers do not show how or in what form.' Finally, the memorandum confirms that there is 'little to indicate the stages by which the negotiations subsequently advanced.'[16]

On 21 August 1917, Philip Kerr, private secretary to the Prime Minister, stated in a note to the private secretary of the Foreign Office that an official statement was 'now under consideration' regarding Zionist aims in Palestine. The memorandum went on to say that Kerr's note was written in relation to a letter from the Jewish Congress at Salonica, who had asked that the declaration be addressed to their own congress while it was meeting on 2 September 1917. The answer of the Foreign Office was that the 'Rothschild message should suffice for all purposes.' The memorandum then concluded that 'it is quite clear that much must have been passing behind the scenes to which the official papers give no adequate clue.'

Early in October 1917, further evidence that the Germans were about to issue their own pro-Zionist declaration reached the Foreign Office. A dispatch from the British consul in Bern, on 2 October, gave an account of a meeting held between Herr Richard von Kuhlmann, the German Secretary of State, Jemal Pasha,[17] and a leading Zionist in Berlin. Its object was to discuss the Palestine question. It was believed that some pledges had been given to the German Jews in order to obtain their cooperation for a new war loan, and that the German government had given safe passage to Jews proceeding from Palestine to America. The Foreign Office commented on this by saying, 'we have already heard that the Germans are frightened of our Zionist propaganda'. The question of the German declaration thus came before the War Cabinet on 4 October 1917, and, according to the official minutes, Balfour relied on three arguments when he presented the case to the cabinet. The first was that the Germans were making great efforts to capture the sympathy of the Zionist movement.[18] The second was that the Zionist movement, although opposed by the majority of wealthy British Jews, had the support of many American as well as Russian Jews and possibly in other countries. His third argument was that the movement was based on the 'intense national consciousness' of Jews who had 'a passionate longing to regain once more their ancient national home in Palestine'. In the end, Balfour read a sympathetic declaration by the French government and added that President Wilson was also strongly in favour of such a policy. At this point, Edwin Montagu[19] objected strongly to the government's pro-Zionist policy, and Lord Curzon opposed the declaration on practical grounds. It was therefore decided that before a final decision was taken, the War Cabinet should hear the views of representative Zionist as well as non-Zionist Jews.[20] In the meantime, the draft declaration under consideration was to be referred confidentially to President Wilson, to the heads of the Zionist movement, and to representative persons in Anglo-Jewry opposed to Zionism. On 31 October 1917, according to the official records, the question came before the War Cabinet once more, but it is not clear from those records whether President Wilson's views had been received. The following additional papers were put before the cabinet at this meeting:

> A long memorandum by Lord Curzon on the Future of Palestine, in which he developed his arguments against the policy of converting Palestine into a Jewish State; a paper written about a year before by the late Lord Cromer [see

below]; notes by a number of representative Jewish leaders; seven variants of the proposed draft Declaration.[21]

According to the official minutes, Balfour again stressed the 'diplomatic argument'. It was his view that 'everyone was now agreed that from a purely diplomatic and political point of view it was desirable that some declaration favourable to the aspirations of the Jewish nationalists should now be made', adding that most American and Russian Jewry were favourable to Zionism, and that if such a declaration were made 'we should be able to carry on an extremely useful propaganda both in Russia and America.' In the end, Lord Curzon seems to have been overwhelmed by such powerful arguments and had finally to admit 'the force of the diplomatic arguments in favour of expressing sympathy', recognizing that 'some expression of sympathy with Jewish aspirations would be a valuable adjunct to our propaganda', although still believing that 'we should be guarded in the language used in giving expression to such sympathy.' The memorandum noted that 'The outcome was the famous Balfour Declaration of the 2 November 1917, the actual text of which was drafted by Colonel LS [Leopold] Amery, MP.'[22]

We now turn to a brief examination of the 'additional papers' put before the Cabinet during this meeting, as mentioned above.

Lord Curzon's memorandum

In this secret cabinet memorandum by Lord Curzon, drafted in February 1923 (five years after the fact), it was asserted that 'It is clear that there was some difference of opinion in the War Cabinet itself at the time when the Declaration was framed', adding that Lord Curzon, who, as noted previously was a member of this Cabinet, had written a memorandum on 26 October 1917 in which he laid down 'the following propositions as representing the maximum that could properly be aimed at.' These propositions were:

1. Set up some form of European administration (it cannot be Jewish administration) in Palestine.
2. Devise a machinery for safeguarding and securing order both in the Christian and the Jewish Holy Places.
3. Similarly guarantee the integrity of the Mosque of Omar and vest it in some Moslem body.
4. Secure to the Jews (but not to the Jews alone) equal civil and religious rights with the other elements in the population.
5. Arrange as far as possible for land purchase and settlement of returning Jews.[23]

Views of Lord Cromer

Evelyn Baring was the first Earl of Cromer. He was a quintessential British colonial administrator and diplomat who spent 24 years (1883-1907) in Egypt ruling the country's rulers through a mechanism called the 'Veiled Protectorate', despite not speaking Arabic or having much liking for the Egyptian people.[24]

Lord Cromer's paper was in the form of an article written in *The Spectator* on 12 August 1916,[25] in which he expressed the view that many British Jews—as opposed to Jews in Eastern Europe, where anti-Semitism was rife—had no reason whatsoever to complain. 'Jews now sit in both Houses of Parliament', he stated 'And yet this answer, plausible though it may appear, is far from disposing of the whole question'. He referred to a series of published essays entitled 'Zionism and the Jewish Future' as 'all the more timely', in that one of the consequences of the war was almost certainly going to be to open the Jewish question. These essays allowed us, he stated, 'to gain some insight into the views current in Jewish circles'. Cromer went on to say:

> What is it that Zionists want? The idea that they wish the Jews of all races to be congregated together in Palestine may at once be dismissed as absurd. Nothing of the sort is proposed. Neither do they want to establish a mere colony in the sense in which that term is usually employed. Zionism stands for a national revival . . . It would be both premature and presumptuous to attempt to forecast the future of the Zionist movement.

Lord Cromer concluded by saying that:

> Enough, however, has been said to show that, although possibly the Jewish question will not mature quite so quickly as some of the more enthusiastic Zionists consider probable, it is rapidly becoming a practical issue, and that before long politicians will be unable to brush it aside as the fantastic dream of a few idealists.[26]

Notes by a number of representative Jewish Leaders

According to the instructions given in War Cabinet 245, Minute 18, the draft declaration on Zionism was submitted to nine—'or, including Mr. ES Montagu, ten'—representative Jews [of the Jewish community in Britain]. The six favourable to Zionism were: The Rt. Hon. Herbert Samuel, MP, Chief Rabbi Gaster, Lord Rothschild, Sir Stuart Samuel (Chairman of the Jewish Board of Deputies), Dr. Weizmann, and Mr. Nahum Sokolow. The remaining three, who were unfavourable, were: Sir Philip Magnus MP, CG Montefiore (President of the Anglo-Jewish Association), and LL Cohen (Jewish Board of Guardians). Hankey noted that Mr. Montagu's anti-Zionist memorandum [Paper No. G.T.2263] had already been circulated, but made no mention of it in his memorandum of 17 October.[27]

The various alternative drafts of the Balfour Declaration

Last but not least, the full set of various alternative drafts of the Balfour Declaration were also included among the 'additional papers' put before the cabinet. The seven drafts are listed below and presented in full in Appendix B.

1. The first draft was submitted by the Secretary of State for Foreign Affairs in August, 1917.
2. A draft was submitted by Lord Alfred Milner to the War Cabinet on 4 October 1917. This was also the draft that was submitted to various Jewish representatives on 6 October, 1917.
3. Amendments to the draft mentioned in No. 2 were proposed by four parties: the Chief Rabbi Gaster, Dr. Weizmann, Mr. Sokolow, and Lord Rothschild.

4. An alternative draft was submitted by Mr. Montagu, MP.
5. A draft was submitted by CG Montefiore. Esq.
6. A draft was submitted by LL Cohen, Esq.
7. A draft was submitted by Sir Philip Magnus, MP.[28]

It will suffice to mention here that Milner's draft, and the Zionist leaders' minor alterations to it, (i.e., items 2 and 3 in the foregoing list) was virtually the same as the draft that was finally approved by the War Cabinet, which we have come to know as the Balfour Declaration.[29]

A PANDORA'S BOX: THE MCMAHON PLEDGE IN BRITISH ARCHIVES, 1922-24

As mentioned earlier, the Colonial Office debate over the Balfour Declaration and the McMahon pledge reached new dimensions between 1922-24, when the Palestine Arab Delegation published parts of the Hussein-McMahon correspondence in the British press, arguing that Palestine was included in the area where Hussein had been promised independence. This debate opened a Pandora's box for the British government.

On 6 August 1922, High Commissioner Herbert Samuel wrote to Shuckburgh from Palestine pressing for the publication of McMahon's explanation (to Shuckburgh) on 12 March 1922, in which he (i.e., McMahon) stated that his intention then was to exclude Palestine from the pledge of 1915. It is possible that Samuel was unaware of the doubts expressed in the Middle East Department as to whether Palestine was included or excluded from McMahon's pledge to Hussein, and he seems to have accepted the interpretation that Palestine was so excluded from the pledge of Arab independence. Therefore, by publishing McMahon's letter, Samuel hoped that the controversy might die down, and that the Palestinian Arabs would finally accept the fact that Palestine was excluded from that pledge as a *fait accomplit*. However, the internal minutes of the Colonial Office regarding this irksome issue reveal a different picture. When Shuckburgh received Samuel's letter on 7 November, he wrote privately, telling him he was 'rather against making any further public announcements on this troublesome question', and that he had 'always felt it to be one of the weakest joints in our armour'. He added that McMahon, in his letter to him (i.e., to Shuckburgh), took 'his stand on rather different ground from that of the original draft (as sent to the Arab Delegation)'. Shuckburgh therefore advised against publishing the letter, explaining that the Middle East Department used the argument that in the pledge of 1915, 'Damascus' meant the 'Turkish Vilayet of Damascus'. He referred to Churchill's reply to Ormsby-Gore's Question in parliament on 11 July 1922, saying that:

> The wording of that reply was drawn up with the most meticulous care and represents, I think, the best that can be said on the subject. I doubt whether anything is to be gained by further publication, and indeed it seems to me that our best policy is to let sleeping dogs lie as much as possible.[30]

In January 1924, King Hussein had made assurances to a Palestinian delegation of his 'firm wish to continue his endeavours for the complete independence of the Arab countries amongst which is Palestine', and for the realisation of their unity and the fulfilment of pledges made to him by the Allies. Hussein had added that the Arab negotiations with the British had not ended, and that he:

> ... would not conclude any treaty contrary to those pledges or to the nation's aspirations for independence. On the conclusion of negotiations, he would call for the nation's opinion prior to the signature of the Treaty. He would not by any means accept but that Palestine should belong to its Arab inhabitants.[31]

The Secretary of State for the Colonies (the British Cabinet member charged with managing Britain's various colonial dependencies), James Henry Thomas, invited his colleagues to agree to adhere to the policy of giving effect to the Balfour Declaration, as interpreted by the late government. The Secretary gave his reasons as to why an early decision was needed. He wrote, in February 1924:

> I think it is important that we should come to a decision on the question of policy at the earliest possible date. The situation in Palestine is now calm, but uncertainty is always dangerous, and if the announcement of our policy is delayed there may be a revival of agitation. My own view is that we have no alternative but to adhere to the policy carrying out the terms of the Balfour Declaration as interpreted by our predecessors. I do not underrate the

difficulties, but I am satisfied that the difficulties of any alternative course would be even greater.[32]

Thus, after a long drawn-out controversy, a memorandum by the Middle East Department of the Colonial Office stated in February 1924 that 'it has frequently been alleged that the Balfour Declaration was inconsistent with previous pledges given to the Arabs during the war', and, referring to the Hussein-McMahon correspondence, added that:

Sir H McMahon, who was consulted personally in March 1922, stated definitely that his intention had been to exclude Palestine ... Whether the actual language to the pledge, if interpreted as a court of law would interpret it, can be held to have given effect to this intention, is more doubtful. The natural meaning of the phrase 'west of the district of Damascus', has to be strained in order to cover an area lying considerably to the south as well as to the west of Damascus city.[33]

In the end, to set the seal on the controversy revolving around the Balfour Declaration as well as the McMahon pledge to Sharif Hussein, a memorandum by the Middle East Department, written before King [Sharif] Hussein's final downfall, gave a hint of the fate awaiting him eight months later. The memorandum implied that, had he approved the Middle East Department's interpretation of McMahon's promises to him in 1915—an interpretation that excluded Palestine from the area within which the British promised independence to the Arabs—he might have retained his position as

King of the Hijaz. His insistence on the original promise, that a single Arab Kingdom including Palestine was to be set up after the war ended, seems to have cost him his throne, for when he was attacked by his rival Ibn Saud, the founding monarch of Saudi Arabia, in the summer of 1924, his British allies failed to come to his rescue as they had always previously done. The memorandum stated that:

> Negotiations have been in progress for about a year for the conclusion of a treaty with King Hussein of the Hejaz, who is the person to whom the McMahon promises of 1915 were given. A draft of the treaty was actually initialled in London in April 1923, but difficulties have since arisen, particularly in regard to Article 2 of the draft, which deals with our position in the Mandated State of Iraq, Palestine and Trans Jordan. The point is simply this. The late Government hoped to obtain King Hussein's assent to a formula which would imply his acceptance of the policy pursued by the British Government in the Mandated territories. This would have been an effective answer to those of our critics who assert that the Zionist policy in Palestine is a contravention of the promise given to King Hussein in 1915. It is now fairly clear that this object is not likely to be achieved. King Hussein is at present at Amman in Trans-Jordan, where he has had long discussions with Sir Herbert Samuel. The latter proposes that he should be authorized to clinch matters by concluding a treaty with the King, omitting Article 2 altogether. This may prove in the end the best issue from the impasse. But there are strong objections

to reaching such a solution at Amman, through the High Commissioner for Palestine. If Article 2 goes, the treaty has little concern for the Mandated territories, and our reasons for acting through the agency of Sir Herbert Samuel would be difficult to explain. The result would be hailed as an open surrender of our position in regard to the Balfour Declaration. It would be represented that the great King of the Arabs had come in person to the gates of Palestine and had imposed his will on the British High Commissioner. The inevitable result would be a revival of Arab agitation, which has lately shown some signs of dying down.[34]

The same memorandum went on to say that it was

> ... unnecessary to enlarge upon the special position occupied by Palestine in the eyes of the world. It is scarcely conceivable that, having re-conquered the Holy Land from the Turks, we could have handed it over to the Arabs. It would have been impossible to justify such a step to the League of Nations or to the civilised world as a whole.[35]

Thus, the controversy surrounding the Balfour Declaration and the McMahon pledge to Sharif Hussein during 1922-24 ended when the Colonial Office, after more than a year's deliberation, decided to stick to its old policy of supporting the Zionist cause. The same policy, with the many doubts and uncertainties that accompanied it, was to last until the final days of the British Mandate in Palestine in May 1948. Scores of White Papers aiming to remedy the impossible situation were produced throughout that period.[36]

It should be noted that the interpretation of the Middle East Department concerning the Balfour Declaration worked out during 1922-23 carried even more weight than the White Paper of June 1922, especially when it is remembered that the Mandate was not ratified by the League of Nations and did not come into force until September 1923. In other words, when in 1917 the Balfour Declaration was issued, it was not exactly clear what was meant by it, and hence, the 1922-23 official British interpretation of it, emanating from the Middle East Department, seems to have been much more decisive than the declaration itself. Moreover, the Balfour Declaration, which hitherto had been considered a political and not a legal document and which could have been revoked by any successive government, was now, thanks to the Middle East Department, incorporated in the text of the mandate. Hence, it acquired a 'legal' status.

OTHER PLAYERS BEHIND THE BALFOUR DECLARATION

Because the Balfour Declaration was a product of the War Cabinet, it seems relevant to explore how and why it was established, who the key players were (beyond Mark Sykes), and how it subsequently functioned, as well as the influence of another quasi-secretive group, The Round Table. Among other archival sources, the diary of the War Cabinet Secretary, Sir Maurice Hankey, provides valuable insights.

In December 1916, following the fall of the Asquith government, new ideas and new systems were introduced into the British system of government. Following the defeat of the Asquith government in December 1916 (which was blamed for 'losing the war' by Northcliffe's press,[37] which succeeded in convincing the British public, through *The Times* and *The Daily Mail*, that the government was preventing the generals from gaining victory), Lloyd George immediately created a War Cabinet. It was composed of Lloyd George, the Prime Minister, Bonar Law, Lord Curzon, Lord Alfred Milner, Arthur Henderson, and Sir Maurice Hankey (its Secretary). All were the Prime Minister's men. The small War Cabinet, which rapidly emerged as an extremely powerful body, became the 'political powerhouse of the country'. At the will of the new Prime Minister, decision making on important political matters could now be practically diverted from the established departments of state, including the Foreign Office. One such area that the prime minister and his cabinet had 'confiscated' from all other departments and placed under the 'exclusive' control of the War Cabinet, at least for a while, was the Near East. Mark Sykes himself was moved from the Foreign Office to the War Cabinet Secretariat.[38]

The creation of the War Cabinet thus fundamentally altered the supreme overall direction of the war effort. In their memoirs, both Leopold Amery and Hankey provide us with rare insight into how the War Cabinet functioned, adding to our understanding of this critical period in British politics that produced the Balfour Declaration.

Amery reveals that, for the first time in the history of the British Empire, two cabinets were sitting in London,

> . . . over each of them the Prime Minister of the United Kingdom presided . . . one of them is designated as the 'War Cabinet', which chiefly devotes itself to such questions touching the prosecution of the war as primarily

concern the United Kingdom. The other is designated as the 'Imperial War Cabinet' which has a wider purpose, jurisdiction and personnel.'[39]

Amery explains that the new cabinet system was a 'complete revolution' in the central body of the British government. It was composed of five men (as opposed to the twenty-three in the old system) who met daily, instead of weekly, and at times 'entirely by themselves'. According to Amery, they were free of all routine administrative duties and could therefore concentrate exclusively on matters of policy. On Milner's counsel, Amery and Sykes were to be the two Political Secretaries to the War Cabinet.[40] 'As such', Amery goes on to say, 'we were to be at the disposal of its members and at the same time free, as a kind of informal "brains trust", to submit our ideas on all subjects for our chiefs'.

Although no such office was formally created, Amery asserts that he and Sykes had the political status of under-secretaries.[41] They were to be attached as assistant secretaries to Sir Maurice Hankey, Secretary to the Committee of Imperial Defence, and now also Secretary to the War Cabinet, 'to be made use of by him at his discretion'. Amery adds that he had to work closely with Milner, whom he regarded as his leader as well as his best friend, and with Hankey, whose 'clear head and practical ability' he had long admired. With Mark Sykes, Amery was to produce a weekly summary of the world situation; for the rest, he was to make himself useful 'as occasion arose', or as he 'might' himself 'suggest'.[42]

But the War Cabinet was not the only quasi-secretive group that steered British foreign policy. Sir Maurice Hankey wrote in his diary for 15 August 1917 (at a time when discussion of the Balfour

Declaration was at its height) that 'among the most influential at the present moment', was what he called *The Round Table* group:

> They dine every Monday usually either at the house of Major Waldorf Astor MP, Sir Edward Carson, or Frederick S Oliver. Milner is the real leader of the Group, which includes Amery, Philip Kerr, and the editor of *The Times*, Geoffrey Robinson (who has just changed his name) as well as the various young men associated with this table, Lloyd George sometimes attends.[43]

The Round Table was founded in 1910 by Lord Milner and others, including Lionel Curtis, founder of the publication *The Round Table Group,* and Philip Kerr. It was a cooperative enterprise conducted by people from all parts of the British Empire who advocated imperial federalism. It was also known as the Garden Suburb. Its members produced a quarterly comprehensive review of imperial policies and developments and analyzed major international developments. Curtis claimed that the British Empire had no choice but federation or disintegration.[44] It is true Hankey makes no mention in his diary whether the men associated with *The Round Table* discussed British-Zionist policy, and does not refer in any way, explicitly or implicitly, to any association between this circle of influential officials and the Balfour Declaration; yet, given the 'life-saving' character bestowed upon that declaration by high-ranking British officials of the time, it seems unlikely that the pro-Zionist declaration was not one of the major topics of discussion among this group of British statesmen. Moreover, Hankey's daily and 'securely guarded' diary does not reveal anything about the early history of the Balfour Declaration. However, it does provide invaluable insight into the inner workings of the Lloyd George government, which, in the final analysis, produced the Balfour Declaration, and hence adds a great deal to our understanding of that period.

The creation of the War Cabinet made it possible for Lloyd George to carry out his Eastern policy without any serious opposition and brought a change of Britain's objectives in the Middle East. Previously, this policy had been determined by Kitchener, Secretary of State for War (1914-1916), who had always thought little of Palestine and advocated control of Alexandretta instead.[45] After he died, and Asquith and Grey lost office (both had opposed the Zionist solution and doubted the wisdom of acquiring new territories in the Near East), there was no one (except Curzon and Montagu) to challenge the prime minister's belief that the East was of primary importance for winning the war. Lloyd George and Milner controlled things as a sort of 'dictatorship of two'. It was Balfour who noted: 'If he [i.e., Lloyd George] wants to be a dictator, let him be. If he thinks that he can win the war, I'm all for his having a try.'[46]

As a consequence of the war, hostility to Turkey had much increased, and Lloyd George's principal war aim thus became the disruption of the Turkish Empire. Early in 1917, the prime minister told the Imperial War Cabinet that he regarded this as the last of the Western-Christian expeditions to wrest Palestine, Syria, and Armenia from the Turks.[47]

Thus, within days of Lloyd George's occupancy of 10 Downing Street, preparations for a military offensive in the Near East were stepped up, along with moves to gain the support of the Jewish world Diaspora for an Allied victory.[48]

It was becoming evident that Lloyd George's interest in the Near East was not just a means of securing the road to India, but rather an end in itself. He sought the destruction of the Ottoman Empire and exclusive British control of the Near East.[49] Lloyd George's motives can be briefly summarized as follows: (1) He loathed the Ottoman Empire for its cruel treatment of its Christian subjects; (2) he sympathized with Greek territorial ambitions in Asia Minor; (3) with his biblical upbringing, Lloyd George supported Zionist aspirations in the Holy Land, and made it clear that the Jewish national home was to develop under British rule.[50]

David Lloyd George had first come into contact with Zionism in 1903 when he was appointed as the British attorney for the Zionist movement and its founder, Theodor Herzl, in connection with an issue that split the Zionist movement in those years, and which revolved around whether a Jewish state should necessarily be located in Palestine. In 1902, Herzl met Joseph Chamberlain, the Colonial Secretary, in the hope of securing a piece of land across the frontiers from Palestine, as a temporary measure until Palestine itself should become available, to serve as a Jewish political community. The Zionist leader had two options in mind, either Cyprus or al-Arish, which were both nominally still parts of the Ottoman Empire, but were in fact under British control. Chamberlain refused the Cyprus option, but promised to help Herzl in securing the consent of British officials in charge of Sinai. It was in this context that Herzl sought the services of a politically oriented lawyer, and chose George, who personally handled the matter on behalf of his London firm 'Lloyd George, Roberts and Co.' The plan, however, never materialized. Hence, the Colonial Secretary at that time, Joseph Chamberlain, made the Uganda proposal. Herzl agreed and Lloyd George immediately drafted for the Zionist leader a charter for the 'Jewish Settlement'. Thus, as a result of his professional representation of the Zionist movement, Lloyd George had a clear idea of its goals and objectives, and when the conquest of Palestine was contemplated in 1917, he was perhaps the only British statesman, as will be seen later, who had a clear idea of what to do with it once it was conquered.[51]

Lloyd George's second encounter with political Zionism came about in 1914, when his closest friend and political confidante, CP Scott, editor of the *Manchester Guardian,* was converted to Zionism by the Zionist leader Chaim Weizmann. Through Scott, Weizmann was able to meet Lloyd George, and the young Weizmann made quite a strong impression on the future Prime Minister. When Lloyd George succeeded Asquith as PM, on 7 December 1916, he was already a convert to Zionism.

Thus, following the capture of Baghdad in 1917, the British Prime Minister was in such high-spirits that he revealed to Weizmann his impatience with French claims in Palestine, telling him that Zionism was 'a matter between the British and the Jews'.[52]

On one occasion, Hankey recorded in his diary one of Lloyd George's many 'unrecorded' conversations and revealed the Prime

Minister's way of 'doing business'. One conversation, which took place on 4 December 1918 between Lloyd George and the French premier, Georges Clemenceau,[53] is of particular importance, and provides us with a rare insight. According to what Hankey had written on that day, after Lloyd George and Clemenceau had driven to the French embassy, and, when they were alone, Clemenceau asked Lloyd George what was to be the topic of discussion, to which Lloyd George replied briefly that it was 'Mesopotamia and Palestine'. The conversation between the two 'dictators', according to Hankey, went as follows:

'Tell me what you want', said Clemenceau.
'I want Mosul', replied Lloyd George.
'You shall have it, anything else?' added Clemenceau.
'Yes, I want Jerusalem too,' continued Lloyd George.
'You shall have it—but Pichon will make difficulties about Mosul.'

Hankey wrote that ' . . . there was absolutely no record or memorandum made at the time, and I believe my diary of December 4th 1918 contains the only record . . . .and that was only second hand from Lloyd George, for I was not present'. Hankey added, 'Thus and thus is history made'.[54] Hankey also describes another important incident that took place later, on 14 May 1919, 'during completely informal talks' between Lloyd George and Philippe Berthelot, Secretary General of the French Foreign Ministry. They were discussing the water needs of Palestine, and he [Hankey], 'immediately infiltrated'—i.e., he immediately sent one of his assistants to 'eavesdrop' on the conversation as soon as he realized that something of importance was being discussed.

> It was a near thing and is a good illustration of Lloyd George's methods of doing business—to produce a maximum of informality; to get a snap decision at the end of a long meeting on a difficult subject; and possibly to have no record. It is most distracting for the Secretaries, unless one is very wide awake.[55]

The significance of what Hankey discloses in his diary is twofold: First, it clearly demonstrates what an important figure Hankey himself was in those crucial years, and how closely in touch he was with the centre of decision-making. This leaves us all the more bewildered as to why he failed to make any mention of the Balfour Declaration in his diary. It is difficult to believe that the issue was too insignificant to merit his attention, and therefore his motives for remaining silent on the subject remain unknown. The second point regards Lloyd George and his carelessness, whether deliberate or otherwise, over having an official record and minutes of important meetings.

This may partially explain the scarcity of recorded evidence on the origins and early history of the Balfour Declaration, but does not absolve the British government's inaccuracies and ambiguities in those wartime statements. Whether these were based on 'misunderstanding or deliberate deception . . . subsequently served to reduce the stature of Britain' in the eyes of all those affected.[56]

As to the role played by Weizmann in securing the Balfour Declaration, there are different interpretations. Many writers dismiss Weizmann's paramount role, but his contemporaries—friends and foes alike[57] —are in no doubt.[58] CP Scott, editor of the *Manchester Guardian,* 'who had intimate knowledge of what transpired behind the scenes', a few days after the pro-Zionist declaration was announced, wrote, in response to a letter from Weizmann: 'Heartiest congratulations on the great step forward of your movement . . . The movement owes almost everything to you'. And Lord Rothschild himself acknowledged that the declaration was the joint personal achievement of Weizmann and Sokolow. As for American Zionists, they saw Weizmann singularly 'as the Zionist most responsible for bringing about the declaration'. Reinharz points out that the Weizmann Archives show that in the months following the Balfour Declaration, Weizmann received 'dozens if not hundreds of letters and telegrams, praising his political and diplomatic acumen'. Moreover, the British historian Sir Charles Webster, who was in 1917 a staff officer of the Intelligence Directorate of the British War Office, stated that 'Weizmann was the main creator of the National Home . . . It was in my opinion the greatest act of diplomatic statesmanship of the First World War'.[59] Reinharz even suggests in his article that the Balfour Declaration may well have been addressed to Weizmann and not to Lord Rothschild, which was Weizmann's preferred choice.[60]

AN ANALYSIS AND INTERPRETATION OF ORMSBY-GORE'S MINUTE OF DECEMBER 1922

Whatever the authors of the Balfour Declaration meant when they were busy drafting it from July to November 1917, it is important to put things in their historical perspective and to keep in mind that the political as well as the military situation had been far from clear when the declaration had been announced at the height of the chaos of World War I.

However, the decisive thing is perhaps not the Declaration itself, as already noted, but the 1922-23 interpretation of it.[61] In a secret memorandum dated 17 February 1923, the Colonial Secretary William Cavendish, the Duke of Devonshire wrote: 'Prior to 1921, no authoritative explanation was ever given of what precisely was meant by a 'National Home' for the Jews.'[62]

As the only 'official' and thorough explanation as yet of the events leading up to the Balfour Declaration, the minute drafted by William Ormsby-Gore on Christmas Eve in 1922 assumed such great importance that the Colonial Secretary thought it expedient to print it as a Cabinet Paper for circulation. All the ideas raised in it deserve serious attention, and its various elements will be dealt with separately in the ensuing pages.

Before examining this note in detail, it is worth noting that because there was no documentary evidence in the official records to prove Colonel Amery's authorship of the Balfour Declaration, Sir John Evelyn Shuckburgh, head of the Middle East Department of the Colonial Office, thought it wise to verify the information in the above-mentioned minute from all the relevant sources before he printed it as a Cabinet Paper for circulation. Thus, in addition to Amery, the memorandum was submitted to the Foreign Office, as it 'deals with matters with which they were concerned and quotes their unofficial notes as well as their secret files.'[63] It was also submitted to Lord Curzon personally, since it referred to his attitudes in the War Cabinet, and to Lord Balfour himself.[64]

On 24 January 1923, EH Marsh[65] sent out the letters of verification as suggested by his chief, the Colonial Secretary (the Duke of Devonshire). The Admiralty answered on 25 January 1923 that, according to Mr. Amery, the 'actual last draft' of the Balfour Declaration was his, 'but, of course, it embodied previous drafts'. The Foreign Office answer came five days later, informing the Middle East Department that the Secretary of State 'has no objection to the circulation to the Cabinet of the memorandum on the Balfour Declaration.'[66]

This means that the Foreign Office concurred that, in 1923, Ormsby-Gore's minute was the *only* comprehensive record to be found in British archives on the origins of the Balfour Declaration. Moreover, all parties involved admitted that documents had existed on the subject, but no one seems to have been able to find them. To say that this lack of documentation on such a significant matter was absurd is an understatement.

Although Zionist sources have provided detailed and comprehensive studies of their version of the events leading up to Balfour Declaration, the British story remains, up to this point, seriously lacking in both narrative and detail. Leonard Stein, the Anglo-Jewish lawyer and leading Zionist who, as Political Secretary of the Zionist

Organization from 1920 to 1929, witnessed the birth of the Balfour Declaration, has written an extensive book on the subject, *The Balfour Declaration,* which has been widely acclaimed and heavily cited since its appearance in 1961.[67]

In his important legal analysis of the Balfour Declaration, WT Mallison asserts that Stein's interpretations 'should be recognized as reflecting an authoritative Zionist perspective and be given thorough consideration'.[68] Indeed, Stein was number two in the World Zionist Organization after Weizmann. Because this work became a seminal foundation for later histories, and because there was no British official version available, it can safely be assumed that historians who have mainly relied on this source have given a largely one-sided story. A statement from Mr. Stein's above-mentioned book demonstrates the point clearly.

> There is an absurd myth to the effect that in the autumn of 1916 the British Government caused it to be intimated to Brandeis that it would undertake to do something for the Jews in Palestine in consideration of Brandeis' using his influence with the President to bring the United States into the War. This 'silly nonsense'... appears to have hatched in the inventive mind of James Malcolm... [69]

Was this a deliberate move to mislead his readers? Or was Stein not better informed? Clearly, historians have since demonstrated that when they issued the Balfour Declaration, the British *did* have imperial motives and strategic concerns—namely, to use the influence that the American Zionists could wield upon the US president to bring the US into the war, particularly as they were under serious pressure from German submarine warfare and the threat of severe famine in 1916. Whatever the answer may be, Stein was not alone in providing a narrative that suited the political needs and requirements of his own party (i.e., to show that this was not a short-term 'deceptive' interest that would evaporate at the end of the war but rather a long-term, considered and committed emotional commitment to a cause). For, in his political memoirs, Weizmann, too, wrote the following:

> The deeper meaning of Zionism must not be lost sight of in the record of practical steps, of day-to-day strategic adjustments, which led up to the granting of the Balfour Declaration, and which accompanied future developments. I am reverting now to the common accusation that Zionism was nothing but a British imperialistic scheme, the Balfour Declaration a *quid pro quo,* or rather payment in advance, for Jewish service to the Empire. The truth is that British statesmen were by no means anxious for such a bargain . . . [70]

The above words stand in sharp contrast to any one of the numerous memoranda prepared by Colonial Office staff in which it was repeated over and over that the Balfour Declaration was the result of prolonged discussions and deliberations in which 'all parties of the State were represented', as well as 'the Overseas Dominions in the person of General Smuts', with a 'definite war object in mind' at a time 'of acute national danger'.[71] It is also important to keep in mind, that when they delayed and wavered—and waver they did—it was always Weizmann who kept them on track.

In his revealing minute of December 1922, Ormsby-Gore unveils a number of important issues surrounding the Balfour Declaration and raises at least 12 main ideas that all deserve to be seriously considered. However, and despite the fact that this minute is essential to our understanding of the early history of the Balfour Declaration, it has been overlooked by distinguished scholars who have had access to it.[72] In doing so, they have neglected a wealth of information, not only about the Balfour Declaration, but also about the whole context of British policy for the period in question. In what follows, I attempt to interpret the whole minute, step by step.

The Balfour Declaration in British Archives

First, Ormsby-Gore mentions that the Foreign Office and Sir Maurice Hankey 'both' have material. It has already been seen that whatever material had originally existed in Foreign Office files seems to have gone missing. In fact, that was the precise reason why Ormsby-Gore himself was asked to submit a memorandum on what he 'recollected' from memory about the Balfour Declaration. Furthermore, although Maurice Hankey was the one who was always present during these discussions, neither Hankey's diaries nor his papers in the Public Records Office (CAB 63) contain anything on the question of the Balfour Declaration either (except for another copy of *The Zionist Movement*, Hankey's secret War Cabinet Paper mentioned earlier). As Hankey fails to mention anything about the Balfour Declaration in his diary entry of 2 November 1917, his biographer, Stephen

Roskill, rightly observes that 'considering that Hankey must have known about this minute [i.e., the Balfour Declaration], and indeed probably had a hand in drafting it, it is odd that he made no mention of it in his diary'. Roskill's implausible explanation is that it was because of Hankey's profound admiration for Sykes that he allowed the latter's 'new born enthusiasm' for a Jewish state in Palestine, as part of his far-reaching scheme for the post-war division of the Ottoman Empire, 'to go through without any careful consideration of the long term consequences'.[73]

Mark Sykes and Zionism

The second point Ormsby-Gore makes in his minute is regarding Sykes' early pro-Zionist activities in 1916, and the fact that he acted 'on his own initiative', making contact with Jewish leaders, such as Herbert Samuel and Rabbi Gaster, adding that Weizmann himself was 'unknown'.

Much of this story has already been told in Chapter One. Here, it should suffice to give a brief account of Sykes' own background and how he came to be regarded as an 'expert' on Near Eastern affairs, and of his early encounter with Zionism. As Assistant Secretary in the War Cabinet Secretariat (1916-19), Sykes won Hankey's affection as the cartoonist of the Secretariat.[74] When the war broke out in 1914, British officials discovered how little they knew about the Near East. Indeed, it is often maintained that the term 'Middle East' itself was coined by Sykes. Sykes, a member of parliament who had travelled in the Near East before the war, although an amateur himself, quickly acquired the status of 'expert' on Ottoman affairs. In 1915, he was brought to the War Office by Colonel FitzGerald, Kitchener's personal military secretary. Because of their ignorance about the region, the members of parliament left Near Eastern matters to Kitchener and his entourage, while Kitchener, in his turn, depended heavily on his staff and was looking for a politician who knew the area. Thus, shortly after arriving at the War Office, Sykes was given his first assignment in the de Bunsen Committee. The other members probably assumed that, since Sykes and Kitchener shared similar views and belonged to the same club, the former spoke with the full weight of Lord Kitchener. Thus, the relatively inexperienced Sykes ended up controlling the Interdepartmental Committee; he was opinionated and outspoken, and the only member of the committee with firsthand knowledge of Ottoman Turkey. Hankey quickly became his friend and supporter. Sykes also made friends with MacDonogh, who proved valuable in advancing his career.[75] Whether Sykes was given a free hand under Lord Kitchener is open to question; it seems more likely that he was given broad instructions and left free to work out the details (though Sykes himself left no written evidence as to how far he had a free hand and how far he simply followed instructions from his superiors). One incident, however, seems to suggest that he managed to have his own way. During the de Bunsen proceedings, while Sykes demanded that the British port on the Mediterranean should be at Haifa, Kitchener insisted on Alexandretta. In the end, FitzGerald, mediating between the two, let Sykes have his way.[76]

Although it is often implied that Sykes acted on his own even during Kitchener's lifetime, there is enough reason to believe that, contrary to Ormsby-Gore's assertion in the minute (that Sykes was acting 'on his own initiative'), at least during 1915-16, he did not depart from the general line of policy drawn by his chief. During negotiations in 1915 between the British and the French, when the future of Palestine became a stumbling block, Sykes wrote: 'I worked ... the Franco-British Agreement on Lord Kitchener's lines, every detail of which I discussed with FitzGerald nightly.'[77] After Kitchener's death in 1916, however, Sykes, continuing to regard himself as 'the' expert on Near Eastern affairs, seems to have increasingly acted on his own initiative.

According to Weizmann, Sykes was first brought into contact with Zionist affairs, and with himself, through Rabbi Gaster. Weizmann asserts that this was somewhat unusual, because Gaster tended 'to keep his finds' (referring to Sykes) to himself, and to play a 'lone hand'. For example, when Weizmann met Herbert Samuel for the first time in November 1914, the Zionist leader asserts that Gaster only told him of Samuel's interest in the idea of a Jewish state after the meeting had already occurred. According to Weizmann, Gaster was not enthusiastic about Zionist negotiations with British officials and statesmen, seeing them as 'pointless'. When the Zionist leader went to meet Samuel, Gaster remarked: 'Ho-ho! So you are going to negotiate with Herbert Samuel!' (Weizmann reveals in his memoirs that Gaster never trusted him, and that he himself had always wondered why the Rabbi looked at him with such 'distrust' and 'roguishness'). In any case, Weizmann confirms that it was Gaster who had first introduced Sykes to Zionism.[78]

Concerning the services 'given with zeal' by Sykes to the Zionist movement, Weizmann states, for instance, that he 'cannot say enough regarding the services rendered us by Sykes', and continues: 'It was he who guided our work into more official channels.' As for the services rendered to Zionism by the War Cabinet Secretariat, including such men as Leopold Amery, Ormsby-Gore, and Ronald Storrs, Weizmann noted that:

> If it had not been for the counsel of men like Sykes and Lord Robert Cecil we, with our inexperience in delicate diplomatic negotiations, would undoubtedly have committed many dangerous blunders.[79]

Thus, the first 'full-dress' conference leading to the Balfour Declaration took place in Dr. Gaster's house, on 17 February 1917. Present were Lord Rothschild, Herbert Samuel, Sir Mark Sykes, James de Rothschild, Nahum Sokolow, Joseph Cowen, Herbert Bentwich, Harry Sacher, and Weizmann himself. Mark Sykes told his hosts that he attended in his private capacity. According to Weizmann, the discussion in Dr. Gaster's house in February 1917 focused on the heart of the Jewish problem, which was to be the main issue for the coming months. First, it was decided that there was going to be no internationalization of the Palestine question, and second, the term 'nation', as applied to the emergent Jewish homeland in Palestine, 'referred to the Jewish homeland alone, and in no wise to the relationship of Jews with the lands in which they lived'. Those were the views of Herbert Samuel, according to Weizmann. In the same meeting, Weizmann added that the Jews who went to Palestine would go there to constitute a 'Jewish nation, not to become Arabs or Druses or Englishmen'. Keeping in mind the international complexities regarding Palestine and the Holy Places, and stressing Sykes' role in promoting the Zionist cause, the Zionist leader went on to say that Sykes 'placed all his diplomatic skill at our disposal, and that without it we should have had much heavier going than we did'. However, Chaim Weizmann also drew attention to the fact that, although Sykes' chief concern at that point was the Powers[80] and international rivalries, the Arab problem did not escape his mind. 'Within a generation', Weizmann quotes Sykes as saying, 'the movement would come into its own, for the Arabs had intelligence, vitality and linguistic unity'. And according to Weizmann, Sykes believed that the Arabs would also come to terms with Zionism, particularly if they received Jewish support in 'other matters'.[81]

Considering Sykes' own misgivings about his own diplomacy and his changing views on Zionism before his death, we may never know what his impact would have been had he lived longer. His contemporaries certainly believed that the history of the Near East would have taken a different course. As Shane demonstrates, Mark Sykes' work was already judged before his death in 1919:

> there were two views as to the soundness and value of Marks' achievement. On his charm and originality there was no difference, but his policy had raised real enmity. Within the Arab Bureau itself views were varied as they touched the superficiality or depth of his work.[82]

DG Hogarth said that he was a 'brilliant amateur' and that 'had he lived longer he would have reconstructed something of more lasting sort, and in any case one cannot but think that some of the shifts, some of pretenses, some of the casuistry, which have marked our peace policy in the Near East, would not have been or need not have been so disastrous'.[83] Major General Sir Gilbert Clayton remarked that: 'Sir Mark Sykes was one of those men of broad vision who—like the late Lord Kitchener—saw the war from the very beginning in its larger aspect . . . ' and adding 'It is permissible to believe that had he lived the situation in the Near East would not be what it is to-day'.[84]

In summary, Ormsby-Gore's minute revealed little more on Sykes' role than we already knew, and the story of Sykes in particular remains one that raises more questions than answers, given that Sykes' role was so pervasive, yet so unclear and so unrecorded. It is even contentious whether he was acting on his own initiative or not. Sykes claimed he was acting on direct orders from his boss Kitchener, but Kitchener, like Sykes, died without leaving records. Because everyone later said it had been Sykes who had all the details of the Balfour Declaration story in his head, we can only attempt to compile as much as we know about this man to enhance our understanding of the history.

Cooperation between Zionism and British Military Intelligence

The next point Ormsby-Gore considered in his minute was the question of intelligence and the services rendered by the Zionists to the British military during Allenby's campaign in Palestine. He stated that after Mark Sykes had made the initial steps to contact the Zionist leaders, it was the Director of Military Intelligence, General George MacDonogh, who took the next step forward.

To explain this point, some light will need to be shed on the activities of the Jewish agronomist Aaron Aaronsohn[85] (who was brought to Palestine at the age of 6 from Romania by his immigrant parents in 1882). For the benefit of the British Intelligence Unit under MacDonogh (Director of Military Intelligence), Aaronson developed a small espionage family network with the code name NILI (Hebrew initials for an acronym that, when fully written out reads *Netzah Yisrael lo Yeshaker*, which translates to 'the glory of Israel will not lie'). This unit provided invaluable information about Turkish defences and local water sources to the British army after its disastrous defeat at the hands of the Turks in the first battle of Gaza in March 1917. Aaronsohn transmitted important information to British warships off the Palestine coast. Moreover, he was a staff officer at British Army Headquarters in Cairo, as well as adviser to General Allenby. His work was part of a plan to realize Jewish aspirations in Palestine and end Ottoman Turkish rule. In mid-October 1917, the NILI group was discovered by the Turks, who executed them all.[86]

Having escaped Turkish revenge, Aaronsohn continued to promote Zionist interests during the Paris Peace Conference in 1919, having also, thus far, succeeded in introducing a number of British officials to Zionism, including Ormsby-Gore himself. His 'astute judgement', and 'encyclopedic knowledge of the East', made him an indispensable advisor to Sykes, Ormsby-Gore, and all those behind Lloyd George's Eastern policy.[87] Aaronsohn subsequently died in May 1919 in an airplane crash over the English Channel in unclear circumstances.

When William Ormsby-Gore joined Sykes and Amery as one of the three assistant secretaries to the War Cabinet, he already had a clear idea of the situation on the ground, because previously, as Secretary to Lord Milner, Ormsby-Gore had been sent to Cairo to work in the Arab Bureau, where he first met and was directly responsible for Aaronsohn, whose information about Turkish defences proved of great value to the British military command in Egypt, and who impressed Ormsby-Gore highly.[88]

Another British official who was persuaded of the merits of Zionism by Aaronsohn was Richard Meinertzhagen,[89] who had taken charge of espionage operations behind enemy lines, under General Allenby.[90] That was the extent of British interest in Zionism from the point of view of the intelligence officers.

However, there were other ways in which Director of Military Intelligence MacDonogh extended help to the Zionists. On 29 May 1917, Weizmann, as president of the English Zionist Federation, wrote to MacDonogh stating that he had written to Ronald Graham of the Foreign Office '. . . with a view to securing exemption from military service for six men without whose assistance the cause of the Zionist movement in this country could not be carried on.' Weizmann told MacDonogh that Graham supported the idea, and that it was he who had referred him to MacDonogh. The Zionist leader added that without these men 'the political work of Zionism in this country would be crippled'. His list included Albert Hyamson, Samuel Landman, Simon Marks, Harry Sacher, Israel Sieff, and Sir Leon Simon. Weizmann's request was granted in full.[91]

However, it is noteworthy that when MacDonogh, once an enthusiastic sympathizer with the Zionist cause, visited Palestine in May 1920, he reported that 'our policy is one fraught with extreme danger'. He also stressed to the government that, should the Jews be given 'unwarranted ascendancy over the other inhabitants', there would be serious local trouble and even 'rebellion throughout our Eastern Empire.'[92]

Another aspect of the intelligence question worth examining, albeit not one of the points made by Ormsby-Gore in his minute, concerns the activities of Captain Reginald Hall, Director of Naval Intelligence (DNI) during the period from 1914 to 1918. Hall, who seems to have enjoyed Balfour's unlimited confidence in his capacity as First Lord of the Admiralty 1915-16, was the first to draw attention to the extreme importance of securing for Britain exclusive control of all railways in the South of Palestine, in order to assure its position in Egypt. Thus, he suggested that in the Brown Area, the question of Zionism and British control of all Palestine railways should be considered. This was in sharp contrast to the terms of the Sykes-Picot Agreement, and Captain Hall did not hesitate to make his point clear when he wrote a memorandum, on 12 January 1916, criticizing the memorandum that Sykes and Picot had prepared following their discussions at the beginning of January.

Throughout the war, it was Naval Intelligence that monopolized the deciphering of the enemy's diplomatic, naval, and military messages. Furthermore, the DNI was in charge of 'Room 40', which deciphered the famous Zimmerman Telegram in January-February 1917—the document that took the credit for finally inducing the hesitant President Wilson to declare war on Germany. The German Foreign Secretary, Arthur Zimmerman, sent a secret cable instructing his Minister in Mexico to seek an alliance with

Mexico against the United States. In return, Mexico was to be given Texas, New Mexico. and Arizona.[93] On 19 February 1917, Hall told an 'appreciative' Balfour that the time had come to make use of the Zimmerman telegram.

Also in January 1916, Sykes was gathering supporters, chief among them being Maurice Hankey, to discuss his proposed Arab Bureau in Cairo, but it was Hall who firmly stood in his way. In order to allay Hall's fears, an interdepartmental compromise was reached and Hall was asked to name his own candidate for the head of the Arab Bureau in Cairo. Hall's choice was Hogarth[94], and Sykes lost the post he had dreamt of. As a result of this incident, Sykes seems to have been convinced that Hall was strong enough to block his way, and that it was better not to oppose him. According to Jacob Rosen, this explains why Sykes 'fell into line', and suddenly discovered the 'glittering light of Zionism'. In a 1988 article in the *Journal of Middle Eastern Studies,* Jacob Rosen demonstrates that it was following Hall's memorandum of 12 January 1916, in which he severely criticized Sykes, that the latter underwent a 'total metamorphosis' and moved to the pro-Zionist track. In the same memorandum, Hall suggested that in the Brown Area, the question of Zionism should be considered. According to Rosen, however, it is difficult to follow Hall's activities beyond this point due to the 'paucity' of documentation, adding that even Hall's biographer, Admiral William James, asserts that 'It is unlikely that there are now any papers in the official archives which would throw any light on his activities. His was not the type of work that could be recorded in reports and letters of proceedings'.

Russian and East European Jewry and the Balfour Declaration

The fourth element in Ormsby-Gore's minute involves the implications of the Russian and East European 'point of view' on the Allied cause, its connection with negotiations leading up to the Balfour Declaration, and the keen interest of one senior Foreign Office official at the time, Ronald Graham, in that aspect of the case.

One of the causes for the restoration of the 'Palestine Idea' to the government's agenda was the wave of anti-semitism and pogroms against Jews sweeping through Russia and Eastern Europe, which, in the view of at least some British policy makers, definitely 'required treatment'. A change in Russian policy towards the Jews could have restored Jewish confidence in Russia. But in British eyes, no such change was likely to be forthcoming.[95]

Moreover, early in 1917, as events on the ground were turning against the Allies, and with the outbreak of the Russian Revolution in March, the British considered it a matter of urgency to arouse the patriotic (i.e., pro-British) feelings of Russian Jews, which were expected to show signs of fading as a result of the Russian Revolution and following the withdrawal of Russia from the war.[96] In 1917, at least some British policy makers became obsessed with the notion that it was the Jewish Bolshevik revolutionaries who were fomenting the demand for a separate peace with Germany and planning to take Russia out of the war. This *idée fixe,* according to one author, an 'almost apocalyptic vision of impending disaster', though not necessarily shared by all cabinet members or senior diplomats, did nevertheless influence all the major protagonists of the Balfour Declaration. William Ormsby-Gore himself had even written in April 1917 that 'In Russia it would appear the Jews are taking the extreme line probably in the hope of splitting Russia into fragments'.[97]

At this juncture, Weizmann convinced Whitehall that all, or most Jews, were Zionists, and that they were a powerful force in Russia who could 'fix things'. And because Britain allied itself to Russia, it was assumed that Russian and American Jews (mostly of Russian origin) were anti-British, anti-Czarist and pro-German. The remedy to gain their support was a British declaration of sympathy with Zionist aspirations in Palestine. 'If you give us a declaration in favour of Zionism', Weizmann told Sykes, 'the declaration will make the Jews of the world understand that you are really friendly and the friendship of the Jews of the world' he went on to emphasize, 'is not a thing to be blown upon, it is a thing that matters a great deal, even for a mighty empire like the British'.[98]

On the other hand, a member of the Rothschild family told Ronald Graham that the emancipation of Russian Jewry threatened the obsolescence of Zionism, and he added, 'the Revolution had knocked the bottom out of the Zionist argument that their plan is the only solution'. On hearing this, Graham turned to Weizmann for more information and advice. The Zionist leader was justifiably alarmed to hear the same old questions being asked once again: How influential were the Jews inside Russia? Where did their sympathies really lie? There had been signs that the information reaching London from the independent sources of the Foreign Office differed from the picture Weizmann had successfully established since the beginning of the war. The British consul in Odessa wrote to the Foreign Office on 10 May 1917 that, in everyone's view, the 'Jews are working against England and are strongly in favor of Germany . . . England is represented as Russia's worst enemy . . .'. On 27 June 1917, Graham minuted that 'our best card in dealing with the Russo-Jewish proletariat is Zionism'.[99] Again on 24 October, Ronald Graham wrote a memorandum to Balfour telling him that 'further delay will have a deplorable result . . . and may jeopardize the whole Jewish situation.' He added that delay in publicly announcing a pro-Zionist declaration would almost certainly lead to losing the cooperation of Russian as well as American Jewry, and might throw the Zionists into the arms of the Germans, who would be more than happy to welcome the opportunity, especially as Zionism itself was originally a German idea.[100]

In the opinion of Albert Hyamson, the Anglo-Jewish historian and civil servant who directed the Department of Immigration in Palestine (1921-34), the Jews in the new Russian government were bitterly opposed to Zionism. Hyamson noted that, as the Balfour Declaration coincided with the outbreak of the Bolshevik Revolution, and as the Jews were seen to be powerful among the revolutionaries, it had been suggested that the declaration should be effective in keeping the new Russian government in the war on Britain's side. However, he dismissed this suggestion as 'worthless', because the influential classes in Russia, as elsewhere, were 'anti-Zionist almost without exception'.[101] But these were not the views of Ronald Graham, who on 1 November 1917 urged the immediate publication of the Balfour Declaration. He stressed the fact that Zionist leaders were prepared to send agents to Russia, America, Egypt, and elsewhere to help work up a pro-Ally and pro-British campaign of propaganda among the Jews. Graham advised that: 'The sooner this starts, the better.'[102]

The Prime Minister held similar views. One of the reasons for the adoption of the Balfour Declaration, noted Lloyd George, was the actions of a section of Russian Jewry, which, he wrote, had been secretly active on behalf of the Central Powers, acting as the chief agents of German pacifist propaganda inside Russia. It was believed that if Britain declared its willingness to fulfill Zionist aspirations in Palestine, this would have the effect of bringing influential Russian Jewry to the side of the Allies. It was also hoped that such a declaration would have a powerful effect upon world Jewry and would secure for the Entente the aid of Jewish financial interests.[103] Furthermore, it was Leopold Amery who noted that the Balfour Declaration was not addressed to British Jews but rather to Russian and Polish Jewry, who were denied citizenship, and who were, in his opinion, a 'separate nation'. By the Balfour Declaration, Amery thought, the Jews were to be offered the chance of 'building their own homeland in Palestine'.[104]

There is a thin line dividing East European Zionism from the German version, and hence it is difficult to discuss one without mentioning the other.

The total population of Imperial Germany in 1910 was 65 million. According to the census of that year, the number of Jews in the country at that time was more than half a million. Eighty-seven percent held German citizenship, while the remaining 12.8% consisted of Yiddish-speaking immigrants from Czarist Russia and the

Austro-Hungarian Empire, essentially known as the *Ostjuden*. It was this East European element among German Jews that traditionally identified with Zionism and supported it.[105]

For this reason, British policy makers were 'justified' in their fear of German Zionism; 'Zionism' itself had always been a uniquely German and East European phenomenon. (Such at least, had always been the case until Weizmann promoted it in England). Up until 1914, the Central Office of the Zionist Organization as well as the powerful Zionist Executive, were located in Berlin, with followers all over Eastern Europe.

The early Zionist movement operated within the sphere of the German *Kulturbereich*.[106] During the war, a new organization under the name *Komitee für den Osten,* (K.f.d.O.), which was also founded in Germany, aimed at placing at the disposal of the German government the know-how of Jews in Eastern Europe (and America) to contribute to the overthrow of Czarist Russia and to secure the national autonomy of the Jews. Naturally, Zionists outside the Central Powers were hostile to the activities of this organization, and it was then, and upon Weizmann's advice, that the decision was made to move the central office from Berlin. Moreover the conduct of Zionist affairs during the war was to be entrusted to a provisional committee for general Zionist affairs in America.[107]

As already mentioned, the Foreign Office was under the impression that Russian Jews exerted great pressure on their government. When the British ambassador in Petrograd, fully aware that the Jews in Russia were a persecuted minority of no political consequence, reported to the Foreign Office his belief that the Jews could not affect the course of the war, he found no one to listen to him.[108]

Of particular importance at this juncture are the American intelligence reports. However, because the views expressed in them fundamentally contradicted those of the British, one may suppose that the American reports might have been referring to German Jews who held German citizenship and who opposed political Zionism, while the British referred to the Yiddish East European pro-Zionist element in German Jewry. This is, however, no more than speculation, as it is difficult to prove the point.

On 1 December 1917, Samuel Edelman, American vice-consul in Geneva, wrote that the German press had simply brushed aside the British declaration on the Zionist question. The *Berliner Tageblatt* 'ignores it completely', although, he maintained, this paper was known to be in Jewish hands. Some papers, he added, declared that it was a British trick to stir up racial antagonism between the Jews of the Central powers, and that, if successful, England desired to organize a buffer state as a further protection for Egypt and the Suez Canal. According to the same American report, the conservative Jewish press, *Die Jüdische Presse* of Berlin, wrote on 16 November, two weeks after the Balfour Declaration was announced, that British sympathy for Zionism was not based on humanitarian grounds but rather in the interest of British world politics. 'Judaism', the German paper continued, 'has no political aims, only moral ones, and hence this British declaration should not be taken seriously.' It further observed that Balfour's declaration did not speak of a 'Jewish State', but of a home in Palestine, concluding that 'it is quite plain that the civil and religious rights of the Arab and Christian populations must be considered'.[109]

In his report to Hugh Wilson, Edelman also spoke of the situation in Eastern Europe: 'From my knowledge of Jewish conditions in Germany and Austria, I do not think that the British note will exercise the slightest influence upon the Jewish masses in the Central Powers'. The American vice-consul believed the Jewish masses to be conservative, their sympathies lying 'entirely' with their own governments where the opportunities for social and religious freedom were 'bound to improve after the war'. Those who may have been 'momentarily enthused by the ideal of freedom offered in a Jewish state' were, in Edelman's opinion, Russian and Romanian Jewish emigrants who were still resentful of their late recent oppression.[110]

It can, therefore, be concluded that the East European point of view, or rather the effect of East European Jewry on the course of the events leading up to the Balfour Declaration, was greatly exaggerated in importance, and for this, in addition to what has been discussed above, Ronald Graham seems to have been largely responsible in giving it concrete shape. When the War Cabinet was still faltering on 24 October 1917, Graham was pressing for no further delay. He pointed out that Weizmann had promised the moment this assurance was given, that Zionist Jews would start an active pro-Ally propaganda campaign throughout the world, and that Weizmann himself, 'a most able and energetic propagandist', Graham revealed, was 'prepared to proceed himself to Russia and to take charge of the campaign'.[111]

One author notes that, while the idea of committing Britain to the Zionist cause was inspired by Gerald Fitzmaurice[112] and Mark Sykes, 'Graham was probably more responsible than anyone else in the government for actually embodying the commitment in an official document'. The role he played, however, 'tends to be passed over by historians—possibly because he failed to leave a significant archive of private papers behind him'.[113] Graham was the first British official to discuss with Vladimir [Ze'ev] Jabotinsky[114] the creation of a Jewish unit in the British army, following his return to England from Cairo, where he had been in service for more than 10 years. He immediately set out to urge the Foreign Office to support Zionism publicly. Thus, Graham's interest in Zionism was twofold. In the first place, he considered it from the angle of the oppressed Jews in Eastern Europe; and by promising them Palestine, it was hoped that they would side with the Allies. And second, he was thinking of what a Jewish unit in the British army might achieve in the conquest of Palestine.[115]

These two objectives, however, seem to have been intimately connected. The Russian-born Jabotinsky, who was the chief initiator of the idea of establishing a Jewish force in the British Army, was naturally going to seek recruits for his Jewish battalions from Russia and Eastern Europe, in addition to the Jews living in England who were also of Russian origin and had not yet been naturalised (about which, more will be said below).

American Jewry and the question of Zionism

The fifth point in the minute concerns American Zionist activities. Ormsby-Gore confirms that early in 1917, 'important representations came from America'. It is not at all clear what he meant by this statement. Did Ormsby-Gore mean that Zionist delegates came from America? Or that American Zionists reflected on the issue and proposed solutions? Or was it rather that they provided certain facts to influence the conduct of the British government? Reference has already been made to the part played by James Malcolm in drawing the attention of Mark Sykes to the important role American Zionists were capable of playing in dragging America into the war on the side of the Allies. The key issue was Palestine. Louis Brandeis, US Supreme Court Judge and President Wilson's confidant, was persuaded to win over the president. In April 1917, the US entered the war to rescue the Allies, as a result of the Zimmerman telegram (noted above), which was decoded by British intelligence.[116] While President Wilson was sympathetic to Zionism, he was suspicious of British designs on Palestine. Although he favoured a Jewish Palestine, he was reluctant to support a British one. When the British War Cabinet was contemplating the Balfour Declaration, one of the first things it sought was US President Wilson's approval. The proposed declaration was presented to the American government as an expression of sympathy for Zionist aspirations, as if it were solely motivated by British concern for the persecuted Jews of Eastern Europe. But to the mind of Colonel Edward House, President Wilson's foreign policy adviser who influenced Wilson against the Balfour Declaration, the declaration basically meant that 'The English naturally want the road to Egypt and India blocked, and Lloyd George is not above using us to further this plan'.[117]

Justice Brandeis, leader of the Zionist movement in America since 1914, was converted to Zionism in 1912. He set out to address the fact that American Jews had hitherto been uninterested in Zionism; in fact, they had distanced themselves from it for fear of accusations that attachment to Zionism might undermine their loyalty to their new country, the great bulk of them having been recent immigrants from Russia and Eastern Europe. What Brandeis sought to do was to provide these immigrants with a new identity. He had noticed that American Jews lacked an important thing, which, in his view, other Americans possessed, and that was a national heritage. He admired Irish-Americans for their strong connection to their 'motherland' and persuaded his fellow American Jews that by identifying with a 'cause' with special significance for their particular group they would be better Americans, and not the opposite, as they had feared. 'Every American Jew who aids in advancing the Jewish settlement in Palestine', Brandeis stated, 'will likewise be a better man and a better American.'[118] In this way, Brandeis tried to win over American Jews to Zionism. It is interesting to mention in this respect that by mid-October 1917, some American suggestions were introduced to the text of the draft declaration. American Zionists conveyed their views to Colonel House that they objected to the draft declaration referring to Jews as a 'race' and that the reference in it of assurances to 'such Jews who are fully contended with their existing nationality' seemed to them to imply an element of discontent, which American Zionists did not share with regard to their country.[119]

Another significant aspect of the case concerns finance and banking. Britain and her Allies had attached prime importance to

Jewish banking firms, due to the fact that money and credit were needed for the war, and all the important international banking establishments of the day conducted major operations in America, through the New York banking house of Kuhn, Loeb, and Company. American Jews detested the Czarist regime and wished to see it destroyed. Jacob Schiff, a highly influential figure at the time in American Jewish life and a senior partner in Kuhn, Loeb, and Co., wrote in 1915: 'It is well known that I am a German sympathizer ... England has been contaminated by her alliance with Russia. I am quite convinced that in Germany anti-semitism is a thing of the past'. To demonstrate the extent of the power, and anti-Czarist animus, exerted by Schiff's firm, it will suffice to mention that it financed Japan in the Russo-Japanese war in 1904-05.[120]

Throughout 1916, Sykes was busy attending a series of meetings in the house of Chaim Weizmann in which Malcolm and Sokolow took part, with the knowledge and approval of Sir Maurice Hankey, secretary to the War Cabinet. It was at this point, in the autumn of 1916, that the triumvirate of Sykes-Weizmann-Sokolow decided to send a secret message to Justice Brandeis to the effect that the British cabinet would help the Jews gain Palestine in return for active Jewish support for the Allied cause. This information was ciphered to Washington through the Foreign Office. Sir Ronald Graham was then one of the principal under-secretaries.[121]

Finally, the matter reached President Wilson in September 1917, when he was approached by the British War Cabinet as to his views on a pro-Zionist pronouncement. According to Leonard Stein, he sought advice, 'not from Brandeis', but from his 'still more intimate confidant, Colonel House'. Upon the advice of the latter, he sent a discouraging reply to the British cabinet. But the British firmly insisted on getting the approval of the American president, and when a few weeks later another enquiry reached Washington from the British, it seems that Brandeis had finally succeeded in changing President Wilson's views. On hearing the news, Weizmann and his colleagues celebrated the happy occasion in London. Leonard Stein asserts that insofar as;

> ... Brandeis helped to swing Wilson from discouragement to approval of a British assurance to the Zionists, he rendered a signal service to the Zionist cause.

Stein adds:

> Wilson's September message had come near to killing the Balfour Declaration. Had his reply to the second British enquiry been equally chilling, it is quite possible that the Declaration would never have seen the light.[122]

The War Cabinet and the Balfour Declaration

That the 'form of the Declaration' and the ensuing policy 'was debated more than once by the War Cabinet' has already been made abundantly clear in Chapter One. Sir Maurice Hankey's War Cabinet Paper of 17 October 1917, mentioned in Ormsby-Gore's minute, has also been discussed at some length and does not need to be dealt with again. It is reproduced in full in Appendix B.

Northcliffe's propaganda machine and the Balfour Declaration

Next, Ormsby-Gore's minute deals with Viscount Northcliffe's Propaganda Department and the 'utmost' use it made of the Balfour Declaration, thus affecting the course of events of the war, or so it was believed. Lord Northcliffe, also known as Sir Alfred Charles William Harmsworth and as the 'Press Lord,' was Britain's greatest newspaper proprietor. In 1918, he was appointed Director of Propaganda in Enemy Countries. Although initially pro-Zionist, he was later known to have become an anti-Zionist when he saw what was happening on the ground in Palestine.[123] Exactly how the 'utmost' use was made of the Balfour Declaration is unclear from the various sources that have dealt with the subject. However, it is not very difficult to apprehend the logic that prevailed in those crucial months, since the main aim of British policy makers at the time was to strengthen the pro-Allied sympathies of the Jewish Diaspora. The Ministry of Propaganda, under Lord Northcliffe, made use of the Balfour Declaration immediately following its publication and during the course of 1918. By owning the two important daily newspapers, *The Times* and the *Daily Mail*, Northcliffe controlled half the London press. Through them, it was said he controlled both the 'classes and the masses'.[124]

During the early days of World War I, following a political crisis on an issue concerning the shortage of artillery shells, known then as the 'shell scandal', Northcliffe was bent on bringing down Kitchener.[125] His propaganda machine was at least partly responsible for the fall of the Asquith government in the final days of 1916, when, as noted above, he used all his power to convince the English public that it was Asquith's government that prevented the generals from winning the war. Following the announcement of the Balfour Declaration on 2 November, the Foreign Office and the government's propaganda machine immediately set out to devise 'the best method of obtaining full political advantage from the new situation created by the Declaration.'[126]

Even a man as powerful as Hankey, the 'keeper of a million secrets' as he was known, felt threatened by the 'power wielded, entirely without scruple, by the Northcliffe press'.[127] On 24 May 1917, he wrote:

> Interesting discussion at morning War Cabinet on subject of the articles on the submarine question in the *Times* and *Daily Mail*, and all the Northcliffe press, which supply valuable propaganda to the enemy, who makes full use of it.[128]

On the other hand, as late as September 1918, the prevalent political mood in London seems to have been a gloomy one. AJP Taylor asserts that Northcliffe, 'presumably a well informed man' told one of his subordinates that 'none of us will live to see the end of the war'.[129] It was through cooperation with British and American Zionist leaders that many top-ranking and influential British statesmen believed salvation [i.e., the end of the war] would come.[130]

Germany and the Balfour Declaration

The statement in Ormsby-Gore's minute that 'remarkable tribute' was received from General Ludendorff is perhaps the most obscure in the whole minute. Erich Ludendorff was the 'presiding military genius' of the then German Chief of the Greater German General Staff, Paul von Hindenburg. Together they controlled German military and civil policy from July 1917 until autumn 1918.[131] In January 1917, Ludendorff believed that the war could be speedily won, without any compromise, after Germany undertook to carry out unrestricted submarine warfare against allied shipping.[132]

However, a few months later, Ludendorff's attitude began to change, and by July 1917, he was constantly speaking of the deterioration of German morale.[133]

In the English translation of his memoirs, Ludendorff makes no mention of the Balfour Declaration, nor does he reveal anything about his own attitude towards the Jewish question, beyond some passing remarks on the state of affairs of Jews in Lithuania and Eastern Europe. But from what can be inferred from his memoirs, the explanation for Ormsby-Gore's remark might lie in the situation in Lithuania. According to the German general, the Lithuanian movement was seeking to unite with its opposite number in Poland. Ludendorff firmly believed that:

> We had no reason to permit these agitations . . . we could no longer consider anything but our own future, and the dangers which might threaten us from Poland . . . the establishment of a Poland that would surround East and West Prussia was incompatible with the security of Germany . . . [134]

According to Ludendorff, German rule in the East needed to be based on the Lithuanians and White Ruthenes (i.e., Ukrainians).[135]

Furthermore, he advocated that Lithuania should be closely integrated into the German Empire and united under the personal sovereignty of the Kaiser, either in his capacity as King of Prussia or Emperor of Germany. In this way, Germany would gain a military base for defence against further surprise attacks by Russia, one that could also provide land for the settlement of German troops after the war.

In one of the very few places in his memoirs where he mentions the Jews, Ludendorff states that:

> Jews were to be found all through Lithuania. . . . My immediate object was to obtain the Imperial Chancellor's consent to a pronounced pro-Lithuanian policy . . . The Lithuanians were to be won over by all possible means, and the White Ruthenes in the northern district to be brought more in touch with them, and Polish propaganda was to be prevented.[136]

He added that although nothing definite resulted from this, it did enable the Germans to follow a settled policy with regard to the Lithuanians. Moreover, Ludendorff does not seem to have held any hostile or anti-semitic attitudes towards the Jews. As for Lithuania, he noted that:

> No restrictions were imposed on anyone in the practice of his religion. We went so far in our toleration as to give the Jews wheaten flour for unleavened bread . . . [137]

Could it be then that, by hailing the Balfour Declaration, Ludendorff was hoping, among other things, to win over Lithuania's Jewish population?

It is important to note that during 1917, the Zionist movement was spreading in Lithuania, as well as in Poland and other parts of Russia, and new groups of pioneers for the colonization of Palestine after the war were being organized among the Lithuanians.[138]

On the other hand, early in October 1917, Balfour pleaded for the speedy announcement of the declaration because, as he informed the cabinet, the Germans were contemplating announcing their own similar pro-Zionist declaration. And when further evidence reached the Foreign Office that the Germans were endeavouring to make use of Zionist aspirations for their own ends, the Foreign Office commented that they were already aware of the Germans' fear of British Zionist propaganda.[139]

Again, it was none other than Weizmann who brought news of the suspected German pro-Zionist declaration to the British. As early as June 1917, he wrote to Ronald Graham enclosing an English translation of an article about a 'Jewish Republic', which he stated appeared in the *Reichsbote*. The German paper was reputed to be a semi-official one; and its author, the writer, Gustav von Dobeler, was said to be a 'well-known right-wing publicist'.[140] On these premises the Zionists founded their conclusions, which they conveyed to the British government, that a German pro-Zionist declaration was imminent.

Dobeler's article, entitled *A Jewish Republic In Palestine,* stated, according to Weizmann's translation of it to Graham, that:

A Jewish Republic upon Palestine soil as intermediary between Egypt and India—the idea is an extraordinarily good one for England but would be destructive to the political future of the Central Powers ... It is thus evident that England ... is about to carry out the cleverest political move by the creation of a Jewish Republic .... The establishment of a Jewish State under Turkish supremacy would be for us a measure of defence .... England in the possession of Palestine would signify the isolation of Central Europe.[141]

A week later, Weizmann again wrote to Ronald Graham that:

... there seems to be very little doubt that the German Government is endeavouring by all means at its disposal to work on the Zionists in Germany with a view to utilize them for purposes of a peace agitation.[142]

On 18 October 1917, in an editorial in the German newspaper *Vossische Zeitung*, Richard Lichtheim urged his fellow Zionists not to give up on Germany and her Ottoman ally, because, as he expounded, while the Entente can only make promises, it was Turkey that was in actual possession of Palestine and could offer 'more tangible concessions'. Alarmed, the London *Times* described the editorial as 'insidious propaganda' and printed a historic leader on 26 October that 'Germany has been quick to perceive the danger to her schemes and to her propaganda that would be involved in the association of the Allies with Jewish national hopes, and she has not been idle in attempting to forestall us'. Two days later, on 31 October, the British war cabinet approved the Balfour Declaration.[143]

However, there is little reason to believe that Palestine, still more a Jewish Palestine, was contemplated in Germany, and it is doubtful whether it had any real significance for the Germans. But to the British, the Palestine campaign was important in raising the 'shaken spirits' of a badly defeated army. Following a series of disastrous defeats on the Western Front, as well as in Mesopotamia and Palestine, the British were intent on a victory in the East. On 9 December 1917, Allenby received the surrender of Jerusalem. Although the British were overjoyed, and Allenby's successful campaign in December 1917 came as a real 'Christmas gift' to the British, the capture of Palestine seems to have caused 'little distress to the Germans'.[144]

The Recruitment of Jewish Battalions in America

The ninth consideration in the minute of Ormsby-Gore is that, as a direct result of the Balfour Declaration, the British government recruited special battalions of 'foreign' Jews in New York with the permission of the American government.

The contribution of William Ormsby-Gore himself to the idea should not be lost sight of. In April 1917, Ormsby-Gore drew up a paper for the Cabinet Office on the question of 'Zionism and the suggested Jewish battalions for [the] Egyptian Expeditionary Force', in which he advocated the idea and frankly linked the two issues. The theme of this paper was that of the possibility of military cooperation between British and Jewish nationalists all over the world. Ormsby-Gore held that the movement of 'Nationalist Jews' was a serious one that was gathering ground not only in Russia and Palestine, but in the US as well. In the paper, Ormsby-Gore went on to say that Zionists were anti-Russian; they were also profoundly anti-German, and were deeply suspicious of the French.[145]

The Jewish Legion, originally the brainchild of Vladimir Jabotinsky and brought to the attention of the War and Foreign Offices with the backing of Chaim Weizmann as early as 1916, was conceived to enlist unnaturalized Jews of Russian origin, resident in England, in the British army. At first, the British responded to the idea with indifference. But as the military situation changed, and once the British invasion of Palestine was in full swing, thanks to the activities of Zionist leaders in Britain, the idea of the 'liberation' of Palestine with the help of a combatant Jewish Legion gained new momentum. The battalion raised in England was attached to the 38th Royal Fusiliers, whereas American Jews who joined later were attached to the 39th and 40th.[146] The roots of Jabotinsky's idea for the Jewish Battalions (which was later conceived in the form of the Zion Mule Corps) may have been inspired, ironically, by a previous plan devised in 1915 by Itzhak Ben-Zvi[147] and David Ben-Gurion to form a Jewish Legion, *ha-Halutz,* whose members would fight with the Turkish army for the defence of Palestine.[148] The idea was at first approved by the Turkish commander (40 men actually volunteered), and the battalion was formed, only to be later disbanded by Jemal Pasha.[149]

In New York, the East Side was the centre of Jewish life, consisting mainly of Russian immigrants who had just reached the New World. There were said to be, according to a famous English historian, whole streets in which nothing but Yiddish was heard; there were synagogues for every Jewish sect, and children were taught in

Hebrew; and the general atmosphere was said to resemble that of the Pale of Settlement[150] (the restricted area in the Western border region of imperial Russia where Jews were required to live from 1791 to 1917). It was here, on East Broadway, that the British opened their recruiting mission offices on 42nd Street to recruit Jewish people from NY for the battalions to fight in World War I. The Jewish Legion Committee office was situated on 23rd Street.[151]

David Ben-Gurion, general secretary of the *Histadrut* (National Workers'[152] Organization) from 1921 to 1935 and future Israeli prime minister and statesman, came to America and was active making speeches for the *Poali Zion* movement (the Labour Movement). When the British started to recruit Jews in New York for the British Army, Ben-Gurion and Ben-Zvi, as members of the Committee for an American Jewish Legion, campaigned vigorously among the rank and file of *Poali Zion* and among American Jews at large, Ben-Gurion himself being among the first to reach Palestine in 1918 as a soldier with the Jewish Legion.[153]

It is questionable whether in 1917 the bulk of American Jews, who were mainly concentrated in New York, supported Zionism. Moreover, it is not known what numbers were recruited there for the British army. While one scholar (Cecil Roth) gives the impression that the East Side of New York was a hotbed of Zionist activity, another (Amos Elon) asserts that the vast majority of the Jews in the lower East Side were far removed from the Zionist cause.[154] The fact that Ben-Gurion was only able to recruit 600 Jewish immigrants from America between 1919 and 1923[155] tends to support the second view.

Moreover, there is no evidence that the Jewish Legion played any significant role alongside Allenby's forces in occupying Palestine. In September of 1917, as General Allenby's expeditionary force was driving out the Turkish army, Ben-Gurion wrote in his diary, as he lay sick in bed: 'I fear our battalion has lost the chance to take part in the conquest of Palestine.'[156]

Similar declarations by the US, France, and Italy

Ormsby-Gore's reference to 'similar declarations by other powers ... including the recent one of the American Senate' refers to declarations made by the US, France, and Italy. Zionist negotiations with the French and Italian governments towards a pro-Zionist declaration were far more difficult than those with the British. In Paris as well as in Rome, the announcement of the Balfour Declaration was met with a distinctly cool reception. This was evident from the extent of Zionist efforts needed to extract an endorsement of the Balfour Declaration, and in both cases, the endorsements were communicated to the Zionists and not to the British government, who issued the declaration.[157]

When studying the early history of these allegedly 'similar' declarations, it will become evident that they were not so much the outcome of an entirely independent decision by each power as the direct result of British-Zionist planning and persuasion. Once again, it was Mark Sykes who was largely responsible for such endeavours, as the following brief sections will show.

The American resolution

During the war, American Zionists in the circle of Justice Brandeis were kept informed by their Zionist friends in London of the talks between them and the British War Cabinet. Through his efforts with humanitarian relief work for starving Jews in Palestine, Brandeis got in touch with State Department officials and had occasion to mention to them Zionist endeavours in London. However, the extent to which Brandeis received from American officials verbal approval for Zionist political aims as opposed to purely humanitarian ones remains disputed. In May 1917, during a trip to the US, Balfour discussed with Brandeis the subject of Zionism and his own declaration. The two were mutually impressed, and Balfour personally pledged his support for Zionism. There is no evidence, however, that Balfour discussed a Jewish Palestine with President Wilson during the same visit. Moreover, it seems that the American State Department did not consider the political implications of the Balfour Declaration prior to its issuance on 2 November. In the following months, when the declaration was being drafted, its drafts were sent to Brandeis to secure the approval of the American government. During the crucial months of September and October, when the critical details of the Balfour Declaration were being debated in London, the British were trying hard to draw in President Wilson as an active partner. But whatever discussions for a Jewish Palestine were conducted on a direct level between members of the Brandeis group and Wilson, or through Colonel House, these were carried out without the knowledge of Secretary of State Lansing, who was hostile to Zionism. And thus, Lansing could later maintain with 'complete accuracy' that the US government had never approved the declaration prior to its announcement. Colonel House himself expressed his personal misgivings about the whole idea by saying: 'If I were the British I would be chary about going too definitely into that question.'[158]

Indeed, as late as 19 September, no specific written approval from Wilson was yet in sight. Weizmann continued to press hard on Brandeis to influence the American president. The formula for the declaration, as has already been seen, underwent a series of changes. The October formula that Weizmann had sent to Brandeis was significantly watered down to meet the approval of anti-Zionist Jews. Whereas in September, the British promised to 'secure the achievement' of the Jewish national homeland, in October, they merely promised to 'facilitate' it. When reminded again by Colonel House, President Wilson left House's original note on this question forgotten in his pocket for more than a month. Eventually, he told House that he concurred with the formula. It is not clear, however, whether President Wilson was aware of the changes that the formula he was approving had undergone. On 16 October, House wrote: 'I will let the British Government know that the formula they suggest as to the Zionist Movement meets with your approval.'[159]

One author, Frank E. Manuel, concludes that the declaration was a minor incident in President Wilson's mind, and that ' ... under the circumstances it is rather far-fetched to consider Wilson one of the progenitors of the Balfour Declaration. The most that can be said is that he allowed it to happen'.[160]

The resolution of the US Congress referred to in Ormsby-Gore's minute of December 1922 had been announced the previous June.

It stated that the outcome of World War I was to enable the Jewish people to re-create and re-organize a national home in the land of their fathers, and afford an opportunity to the House of Israel to re-establish its Jewish life in the ancient Jewish land, therefore be it:

> Resolved by the Senate and the House of Representatives of the United States of America in Congress assembled, that the United States of America favors the establishment in Palestine of a national home for the Jewish people, it being clearly understood that nothing shall be done which may prejudice the civil and religious rights of Christians and all other non-Jewish communities in Palestine, and that the holy places and religious buildings and sites in Palestine shall be adequately protected.[161]

The French declaration

As soon as a declaration of sympathy with the Jewish people was contemplated by the British government, Mark Sykes began working to obtain the approval of the French, and while Weizmann was busy presenting the Zionist case to British officials, Sykes had Nahum Sokolow sent to Paris with the mission of persuading the French government to issue a pro-Zionist declaration similar to the Balfour Declaration. In the eyes of Balfour too, it was expedient that the French declaration should precede the British one chronologically, as a means of persuading the less enthusiastic members of the British cabinet.

On 4 October 1917, the question of the German declaration came before the War Cabinet. Balfour, in presenting the case to the cabinet, relied on three main arguments, and at the end of his speech read a 'very sympathetic declaration' by the French government. (Balfour's description of the French announcement as 'very sympathetic' was a considerable exaggeration, to say the least). To further convince the cabinet, Balfour stated that 'he knew' that President Wilson was 'extremely favourable to the movement.'[162]

It is significant that Balfour needed to read out to the cabinet similar declarations of sympathy in order to persuade his own government that other major powers had already committed to the Zionist cause. When Sokolow went to Paris, on Sykes' advice, he set out to convince Picot (this seems to have been one of Sykes' manoeuvres to get rid of the Sykes-Picot Agreement) that the 'Jews are in a position of a child who cannot tell whether he likes his father or mother best', and that 'it is hardly for them [i.e., the Jews] to say whether they would prefer England or France as suzerain power, and that therefore the question must be settled between the governments themselves.'[163]

Thus, the declaration made by Jules Cambon[164] came earlier than the Balfour Declaration and indeed was thought to have favourably 'influenced' it. Mark Sykes was very satisfied with the results of the 'Declaration Cambon', for it served his plans in two ways; First, after having the French, who were the main competitors of Britain in Palestine, declare their sympathy with Zionism, he could now openly reveal British sympathetic views towards the Zionist cause; and second, he could now use the French declaration to persuade the hesitant and silent members of the British cabinet to follow the French lead. The French, however, preferred to keep their declaration unpublished, and the Quai d'Orsay only circulated it internally to some of its embassies. For different reasons, neither the Zionists nor the French made the declaration public in France itself.[165] In retrospect, the 'Declaration Cambon' seems to have been especially tailored for the British cabinet.[166]

For his part, whenever he found it necessary, Balfour continued to stress the 'other' declarations by 'other powers' long after 1917.

In the spring of 1919, Balfour wrote to Curzon from Paris that it might be useful to remind the military authorities in Cairo how the 'French, United States and Italian Governments have approved the policy set forth in my letter to Lord Rothschild'.[167]

However, Leonard Stein (who, it will be recalled, served as Political Secretary of the World Zionist Organization for a decade and thus wrote from a Zionist perspective) asserts that, as far as France and Italy were concerned, the only evidence to support Balfour's statements were Cambon's letter of 4 June and Pichon's letter of 14 February 1918, in the case of France, and they were both addressed to Sokolow and not to the British government, or any other international entity. Stein also observes that Sokolow's translation of the French statement was inaccurate. The French used the term *un établissement juif*, which Sokolow rendered as 'a Jewish national home'. Stein's translation of the French statement, which had never been, up to that point, translated into English and had always been officially quoted only in French, reads as follows:

> Monsieur Sokolow, representing the Zionist Organizations [sic] was this morning [9 February] received at the Ministry of Foreign Affairs by Monsieur Stephen Pichon, who was

happy to confirm that there is complete agreement between the French and British governments in matters concerning the question of a Jewish establishment in Palestine.[168]

Indeed, two years later at the London and San Remo Conferences, the Zionists, who had so far made the most out of Pichon's assurances, were brushed aside by French representatives who firmly stated that there had never been any French endorsement of the Balfour Declaration.[169]

In addition to Sokolow's influence, one of the most important external factors influencing the decision of the French to make a pro-Zionist declaration may well have been the influence of the New York Zionist organisations. Tardieu, the French High Commissioner there, had become interested in the American Zionist movement and was closely in touch with Justice Brandeis. Moreover, it was Weizmann who had indicated to Brandeis the importance of maintaining this relationship with the French official. Tardieu justified a pro-Zionist declaration in that it secured for France the support of the 400,000 Jews who lived in the French colonies in North Africa.[170]

By putting emphasis on all those other pronouncements, it was as if Ormsby-Gore was once again, just as Balfour before him had done in 1917, trying to convince a sceptical government in 1922 of the wisdom of continuing the policy begun in 1917.

The Italian pronouncement

The Italian pronouncement also came in the form of a letter from the Italian ambassador in London, the Marquis Imperial, by order of

Baron Sidney Sonnino, the Italian Foreign Minister, to Sokolow, on 9 May 1918. It read:

> In connection with the requests which have been made to it His Majesty's Government is happy to confirm the previous statements made through its representatives in Washington, the Hague and Salonica, that is to say that it is prepared to take steps with pleasure in order to facilitate the foundation in Palestine of a Jewish national centre, on the understanding however that no prejudice shall arise through it to the legal and political status of existing religious communities and to civil and political rights already enjoyed by Israelites in any other country.[171]

However, when Sokolow translated the Italian text into English, which was also quoted in the British official documents only in its original language, he seems to have put his own interpretations on it. Leonard Stein once again notes a number of inaccuracies in his translation.[172]

In Italy, Zionism had, until the British government's issuing of the Balfour Declaration, received only a lukewarm response. The Jews there were an elite group in a country where anti-semitism was non-existent, and Italian Zionism had thus far been a sentimental, philanthropic movement with no political force. All of a sudden, the delegate of the international Zionist Organization, Nahum Sokolow, became a factor within Italian diplomatic circles while he was abroad in Italy for negotiations, after the Italian Foreign Minister, Sonnino, received intelligence information of a meeting between Sokolow and the pope, who was said to have given the Zionist leader certain assurances. 'With the holy father pro-Zionist, could the Italian government be more Catholic than the Pope?' reflected the Italian Foreign Minister.[173]

Soon after, Sokolow achieved his goal of getting a pronouncement from the Italian government. Nevertheless, the Italian pronouncement was not another Balfour Declaration; as Jeffries notes, the Italian government put in the missing words, which made all the difference. And by 'inserting' the words 'legal and political status',

> the Italian Government guaranteed that the National Home should not prejudice those very fundamental rights of the Arabs which the Balfour Declaration deliberately had excised.... with entire politeness it indicated that it was not deceived by the terms of the Balfour document, and that it would not be party to the suppression of native rights.[174]

Zionist Funds and the Jewish National Home

By focusing on the things that had 'been done by the Jews already in Palestine', such as the 4 millions in money and the establishment of schools, Ormsby-Gore suggests that great achievements had been made in Palestine. A closer examination of the record, however, reveals a different picture. The High Commissioner, Herbert Samuel, during the first few months of his Civil Administration in Palestine, constantly complained that the expected Jewish funds for the development of Palestine were insufficient. Indeed, the main obstacle in the winter of 1920-21 seemed, in his view, not to be Arab opposition, but Jewish reluctance to provide the Zionists with the necessary funds to make the 'national home' a reality.

The development loan that Samuel and Weizmann had envisaged was repeatedly delayed as it became increasingly evident that Jewish financiers were opposed to Zionism. And when Weizmann visited America in 1921 and 1923 to raise funds, only a small fraction of what had already been anticipated was achieved. Thus, 'the fund-raising failure had a direct impact on the Zionist enterprise in Palestine'. As early as October 1920, Zionist cash resources for the development of Palestine were so inadequate that Zionist officials asked for the number of Jewish immigrants to be reduced from 16,500 to a mere 1,000 immigrants per month.[175]

At the same time as Ormsby-Gore was making such claims, a revealing article by the journalist JMN Jeffries on the question of Jewish funds appeared in the *Daily Mail* on 24 January 1923. Jeffries, who had been on a three-month investigative mission in Palestine and had met many Arabs, Jews, and British officials on the spot, reported the following conversation between himself and a prominent Jewish man in Jerusalem, who, he said, was at the point of abandoning political Zionism. Upon asking him 'what on earth did you want the Balfour Declaration for at all?', the man replied frankly that it was 'the power of a statement of that sort which enabled us to reach the people's hearts and pockets'. Jeffries adds that the sum of £8 million had been collected in donations and he cites, from the papers of the Jewish Reorganization Commission, a report written to Weizmann in 1921 (before the £8 million had been raised), to the effect that:

> The vast amounts expended have contributed in slight degree towards the establishment of a self-supporting Jewish community . . . It is with deep regret we were obliged to conclude that the farms of the Jewish National Fund of which all Zionists have been taught to speak with pride were, from the standpoint of future national colonization, of little value.

The *Daily Mail* correspondent then poses the question: 'Who provided these great sums?' and answers that it was the poor Jews of Eastern Europe, and ordinary Jews around the world. Since, he adds, these resources have to be constantly renewed, and the resources of the East European Jewish communities have already been largely exhausted, further funds must be 'wrung' from American Jews (and Dr. Weizmann was already on his way there), otherwise 'the whole movement will collapse'.[176]

The Final Draft of the Balfour Declaration

That the final draft of the declaration was written by Leopold Amery and Ormsby-Gore himself has already been verified.

Although Amery's authorship of the declaration was well-known (the Milner-Amery draft was the one that was finally approved by the War Cabinet), yet, when Shuckburgh read Ormsby-Gore's minute in December 1922, he thought it wise to verify this with Amery himself, before printing the minute for circulation as a Cabinet Paper. Shuckburgh reveals that he had not known of Ormsby-Gore's help in writing the last draft. Amery's answer to the inquiry made by

Shuckburgh was that the last draft was 'actually' his but that 'it of course, embodied various previous drafts'. Amery is here referring to the fact that, for at least the preceding five months, the declaration was being drafted and redrafted, receiving the most careful scrutiny by Zionist leaders as well as British officials, to the extent that it travelled back and forth across the ocean (for Brandeis to participate in the redrafting process), the first of these drafts being the one submitted by Weizmann upon Balfour's invitation, as already discussed at some length.

Leonard Stein gives a thorough account of this aspect of the declaration. He also reveals a letter that he had written to Harold Nicolson on 19 March 1952, which contains some interesting details. Nicolson was in 1917 a young Foreign Office official who had assisted Sykes in handling the Zionist question. Stein wrote to him 35 years later to verify whether the course of events was as he remembered it and whether the Rothschild draft was, in fact, Nicolson's (or, as Stein himself believed), that of Sykes. Leonard Stein's account went like this: While the Zionist Committee members were busy drafting a formula to be submitted by Rothschild to Balfour, Nicolson was instructed by Sykes to draft a reply to Rothschild, to be submitted to Balfour for approval. Sokolow was shown Nicolson's successive drafts; the idea was that the Rothschild draft should be one known in advance to be acceptable to Balfour and Sykes. When Nicolson's formula was finally completed, and Sokolow 'knew what formula might be expected to be acceptable', he went back to the Zionist Committee and arranged for a draft on Nicolson's (or Sykes') lines to be submitted to the British government. When Rothschild wrote a draft on 18 July, Stein asserted that 'Balfour's approval of the formula had already been obtained'. Harold Nicolson answered Stein's letter a week later, telling him that he [i.e., Stein] had 'attributed much more importance to his [i.e., Nicolson's] part in the Declaration than is really justified', adding that, although he could not assure him that was what had occurred, nevertheless it was more or less correct, and Stein's 'sequence of events is probably accurate.'[177]

In the same letter, Nicolson (whose name is mentioned only rarely but who was all along a scribe throughout) mentioned that he was only 'attached to Mark Sykes to see that he did not lose documents'.[178] This last remark is particularly interesting in view of the admitted absence of all relevant material on the declaration, and of suggestions by some scholars that the absence of documentation may be due to the way Sykes handled the case, to his inexperience, and to his particular character as a negotiator who depended on verbal communication, leaving no written records.[179] To the contrary, this comment suggests that there *were* documents at some point. The perplexing question is, as this work has asked many times, what happened to them?

It is also interesting to add that Nicolson maintained that without Sykes' persistence on Lloyd George and Balfour, the Declaration might not have gone through.[180] Indeed, it might as well have been called the Sykes Declaration. When the British war cabinet finally adopted the Balfour Declaration after much delay and hesitation, it was Sykes who announced to the Zionist leader: 'Dr. Weizmann, it's a Boy!'.[181]

Moreover, it is significant to note that Nicolson himself was quoted saying in 1947: 'We never promised a Jewish State. All we ever promised was 'a' national home 'in' Palestine; and that promise was explicitly conditional on the maintenance of the rights of the Arab'.[182]

Finally, a minor but perhaps significant detail regarding the actual wording of the last draft of the Balfour Declaration may be added here. Foreign Office files reveal that the carbon copy of the letter finally sent to Lord Rothschild on 2 November contained a final sentence that appears to have been omitted at the very last minute. The final part of the last draft of the Balfour Declaration (which was written by Amery and Ormsby-Gore as we have seen and was sent for the 'immediate' signature of the Secretary of State) read as follows: ' . . . I should be grateful if you would pass on this declaration to the Zionist Federation *and secure that it is given the necessary publicity*' [italics added]. Thus, 'pass on' was replaced by the word 'bring', and 'to the Zionist Federation' became 'to the knowledge of the Zionist Federation'. The declaration was ended here with a full stop. The word 'secure' was at first replaced by the less forceful 'see'. But in the end, the Secretary of State seems to have decided against letting the Zionist Federation, (or at any rate, Lord Rothschild, because the letter was addressed to him), 'secure' the 'necessary publicity' for the Balfour Declaration and the sentence was omitted altogether for unknown reasons.[183]

Ormsby-Gore's Article in The XIXth Century

Finally, Ormsby-Gore ends his minute by mentioning an article that he himself had written in 1920 in *The XIXth Century*, and which he claimed 'has some interesting data'.

The article referred to is entitled *Great Britain, Palestine and the Jews*. About the history of the Balfour Declaration, it has absolutely nothing to add, and in this respect, it is disappointing. However, it does contain a number of revealing misconceptions. Coming from Ormsby-Gore, Under-Secretary for the Colonies 1922-24 and future Colonial Secretary (as Lord Harlech),[184] these inaccuracies take on a particular significance. Not only was he a wholehearted Zionist who was instrumental in bringing about the Balfour Declaration and who took practical steps towards achieving those ends (he was appointed in 1918 to the Zionist Commission to Palestine to secure every facility for the movement and its members), but he was actually in a position to see his own ideas being realized. In *The XIXth Century*, Ormsby-Gore discloses his biased views:

> Only twice in its long eventful history has [Palestine] formed a separate State, first under the Jews, and then for nearly a century as the kingdom of the Latin Crusaders.

He goes on to dismiss its Arab past as merely 'part of successive empires', then argues that 'the bulk of the present Mahommedan population are probably of Canaanite or Phoenician stock'.

On the agricultural situation of the country, Ormsby-Gore makes the sweeping remark that 'potentially it is a rich, very rich, agricultural country which has been allowed to go to ruin since Roman times'. Here it is interesting to add that it was Aaron Aaronsohn who had first introduced Ormsby-Gore to Zionism during his time at the Arab Bureau in Cairo, and convinced him that 'the Palestinian wilderness could be made to blossom like the rose by Jewish skill and industry'.[185]

It is odd to suggest that this supposed lamentable situation in Palestine had gone on uninterrupted for such a long stretch of time. Ormsby-Gore completely disregards the catastrophic effects of World War I on the agriculture of Palestine (largely due to the Turkish policy of felling huge numbers of trees as an energy source for their army—(the depredations of war were in fact one of the factors underlying the disastrous famine which swept the area).

A balanced view of the situation in Palestine on the eve of World War I could have been gained by looking at the situation from an unbiased historical perspective. The region's general agricultural backwardness can be reasonably attributed to the decline of the Ottoman Empire in the latter part of the nineteenth century, rather than to Ormsby-Gore's absurd notion that, once the Romans had ceased to rule Palestine, the native element allowed the land to rot and go to ruin. There are many further implications behind Ormsby-Gore's statement. For one, he was hinting that the native dwellers of Palestine had been such 'inferior' farmers, throughout so many centuries, that they could not even manage to keep their land fertile; and that because of this, they had no valid claim on the country, which should therefore now be handed over to the Jews who would make the ancient land flow with 'milk and honey' once again.

This notion that Palestine had been neglected over many centuries, and that the Jewish colonizers had made it bloom was prevalent in Zionist literature and propaganda at the time, and this Zionist reasoning was fully shared and seems, on this evidence at least, to have been fully endorsed by Ormsby-Gore.

In the same article, Ormsby-Gore makes the curious remark that 'It is conceivable that in a Jewish Palestine there could exist Mahommedan Jews'. Finally, he quotes a passage from Ezekiel Chapter 36, which, he says, perhaps more than any other passage in the Bible, 'illustrates' the ideas 'which underlie the Zionist movement', adding that 'nothing can now stop the Zionist movement.'[186]

Whatever else might be said about Ormsby-Gore's actions, the firmness of his convictions about Zionism is indisputable. When he met with the London Zionist Political Committee in 1918 and reported on his five months abroad [with the Zionist Commission in Palestine], he stated his conviction that 'sooner or later' there would be a Zionist Palestine, advocating 'peaceful penetration' by Zionist Jews from the coastal areas towards the hills.

As for the Palestinian Arabs, he looked down on them with contempt; to him, they were not even Arabs, but merely 'Arabic-speaking vice-ridden' people.[187]

Even though a Zionist lobby is not one that is usually mentioned in connection with British politics, that is what it was,[188] and during the early 1920s, it can safely be said that William Ormsby-Gore was the effective leader of that lobby.

SUMMARY AND CONCLUSION

The Balfour Declaration was carefully and ambiguously worded to mean anything, from a Jewish cultural centre in Palestine—such as a Hebrew University—to a fully fledged state; it was left for time to tell what the final outcome would be.

'Nobody knows why the Balfour Declaration was made', wrote Christopher Sykes in 1965, adding that Leonard Stein devoted years to study its origins, yet after reading his masterly book, the reader still 'cannot say for certain precisely why the coalition government of Lloyd George authorised Balfour to write to Lord Rothschild as he did'.[1] And the story of the Balfour Declaration, as Mayir Vereté wrote in 1983, 'continues to cast its spell'.[2]

In effect, the inherent ambiguity that has been the focus of this study gave British officials the liberty to explain it each according to his own understanding, and this was to last throughout the early 1920s and beyond, causing much confusion along the way. Future historians may still uncover what really happened to all those lost papers and files mentioned in this narrative. Or we may never know, and William Ormsby-Gore's version of events may remain the only official British interpretation of the origins and early history of events leading up to Balfour's declaration.

In any case, given all the complications surrounding the Balfour Declaration, there is sufficient reason to believe that, as this study has shown, had it been postponed for a few months, or perhaps even weeks, it might never have materialised; and Weizmann himself attests to this. In his reflections on the declaration 10 years after it was issued, Weizmann noted that its foundations had to be laid through years of hard work:

> The Balfour Declaration of 1917 was built on air ... every day and every hour of these last ten years, when opening the newspapers, I thought: Whence will the next blow come? I trembled lest the British Government would call me and ask: 'tell us, what is this Zionist Organization? Where are they, your Zionists?' For these people think in terms different from ours. The Jews, they knew, were against us.[3]

In the light of all the above arguments, we can reiterate some conclusions. First, in 1917, it was not clear what exactly was meant by the Balfour Declaration, and hence the 1922-24 official British interpretation of it seems to have been much more decisive than the declaration itself. It will be recalled that when, on 31 October 1917, Balfour recommended the pro-Zionist declaration to the War Cabinet, he had no clear idea as to what exactly was to be done, since he advocated 'some form of British, American or other protectorate'.[4] Again in August 1919, Balfour wrote: 'I am an ardent Zionist ... but, I should personally like someone else to take the Mandate'; in 1922, he wrote to CE Hughes, the American Secretary of State: '... At Paris [i.e., at the Peace Conference] I always warmly advocated that it should be taken, not by Great Britain, but by the United States.'[5]

Indeed, according to Leonard Stein, 'neither on the British nor on the Zionist side was there any disposition, at the time, to probe deeply into its meaning—still less was there any agreed interpretation'.⁶ In addition, Stein reveals that this was not inconsistent with Lord Hankey's impression. In a private conversation with Stein, Hankey told the Zionist historian that his own recollection from many conversations with Balfour was that:

> When asked privately what he understood by a Jewish National Home in Palestine, his answer would be, in effect, that he could give no exact definition—it might turn out to be anything from a religious and cultural centre, a kind of Jewish Vatican, to a Jewish State; time alone would show.⁷

When, in 1923, the Colonial Secretary sought to arrive at a final decision on Palestine and whether the pro-Zionist policy was to be maintained or reversed, the Middle East Department of the Colonial Office advocated its own version of events leading up to the Balfour Declaration and defended the government's pro-Zionist policy in the face of considerable opposition at home, with disastrous consequences for the Palestine Arabs.⁸

Second, the official documents worked out during 1923 stress that the short-term war measure was a decidedly more important factor than the long-term strategic considerations in the minds of British officials at the time the declaration was issued.⁹ For this, one man—Ronald Graham—was largely responsible. Ormsby-Gore's minute of December 1922 stressed the importance to the Allied cause of the role played by international Jewry, at a time, he suggested, of great peril to the Allies. As this was the only official interpretation of events leading up to the Balfour Declaration to be found in British archives, and as the decision to continue a pro-Zionist policy was based on this particular interpretation, its significance multiplies. However, whether the account of events in this minute is consistent with what actually occurred is more open to question. The documents reveal that this view had been contested by at least some high-ranking policy makers during the crucial months when the Balfour Declaration was debated. However, their views went unheeded.

The notion that the pro-Zionist Declaration 'saved' the empire in its moment of crisis is a very doubtful one. The international power of world Jewry turned out to be greatly exaggerated, and the Foreign Office subsequently received information that Zionist strength within the international Jewish community was now thought to be considerably weaker than official circles in London had at first believed. Although positive reports of the Declaration's impact were received in London in November and December of 1917, with accounts of happy demonstrations throughout the Jewish world, more realistic views emerged shortly afterwards.[10]

Moreover, the Committee of Imperial Defence seems to have held the view that Palestine was not as strategically important as was often suggested. It will be recalled, that in July 1923, Shuckburgh had written to the Secretary of State:

> ... You will remember that it was decided to refer to the Committee of Imperial Defence the question of how far Palestine, quite apart from pledges and commitments of every kind, is to be regarded as of strategic value to the British Empire. I understand that the CID have now received papers on this subject from all the Departments concerned ...[11]

SUMMARY AND CONCLUSION

By pushing its own interpretation of events, as the future of Palestine was being debated between 1922 and 1924, the Middle East Department of the Colonial Office was largely responsible for continuing the government's pro-Zionist policy in face of strong internal opposition, especially in the light of the Geddes Act,[12] which exerted strong pressure to cut down on expenditure all over the British Empire, and of the opposition in the House of Lords and other governmental circles. It was here again that Weizmann and the Zionist leadership stepped in to convince high-ranking British officials that the 'national home' policy was cheaper for the British government than the maintenance of a large garrison in the country. The Middle East Department moreover, drove home the notion that the mandate itself was linked to the idea of a Jewish national home, as if it was its *raison d'être,* and as if the two were irreversibly and inextricably linked together.

In her seminal work, British historian Elizabeth Monroe maintained that the declaration was 'one of the greatest mistakes in our imperial history'.[13] In 1945, Winston Churchill was quoted as saying that he was 'not aware of the slightest advantage which has ever accrued to Great Britain from this painful and thankless task.'[14]

It has been made abundantly clear throughout the pages of this book, in answer to the often-posed academic question of whether this policy was in the best interests of Britain or not, that it was one of the most unwise policies the British Empire has undertaken. But more to the point, the Colonial Office did in fact imply in 1923 that this policy was imprudent, even though it was decided in the end, after a year's deliberation, to carry on with this misguided policy. The

Cabinet Committee's final report on 27 July 1923 concluded that it was difficult to argue with those who held that the 'entire Mandate is built on the fallacy of attempting to reconcile the irreconcilable', nevertheless, in the end, it was resolved that whether the policy had been 'wise or unwise, it is well nigh impossible for any Government to extricate itself without a substantial sacrifice of consistency and self respect, if not honour'.[15]

'With feelings of shame and contrition', the eminent British historian Arnold Toynbee expressed his firm belief that throughout World War I and after it, the British government, by 'using deliberately ambiguous language', was playing a 'double game'. In his Foreword to *The Palestine Diary 1914-1945*, Toynbee wrote that the Palestine story is a 'tragedy', the essence of which is that about 1,500,000 Palestinian Arabs 'have now become refugees as a result of the intervention of foreign powers in their country's affairs', adding that 'the might of these foreign powers has been irresistible, and the evicted Palestinian Arabs have been forcibly deprived of their country, their homes, and their property without having been allowed to have a voice in the determination of their own destiny'. Toynbee asserted that 'The tragedy in Palestine is not just a local one; it is a tragedy for the World; because it is an injustice that is a menace to the World's peace . . .'. The historian solemnly concluded:

'As an Englishman I hate to have to indict my country, but I believe that Britain deserves to be indicted, and this is the only personal reparation that I can make . . .'.[16]

APPENDIX A: THE BALFOUR DECLARATION

> Foreign Office,
> November 2nd, 1917.

Dear Lord Rothschild,

I have much pleasure in conveying to you, on behalf of His Majesty's Government, the following declaration of sympathy with Jewish Zionist aspirations which has been submitted to, and approved by, the Cabinet

"His Majesty's Government view with favour the establishment in Palestine of a national home for the Jewish people, and will use their best endeavours to facilitate the achievement of this object, it being clearly understood that nothing shall be done which may prejudice the civil and religious rights of existing non-Jewish communities in Palestine, or the rights and political status enjoyed by Jews in any other country"

I should be grateful if you would bring this declaration to the knowledge of the Zionist Federation.

APPENDIX B: WAR CABINET MEMORANDUM, OCTOBER 1917. SECRET, G-164. CAB 24. PRO

[This Document is the Property of His Britannic Majesty's Government.] **41**

Printed for the War Cabinet. October 1917.

SECRET.
G.—164.

WAR CABINET.

THE ZIONIST MOVEMENT.

(Note by the Secretary.)

IN accordance with the instructions given in War Cabinet 245, Minute 18, the draft declaration on Zionism was submitted to nine—or, including Mr. E. S. Montagu, ten—representative Jewish leaders.

Mr. Montagu's memoranda have already been circulated.

The following are the replies of the remaining nine. (Appendix I.) Of these, six may be regarded as on the whole favourable to the declaration, or to the declaration with slight amendments, while three are opposed to a form of declaration acceptable to the Zionists, and submit alternatives. The six favourable to a Zionist form of declaration are:—

1. The Rt. Hon. Herbert Samuel, M.P.
2. The Chief Rabbi.
3. Lord Rothschild.
4. Sir Stuart Samuel, Bart., Chairman of the Jewish Board of Deputies.
5. Dr. Weizmann.
6. Mr. Nahum Sokolov.

The three unfavourable are:—

7. Sir Philip Magnus, M.P.
8. C. G. Montefiore, Esq., President, Anglo-Jewish Association.
9. L. L. Cohen, Esq., Jewish Board of Guardians.

The various alternative drafts submitted are collated in the attached Appendix II.

Appendix III contains a selection of extracts from documents submitted by the leaders of the Zionist organisation. The latter have not seen Mr. Montagu's Memorandum (Paper No. G.T.—2263), nor have they had an opportunity of replying thereto.

M. P. A. HANKEY, *Secretary, War Cabinet.*

2, *Whitehall Gardens, S.W.,*
    October 17, 1917.

APPENDIX I.

(1.)

From the Rt. Hon. Herbert Samuel, M.P.

The policy embodied in the draft declaration, which is now under the consideration of the Cabinet, seems to me to be right.

If the Turks are left ostensibly in control of Palestine, the country is likely to fall, in course of time, under German influence. If Germany, or any other continental Power, is dominant there, Egypt would be exposed to constant menace. The best safeguard would be the establishment of a large Jewish population, preferably under British protection.

I feel no doubt that the policy expressed in the declaration is that which is desired by the mass of the Jewish people, both in this country and throughout the world. Those who oppose it, though individually influential, are few in number, and, I believe, not representative. The officers of the Jewish Board of Representatives, which is the nearest approach to a democratically elected body in the Jewish

[1074]   B

2

community in England, having recently issued a pronouncement in a hostile sense, were censored by their constituents and obliged to resign.

If the policy were carried into effect through British influence it would be calculated to win for the British Empire the gratitude of Jews throughout the world, and, wherever the interests of the country of which they were citizens was not involved, to create among them a bias favourable to the Empire.

I presume that such a declaration would not be made public until a favourable military situation had been brought about in Palestine. Otherwise it might lead to the persecution of the Jewish colonists there at the hands of the Turks. It might also prove an embarrassment at home, as it might be represented that one of the reasons for the continuance of the war was the pursuit of subsidiary aims, of which this was one. But the adoption of the declaration now, and its confidential communication to those who are interested, would clear the air, and would be, I think, a wise step.

(2.)

From the Chief Rabbi (Dr. J. H. Hertz).

It is with feelings of the profoundest gratification that I learn of the intention of His Majesty's Government to lend its powerful support to the re-establishment in Palestine of a national home for the Jewish people. The proposed declaration of His Majesty's Government that it " will use its best endeavours to facilitate the achievement of this object " will mark an epoch in Jewish history To millions of my brethren throughout the world it will mean the realisation of Israel's undying hope of a restoration—a hope that has been the spiritual lodestar of Israel's wanderings for the last 1,800 years.

The draft declaration is in spirit and in substance everything that could be desired. I welcome the reference to the civil and religious rights of the existing non-Jewish communities in Palestine. It is but a translation of the basic principle of the Mosaic legislation: " And if a stranger sojourn with thee in your land, ye shall not vex (oppress) him. But the stranger that dwelleth with you shall be unto you as one born among you, and thou shalt love him as thyself." (Lev., xix, 33, 34.)

I would suggest one minor alteration in the wording of the last three lines. I am anxious that the phrase:

" . . . or the rights and political status enjoyed in any other country by such Jews who are fully contented with their existing nationality and citizenship "

be shortened to:

" . . . or the rights and political status enjoyed by Jews in any other country."

In conclusion, I must, as Chief Rabbi, thank the Prime Minister, the Secretary of State for Foreign Affairs, and the members of the War Cabinet for their striking sympathy with Jewish aspirations, and assure them that the overwhelming majority of Anglo-Jewry, as well as of the Jewries of His Majesty's Overseas Dominions, will rejoice with me at this broad humanity and far-sighted statesmanship of the men who guide the destinies of the Empire.

(3.)

From Lord Rothschild.

I would welcome a declaration on the lines of the draft you send me, for I think it will to a great extent meet the objections raised by the anti-Zionists.

Personally, I think that the proviso is rather a slur on Zionism, as it presupposes the possibility of a danger to non-Zionists, which I deny. However, I welcome this declaration because it would show that His Majesty's Government is benevolently disposed towards and would lend its potent support to the aspirations of the great mass of the Jewish people, these aspirations being to have a home where they could speak their own language, have their own education, and have their own civil and religious institutions under the protection of the Allied Governments. I should like

APPENDIX B

3

to point out that the opponents of Zionism have almost entirely framed their opposition on the false hypothesis that the possession of a national home and status by one body of Jews would necessarily react on those Jews who preferred to remain citizens of the countries they now live in. In expressing my opinion that this belief is wholly unfounded, I would like to indicate that of the 12,000,000 Jews in the world, at least 10,000,000 are either active Zionists or else pro-Zionist. The greater part of these 10,000,000 hold that they, as Jews, have a historical and inviolable right to a national home, and moreover, a home in Palestine, the land of their forefathers. One of the chief aims of the Zionist Federation, when the settlement in Palestine takes place, is to see that while obtaining as large a measure of autonomy as possible, no encroachment on the rights of the other inhabitants of the country should take place. The relations between the Palestine Jews and their neighbours have hitherto been scanty and spasmodic, which is mainly due to mutual ignorance and indifference, but I have no fear that this would continue if a settlement under the ægis of the Allied Powers is carried out. I feel sure that this hour of crisis offers a great opportunity for a most beneficial development of a country rich in possibility, and a broad basis for permanent and cordial relations between Jews, Armenians, Arabs, and the other inhabitants of the country. Among the 450,000 Jews of the British Empire only some 10,000 or 15,000 are opposed to Zionist aspirations.

I would conclude by once again welcoming the declaration as an expression of the benevolence of His Majesty's Government towards the Jewish people.

(4.)

From Sir Stuart Samuel, Bart., Chairman of the Jewish Board of Deputies.

1. I think that Jews resident in Great Britain are by a large majority favourable to the establishment of a national home for Jews in Palestine, under proper safeguards.

2. English Jews generally have held aloof from the Zionist movement because they were not convinced that Palestine could support a greatly increased population, and should they approve a large immigration into that country they might be faced by the problem of a starving population requiring to be removed to another destination. Consequently, it would be necessary to provide a Jewish settlement in Palestine with the funds required for public works, irrigation, roads, loans to agriculturists, &c. In my opinion, 20 millions sterling would be required to give such a settlement the start that would likely ensure success. This amount would, I think, be provided by the Jews of the world if the settlement were under the auspices of the Allied Powers.

3. A second reason for the aloofness previously alluded to is that many English Jews resented the suggestion that they could be faithless to the country in which they had been settled over 200 years, and adopt, or as it has been put, return to another nationality. Regarded generally, their attitude is that whilst they would be favourable to the project that those Jews who wish to go to Palestine being enabled to do so, and willing to regard it as a restoration of their land to the Jews, it would be necessary to make it clear that any State, if founded, would be a modern State, having no claim upon Jews outside it to be regarded as its nationals. Hence, in my opinion, the draft declaration is susceptible to amendment, and suggest that in line 8 the words after " non-Jewish communities in Palestine " be deleted, and in their place substituted " or the nationality or rights, or political status enjoyed in any other country by Jews." You will observe that Jews who are not " fully contented with their existing citizenship " are not protected by the proposed formula. In my opinion, not 10 per cent. of British-born Jews would go to Palestine.

4. It must be within the knowledge of His Majesty's Government that German and Austrian influence in Palestine has grown largely in recent years. Applications for assistance formerly written in Hebrew and English are now in Hebrew and German. Are the German and Austrian Jews to remain there, or if expelled to be allowed to return as Zionists? They should be made ineligible for 20 years.

5. Non-Jewish opinion would, I think, be conciliated if a statement were made simultaneously that the Holy Places in Jerusalem and vicinity would be internationalised, or at any rate not be placed under entirely Jewish control.

4

(5.)

From Dr. Weizmann, President of the English Zionist Federation.

It is my deep conviction that the declaration framed by His Majesty's Government will, when announced, be received with joy and gratitude by the vast majority of the Jewish people all over the world. It will supply a powerful impetus towards the regeneration and rejuvenation of an ancient country and an ancient people, and will thus form a notable step forward on the path of human progress and display anew the magnanimity of the British Empire.

I must abstain at this stage from entering upon a discussion of the views on the Jewish problem held by Zionists and Jewish Nationalists. These views have been fully expounded in the press and literature in this and other countries, and I personally have had the honour to lay the Zionist view before prominent members of His Majesty's Government. But as your letter refers to the divergence of view existing in Jewry on the subject of Zionism, I beg leave, shortly, to refer to this point.

Although it is unfortunately true that a certain number of Jews, chiefly in Western countries, are opposed to the idea of a Jewish national home in Palestine, it is no less true that these opponents, who are comparatively few in number, are almost exclusively to be found amongst those Jews who by education and social connections have lost touch with the real spirit animating the Jewish people as a whole. Our opponents, therefore, are entitled to speak in their own name only, but have no right to speak for the Jewish masses whose hopes, aspirations, ideals, and sufferings they do not share. The real motive underlying their opposition is of an eminently individual nature. Our opponents are overcome by fear lest the existence of a Jewish national home compromises to a certain extent their own position in the eyes of the peoples in whose midst they are living and with whom they desire to be totally identified. This motive, which they do not conceal, is in itself an indication that they are conscious of being an isolated minority in Jewry and of having the bulk of the Jewish people not with but against them. Had it been really their sincere conviction that the great majority of the Jewish people does not sympathise with the establishment of a national home, they would have no reason to be afraid of a scheme which can only be realised by the whole-hearted and enthusiastic collaboration of all living forces in Jewry. They would, on the contrary, be content to let the experiment pass unhindered, in order to show by its certain failure how correctly they had interpreted the mind of the Jews in general.

As to the wording of the declaration, may I be allowed respectfully to suggest one or two alterations?

(*a.*) Instead of "establishment," would it not be more desirable to use the word "re-establishment"? By this small alteration the historical connection with the ancient tradition would be indicated and the whole matter put in its true light.

(*b.*) The last lines of the declaration could easily be interpreted by ill-wishers as implying the idea that, with the re-establishment of the Jewish national home, only those Jews will have a right to claim full citizenship in the country of their birth who in addition to being loyal and law-abiding citizens would also totally dissociate themselves from the Jewish national home, showing no interest in, or sympathy with, its successful development. This unnatural demand is surely not in the mind of His Majesty's Government, and in order to avoid any misunderstanding I respectfully suggest that the part of the declaration in question be replaced by the following words:—

"the rights and political status enjoyed by Jews in any other country of which they are loyal citizens."

(*c.*) May I also suggest "Jewish people" instead of "Jewish race"?

(6.)

From Mr. Sokolov, Chief London Representative of the Zionist Organisation.

I received with profound pleasure and satisfaction your letter of the 6th instant, and I wish to express to His Majesty's Government the deep gratitude of the Zionist Organisation for the spirit of sympathy and justice manifested in the proposed declaration. With regard, however, to the wording of the draft, I beg leave, in accordance with your suggestion, to submit the following observations on behalf of the Zionist Organisation.

I understand that it is the desire of His Majesty's Government to express its sympathy with Jewish national aims in Palestine in a formula which will, at the same time, meet with the approval of all sections of British Jewry, including those who have not accepted the programme of Zionism. This desire is, no doubt, responsible for the inclusion of a proviso safeguarding the interests of non-Jewish communities in Palestine and the status of Jews who enjoy political rights in other countries.

While the Zionist Organisation would naturally prefer a declaration on the lines of the draft which my friends and myself had the honour to submit some weeks ago, it is not desirous of raising new questions. His Majesty's Government is aware that it is the Zionist movement which is responsible for such steps as have been taken towards the realisation of Jewish national aims in Palestine, and that the future prosecution of these aims, with the invaluable aid which His Majesty's Government so generously offers, will be the particular charge of the representatives of the Zionist movement. The safeguards mentioned in the draft are not open to any objections, since they are and always have been regarded by Zionists as a matter of course.

The following alterations, however, in the wording of the declaration I venture to suggest as most desirable:—

(1.) Line 2. "The establishment in Palestine of a national home." I would suggest the substitution of "re-establishment" for "establishment." By this slight change the real character of the movement and its historic basis would be recognised.

(2.) Line 3. "The Jewish race" I would suggest to be altered to "the Jewish people." The definition of "race" is a much-disputed question. It would also be questionable whether the word refers to all persons of Jewish origin or only to Jews. "Jewish people" is the best definition.

(3.) I would also suggest in substitution for the concluding phrase, " or the rights and political status . . . . nationality and citizenship," the following more comprehensive expression: "or the rights and political status enjoyed by Jews in any other country of which they are loyal citizens."

These alterations I recommend to your consideration, as I think that in this form a more adequate expression will be given to the principle.

The Zionist Organisation has always looked to Great Britain for sympathy and assistance, and it will hail with gratitude and enthusiasm the proposed declaration of His Majesty's Government. The millions of Zionists and their supporters all over the world are keenly aware of the immeasurable services which Great Britain has rendered and is rendering to the liberation of oppressed nationalities, and they confidently hope that His Majesty's Government will be instrumental also in the liberation of the unfortunate masses of the oldest and most hard-tried of living nationalities.

(7.)

From Sir Philip Magnus, M.P.

In replying to your letter of the 6th October, I do not gather that I am expected to distinguish my views as a Jew from those I hold as a British subject. Indeed, it is not necessary, even if it were possible. For I agree with the late Chief Rabbi, Dr. Hermann Adler, that "ever since the conquest of Palestine by the Romans we have ceased to be a body politic"; that "the great bond that unites Israel is not one of race but the bond of a common religion"; and that we have no national aspirations apart from those of the country of our birth. Holding these views, I venture, in compliance with your request, to offer a few remarks on the wording of the proposed declaration of policy with respect to the Zionist movement and its relation to the future of Palestine. I cannot agree that the Jews regard themselves as a nation, and the term "national" as applied to a community of Jews in Palestine or elsewhere seems to me to beg the question between Zionists and their

6

opponents, and should, I suggest, be withdrawn from the proposed formula. Indeed, the inclusion in the terms of the declaration of the words " a national home for the Jewish race " seems to me both undesirable and inferentially inaccurate.

On the other hand, a statement to the effect that the British Government would take steps to secure to the Jews now or hereafter resident in Palestine freedom to develop their religious culture and to observe their religious rites would be welcomed by the Jews and would be consistent with the traditional policy of the British Government. It is essential, however, as stated in the proposed formula, that any privileges granted to the Jews should be shared by their fellow-citizens of other creeds.

It should be remembered that under Turkish rule the Jews have latterly enjoyed many advantages. They have been permitted to found agricultural and commercial colonies, to establish schools, and to teach in those schools through the medium of the ancient Hebrew language. Any pronouncement on the part of His Majesty's Ministers to the effect that they would be prepared to take steps to establish for Jews, and for Jews only, a " national home in Palestine " might be interpreted as implying that the government of that country would, under certain conditions, be transferred to the Jews; and such a pronouncement would certainly arouse considerable opposition from other Palestinian communities, and might result in the Jews now resident in Palestine being exposed to the same treatment at the hands of the Turks as has been unhappily experienced by the Armenian Christians.

The Zionist agitation is a movement of comparatively recent date. The Jews of Spain and Portugal, at the height of their prosperity, made no attempt to use their influence to secure for themselves a " national home in Palestine," nor did they subsequently, when they fled from Spain to Holland and to other countries. If the Jews of Russia had been permitted to observe their religion, and had enjoyed equal civil rights with their fellow-citizens, the Zionist movement would not have developed, and it is more than probable that the agitation will not long outlive the avowed objects of the Revolution.

I know not what may be the real objective of the War Cabinet's military operations in Palestine. It is, however, rumoured in Zionist circles that the conquest of Palestine by Great Britain is desired in order that Palestine may become an independent buffer State between Turkey and Egypt; and that having regard to the declared policy of the Allies to annex no new territories, the country would be restored to the Jews under a British protectorate. Whether this be so or not, I feel sure that our Government, in accordance with its repeated declarations, would deem it necessary to consult the existing inhabitants of Palestine as to the ruling power under which they would desire to live; and, in all probability, they would elect to be governed by Great Britain or by one of our Allies, who would hold the balance fairly between the Christian, Jewish, and Mahommedan communities.

There is only one other remark which I desire to offer. The words " who are fully contented with their existing nationality " fail to express the devotion of Jews to the country of their birth, where they enjoy equal rights with their fellow-citizens. It is not, as has been unwisely suggested, for any distinctly Jewish ideals that Jews are fighting in the present war. They need not the offer of a national home in Palestine to excite their ardour or to stimulate their courage. They are fighting for the attainment of the self-same objects which His Majesty's Ministers have so unmistakably defined.

The wording of the proposed draft declaration of policy, if modified in accordance with the suggestions I have offered, would read as follows :—

" His Majesty's Government views with favour the establishment in Palestine of a centre of Jewish culture, and will use its best endeavours to facilitate the achievement of this object; it being understood that nothing shall be done which may prejudice the civil and religious rights of existing non-Jewish communities in Palestine or the rights and political status now enjoyed by Jews in any other country."

(8.)

From Mr. C. G. Montefiore, President of the Anglo-Jewish Association.

1. In common with all other members of the Jewish community, I am grateful to His Majesty's Government for its interest in the welfare of the Jews.

APPENDIX B

2. I deprecate the expression "a national home." For it assumes that the Jewish race constitutes a "nation," or might profitably become a nation, both which propositions I deny. The phrase "a national home for the Jewish race" appears to assume and imply that the Jews generally constitute a nationality. Such an implication is extremely prejudicial to Jewish interests, as it is intensely obnoxious to an enormous number of Jews. There can be no objection to Jews who *want* to form themselves into a nationality going to Palestine and forming themselves into a nationality in that country, but it must be effected without any prejudice to the character and position of the Jews as nationals of other countries.

3. The idea of a "home" for the Jews was started by the late Dr. Herzl, the founder of Zionism, because (as he himself told me) he believed—

(*a*.) That anti-Semitism was eternal, and that it was hopeless to expect its removal.

(*b*.) That the Jewish problem in Russia was insoluble in Russia.

I told him that (*a*) was a libel upon (1) the Jews and (2) human nature, and that even (*b*) was too pessimistic.

4. I was not wrong. For if the Revolution in Russia holds and reaction does not set in, the Jewish problem *has* been solved in Russia, and already the majority of the Russian Jews desire cultural autonomy *in* Russia, but not exile *from* Russia. (An indication of this condition of things—which will grow—was shown as early as April at the conference of party delegates to organise an all-Russian Jewish conference. The Zionists proposed to place the Palestine question on the programme of the conference, but were unable to carry their resolution. A conciliation committee was appointed, and it was resolved to recommend to the conference, as an optional subject of discussion, the question of civil and national rights in other countries, without special reference to Palestine.)

5. A national home for the Jews on the score of the oppressed condition of the Jews is no longer necessary. A vast majority of the Jews are free citizens of the countries in which they dwell. The Polish Jewish question will, with the co-operation of the Allies, be doubtless settled as favourably as the larger Russian Jewish problem has already been settled. The Rumanian Government will also not be able to resist the pressure of events. When five million Jews have been fully emancipated in Russia, 250,000 Jews in Rumania cannot much longer remain pariahs and aliens.

6. For the true well-being of the Jewish race emancipation and liberty in the countries of the world are a thousand times more important than a "home." In any case only a small fraction of the Jews could be collected together in Palestine.

7. Phrases such as a "national home," however carefully guarded, are likely to injure the newly won liberty of the Jews in Russia and to prevent full liberty in Rumania and Poland. If a "national home" *has been* provided all reactionaries will urge that nothing should, or need, be done in the direction of emancipation and of liberty, for the Jews now have a "national home" of their own. It is very significant that anti-Semites are always very sympathetic to Zionism. It is no wonder.

8. I and my friends do not desire to impede colonisation and immigration into Palestine; on the contrary, we desire to obtain free facilities for them. We are in favour of local autonomy wherever the conditions allow it. Whoever the suzerain Power of Palestine may be, we are in favour of the Jews, when their numbers permit it, ultimately obtaining the power which any large majority may justly claim.

9. The words "who are fully contented with" ill expresses the facts. When thousands of Jews are fighting with passion and ardour for their respective countries they are not merely "*contented* with their nationality." It is bone of their bone and spirit of their spirit.

10. For the reasons given, I earnestly hope that the first part of the declaration, up to the words "this object," may be omitted, and that words to the following effect may be substituted for them, viz. :—

"His Majesty's Government is anxious that free and unimpeded Jewish immigration into Palestine should be established. It views with favour unrestricted Jewish colonisation in that country. It will do its best to facilitate such immigration and colonisation. It will also seek to secure such municipal and local autonomy for the Jews as may be possible, and as the circumstances of the case may demand; it being clearly understood," &c.

8

11. For the words " who are fully contented with " I should wish to see substituted the words " who have no desire to relinquish their existing nationality and citizenship."

12. If the present words of the draft declaration are, for some reason or reasons unknown to me, believed by His Majesty's Government to be in the interests of British policy, and if His Majesty's Government is anxious to publish this formula for the sake of *this* country as well as for the Jews, I would, of course, subordinate my Jewish feelings, wishes, and interests to the interests of England and the Empire.

13. The position of many Jewish institutions and charities in Palestine which may not desire to be disconnected with their present relationship to Jewish (but non-Zionistic) organisations in European countries must be safeguarded. No Jew residing in Palestine should be compelled to come into, or join, a new Jewish " nationality."

Up to the opening of the war, the most influential Zionists were Germans and Austrians. There is only too much reason to fear that any " national home " of the Jews in Palestine will be a centre and a hotbed for German intrigue.

15. I venture to express the hope that His Majesty's Government has earnestly weighed, and will earnestly weigh, the possible effect of the proposed declaration upon the situation of the Jews in Turkey. Even if the declaration be not issued till the British army is in occupation of Palestine, there will still be a large number of Jews in the rest of the Turkish Empire. These may denounce the declaration, and so obtain protection. But they may become the victims of massacres hardly less atrocious than the massacres of the Armenians.

16. I have assumed that this memorandum will not be shown to anybody except the members of the War Cabinet and the Secretary of State for Foreign Affairs.

(9.)

From Mr. L. L. Cohen, Chairman, Jewish Board of Guardians.

1. The establishment of a " national home for the Jewish race " in Palestine, presupposes that the Jews are a nation, which I deny, and that they are homeless, which implies that, in the countries where they enjoy religious liberty and the full rights of citizenship, they are separate entities, unidentified with the interests of the nations of which they form parts, an implication which I repudiate.

2. The expression " by such Jews who are fully contented with their existing nationality and citizenship " is open to a similar objection. The British Jew, for instance, is not merely " contented " to enjoy his rights as a national and citizen, but is prepared (as he has shown) to fight for them, and to join in any constitutional movement to secure thier preservation.

3. I suggest that the promulgation of a declaration in the terms indicated will prejudicially affect the present prospects of the Jews in Russia and Rumania. His Majesty's Government has always exercised its beneficent influence to improve the lot of the Jews in both these countries, and has endeavoured to secure for them equality of treatment with other communities in these countries.

4. In Russia, through the revolution, the Jew has been released from the shackles which have oppressed him for generations, and he is working, so it is reported, to strenghten the foundations of the new Government. Are his enemies in Russia, still numerous, if quiescent, to be furnished with the argument against the Jew's freedom, that he is not a Russian, but a member of a nation, which is to be established elsewhere?

5. In Rumania, the Jew has had to content himself with promises up to the present, but these promises are taking a more definite shape, and the fulfilment of the hopes of the Rumanian Jew may be accomplished before the end of the war.

I conceive a great danger to the Rumanian Jew in the draft declaration, which will be used as a weapon by the opponents of the concessions promised him.

6. In my view a stimulus would be given to anti-Semitism everywhere by a draft declaration, and British Jews, equally with others, would suffer from this attempt to settle " the Jewish question." What is now proposed is optional emigration to the new State; with a revival of persecution, always possible, the Jews might be compulsorily emigrated; the words in the declaration, relating to the preservation of the political status of the Jews in other countries, would not protect them in such eventuality.

APPENDIX B

7. Given the realisation of the hopes and aspirations of the Russian and Rumanian Jews, " the Jewish question " disappears.

8. The pre-war population of Palestine was, I believe, under 400,000; the number of Jews in Europe is estimated to be nine and a quarter millions; if it is contended that there is a " Jewish question," the creation of a Jewish State in Palestine will scarcely solve it.

9. It must also be acknowledged that the new Jewish population to be attracted to Palestine will consist largely of Jews from the Near East, and, consequently, Jews at present belonging to enemy belligerent nations will be very numerous amongst the population.

There will be thus established foci of intrigue on the flank of British interests in Egypt.

10. A pronouncement on the part of His Majesty's Government in the sense indicated in the draft declaration of its attitude towards the Zionist movement will, I fear, further accentuate the divergence of opinion, to which reference is made in the letter now under reply, and is not demanded by British Jews, whose interests have always met with consideration from His Majesty's Government.

11. If, however, a formula *has* to be devised, the following amended declaration is submitted:—

"His Majesty's Government, viewing with favour the settlement of Jews in Palestine, will use its best endeavours to facilitate their immigration and colonisation, and to secure for them the enjoyment of civil and religious liberty, and municipal privileges in the towns and colonies inhabited by them; it being clearly understood that nothing shall be done which may prejudice the rights and privileges on non-Jewish communities in Palestine, or the rights and political status enjoyed in any other country by such Jews who determine to retain their existing nationality and citizenship."

12. I assume that this letter is to be treated as confidential, and will be submitted only to the Members of the War Cabinet and to His Majesty's Secretary of State for Foreign Affairs.

APPENDIX II.

Draft Declarations.

1. Draft submitted by the Secretary of State for Foreign Affairs, August 1917:—

"His Majesty's Government accept the principle that Palestine should be reconstituted as the national home of the Jewish people, and will use their best endeavours to secure the achievement of this object, and will be ready to consider any suggestions on the subject which the Zionist Organisation may desire to lay before them."

2. Draft submitted by Lord Milner to the War Cabinet, the 4th October, 1917. (Draft submitted to various Jewish representatives, the 6th October, 1917):—

"His Majesty's Government views with favour the establishment in Palestine of a national home for the Jewish race, and will use its best endeavours to facilitate the achievement of this object; it being clearly understood that nothing shall be done which may prejudice the civil and religious rights of existing non-Jewish communities in Palestine, or the rights and political status enjoyed in any other country by such Jews who are fully contented with their existing nationality."

3. Amendments to No. 2, proposed by (*a*) the Chief Rabbi, (*b*) Dr. Weizmann, (*c*) Mr. Sokolov, and (*d*) Lord Rothschild:—

Paragraph 1. For " Jewish race " substitute " Jewish people."
Paragraph 3. Substitute the following phrase: " or the rights and political status enjoyed by Jews in any other country."

4. Alternative draft submitted by Mr. Montagu, M.P.:—

"His Majesty's Government accepts the principle that every opportunity should be afforded for the establishment in Palestine of those Jews who cannot, and will not, remain in the lands in which they live at present, will use its best endeavours to facilitate the achievement of this object, and will be ready to consider any suggestions on the subject which any Jewish or Zionist organisations may desire to lay before it."

5. Draft by C. G. Montefiore, Esq.:—

"His Majesty's Government is anxious that free and unimpeded Jewish immigration into Palestine should be established. It views with favour unrestricted Jewish colonisation in that country. It will do its best to facilitate such immigration and colonisation, and will also seek to secure such municipal and local autonomy for the Jews as may be found possible, it being clearly understood," &c. (Paragraphs 2 and 3 of Draft No. 2.)

6. Draft by L. L. Cohen, Esq.:—

"His Majesty's Government, viewing with favour the settlement of Jews in Palestine, will use its best endeavours to facilitate their immigration and colonisation in that country, and to secure for them the enjoyment of civil and religious liberty, together with municipal privileges, in the towns and colonies inhabited by them; it being clearly understood that nothing shall be done to interfere with the rights and privileges of non-Jewish communities in Palestine, or the rights and political status enjoyed in any other country by such Jews who determine to retain their existing nationality or citizenship."

7. Draft by Sir Philip Magnus, M.P.:—

"His Majesty's Government views with favour the establishment in Palestine of a centre of Jewish culture, and will use its best endeavours to facilitate the achievement of this object; it being understood that nothing shall be done which may prejudice the rights of existing non-Jewish communities in Palestine, or the rights and political status now enjoyed by Jews in any other country."

APPENDIX III.

VIEWS OF THE LATE EARL CROMER.

"*Spectator*," *August* 12, 1916.

It is believed that on the eve of the French Revolution there were less than three million Jews in Europe. There are now some nine million, besides about two million in North America and smaller communities in other parts of the world.

From the earliest days of the Dispersion the Jews have, for different reasons, been viewed with dislike and suspicion by the rest of the world. Juvenal, who regarded the Jews as magicians, inveighed against them, and attributed their faults to the fact that they set aside every seventh day as a day, not of rest, but of "sloth." The fifth-century poet, Rutilius (*Itiner.,* V. 386), regretted the Dispersion as he feared that the subjugated nation would conquer their conquerors. *Victoresque suos natio victa premit.* The prejudices of the pagan world were inherited in an intensified form by Christians and Moslems alike. Those of the Christians led to the comprehensible but wholly irrational conclusion that future generations of Jews for all time should be persecuted because some of their predecessors had crucified Christ. Those of the Moslems were based on the personal history of Mohammed. They still survive. Among the most civilised nations of the world, dislike based on religious prejudices, if it has not wholly disappeared, has been greatly mitigated, but other causes have supervened which have kept anti-Semitic sentiments alive.

In England there has never been any "Jewish question" properly so called. This is due partly to the fact that religious toleration, both in the letter and the spirit, has established a firm hold on English public opinion, and partly to the further fact that the relatively small number of Jews in the United Kingdom—there are at present only some two hundred and forty-five thousand—has prevented them

APPENDIX B

11

from exercising so commanding an influence over national life as has been the case in some other countries. There is not, as in Austria, a Jew moneylender in almost every village in the country, who often holds the future welfare of the noble in his castle and of the villager in his cottage in the hollow of his hand. An incident such as that which came within my personal knowledge whilst residing in Styria would be impossible in this country. I was asked by an Austrian friend to make enquiries as to whether he could rent a country house in the neighbourhood of Gratz. After visiting one house, the proprietor asked me whether my friend was a Jew. I replied in the negative. He then explained to me that he was an ardent anti-Semitic, and that he would not, for any pecuniary consideration whatsoever, let his house to a Jew. In no country has the Jew fewer causes for complaint than in England. He is under no civil disabilities. After a struggle, which never excited more than a somewhat languid interest, he was given full rights of citizenship. Jews now sit in both Houses of Parliament. They occupy important public positions. A distinguished man of Jewish origin ruled for some years the destinies of England. The faith of his ancestors and his hereditary proclivities have not prevented him from being regarded to this day by a large section of the community as a typical British patriot. When, therefore, Dr. Weizmann says that what the Jew wants is "to find a place in the social structure of the world which shall enable him to live as a human being without demanding that he cease to be a Jew," the average Englishman will reply with much reason, and perhaps with some slight indignation and amazement, that he has given the Jew all that he asks; that Judaism is a cult like any other, which he is free to exercise in this country; that the British conscience is clear; and that the Jewish question may be dismissed from the minds of British politicians and the British public. And yet this answer, plausible though it may appear, is far from disposing of the whole question.

Whatever sentiments may be entertained towards the Jews, and whatever opinions may be held as to the wisdom of affording encouragement to their present aspirations, it is surely desirable that those aspirations should be understood. It may well be doubted whether they are generally understood in this country. The very useful series of essays now published under the title of "Zionism and the Jewish Future" enables us to gain some insight into the views current in Jewish circles, and the aims which the leading members of the Jewish community seek to attain. The publication is all the more timely because one of the consequences of the war will almost certainly be that the whole Jewish question will in the future have to be approached under auspices which differ widely from those which have hitherto obtained.

The first point to be grasped in order to arrive at a true comprehension of the meaning of the movement known as Zionism is to recognise the fact that for many years past there have been two main currents of Jewish thought which have been moving in divergent directions. It is natural that it should be so. To use an expressive phrase employed by that talented novelist, George Eliot, Judaea—and, consequently, the Jews—is "poised between East and West." The tendency of the Western Jews has been to Westernise Judaism. Moses Mendelssohn (1729-86), who may be said to be almost the founder of this school of thought, held that the best solution of the Jewish question was that "the Jew should become as like as possible to the Gentile." The predominating note of Western Jewry has, therefore, been a movement from the Jewish to the non-Jewish. This movement received a great stimulus from the French Revolution, which broke down the walls of the Ghettos and thus emancipated the Jews, but which, at the same time, went far to denationalise Judaism. Toleration has produced its natural and inevitable result. It has tended to break up the solidarity of the Western Jews, and to facilitate assimilation with the non-Jewish communities to which they belong.

The thought of Eastern Jewry has developed on precisely opposite lines. The inefficacy of persecution, unless it be conducted on a scale and after a fashion which have now become practically impossible, has been clearly demonstrated. It has served to foster the movement which it was intended to stifle. The most passionately ardent Jews prefer persecution, which keeps alive the flame of nationalism, to emancipation, which tends to quench it. The following extract from the works of Asher Ginzberg, who adopted the synonym of "Achad-ha-'Am" (One of the People), is characteristic of their views. Speaking of the Western Jews, he said—

"Do I envy these fellow-Jews of mine their emancipation? I answer in all truth and sincerity, No! A thousand times No! The privileges are not worth the price! I may not be emancipated; but at least I have not sold my soul for emancipation. I at least can proclaim from the housetops that my kith and kin are dear to me wherever they are, without being constrained to find forced and unsatisfactory excuses. I at least can remember Jerusalem, mourn for its loss in public or in private, without being asked what Zion is to me or I to Zion. . . . . And this spiritual freedom—scoff who will!—I would not exchange or barter for all the emancipation in the world."

Zionism, which in its present form may be said to have been born in 1896, is the outcome of Eastern Jewish thought and action. Its headquarters until recently have been in Poland. Whether the centre of gravity of Jewish activity will now be shifted remains to be seen. Dr. Weizmann says: " It is too early as yet to estimate even approximately the effect of the war on the great Jewish centres in which a part of it is being waged, but it is already obvious that it will deal a shattering blow at what has been for centuries the great reservoir of Jewish strength."

What is it that the Zionists want? The idea that they wish the Jews of all races to be congregated together in Palestine may at once be dismissed as absurd. Nothing of the sort is proposed. Neither do they want to establish a mere colony in the sense in which that term is usually employed. Zionism stands for a national revival. Its aim and goal, the Very Rev. Dr. Gaster says, " is to create for the Jew a new home, not so much for physical as for spiritual life. This must be borne in mind and never lost sight of—that the Holy Land is to become the spiritual centre of the Jews. This stands far above any political or economic consideration." It should be added that Dr. Gaster's idealism soars very high. He holds that the re-establishment of Jewish national life in the ancient home of Judaism will help to solve many of the burning questions of the day. Such are " the problem of tenure of property, the problem of commercial dealing, the protection of the labourer, the purity of food, simplified procedure in the Courts of Justice protection against usury, against rings and monopolies, democratic organisation, and the principles of equitable taxation. . . . . The Jewish regathering is to be of great moment in the history of the emancipation and progress of mankind. Only from this point of view has Zionism a meaning and Judaism a justification." Mr. Nahum Sokolow quotes the pathetic question propounded to him by an enthusiastic youth, who may be regarded as a typical " New Jew," to the following effect: " Are we still a people to whom youth and health may return, or a bleached and scattered heap of bones? Are these bones never again to live and move?"

It would be both premature and presumptuous to attempt to forecast the future of the Zionist movement. All that can at present be done is to state the nature of the problem, and to note that some slight practical progress has been made towards the realisation of the Jewish ideals. For some years past a steady stream of Jewish immigration to Palestine has set in. There are now forty-five Jewish colonies, having a population of about fifteen thousand souls and covering an area of about one hundred and ten thousand acres. Good roads have been made. Numerous elementary schools in which Hebrew is taught have been established. "That Hebrew as a living language has come to stay," Dr. Selig Brodetsky says, " that, in fact, Hebrew is well on the way to becoming the mother-tongue of Palestine Jewry, is obvious." From a material point of view, the Jewish colonies thrive. The very common idea that the Jews can never be successful agriculturists has been completely disproved. They export fruit and wine in large quantities. In one colony the value of the irrigable land has risen from 3*l*. 12*s*. per acre in 1890 to 36*l*. an acre. The trade of Jaffa, which in 1904 was valued at 760,000*l*., had in 1912 reached the figure of 2,050,000*l*. Liberal encouragement has been given to arts and industries.

Enough, however, has been said to show that, although possibly the Jewish question will not mature quite so quickly as some of the more enthusiastic Zionists consider probable, it is rapidly becoming a practical issue, and that before long politicians will be unable to brush it aside as the fantastic dream of a few idealists.

VIEW EXPRESSED BY SIR ALFRED MOND, M.P.

Extracts from an Article by him in the " Weekly Dispatch," April 8, 1917.

As for the Palestinian ideal, which the British advance in South Palestine has quickened in the hearts of many of the Jewish people, the question which the average man will ask himself is: Are the Jews suitable for the agricultural life

APPENDIX B

which must be the basis of the development of this sun-enriched soil? He may be answered by reference to the Jewish agricultural colonies established in Palestine in recent years. These colonies have achieved remarkable results and seem to point to the survival of the old pastoral instinct of the Jews.

Arid and unhealthy land has been made fertile and habitable by the work of the tillers of the soil and by the skilful cultivation of eucalyptus trees. Several centres have also been started for the treatment of disease, particularly blindness, which is so unfortunately prevalent among children in the East owing to crude notions of hygiene.

In studying the future of Palestine and the practicability of an autonomous Jewish State there, it is fair to remember that the Jew on the whole gets on quite well with the Mahommedan, with whom he has racial affinities—both represent branches of the Semitic race—and between whose religion and Judaism there is much in common, as one would expect from a like derivation.

But many difficulties immediately suggest themselves. The ancient Temple of Solomon, for instance, is to-day the second Holy Moslem place after Mecca. The Jews would not interfere, but some might remember that it was once the Temple of Solomon.

To be quite frank, I have yet to be convinced that the foundation of an independent Jewish State comes within the domain of practical politics, but I see no reason why guarantees, if they were desired, should not be given to the Jews of the fullest liberty to manage their own local affairs and for the protection of the results of their labour, and I do not doubt, whatever the future of Palestine, that this condition could be obtained. Whether this would satisfy the aspirations of the Zionists who desire the foundation of an autonomous Jewish State is another matter.

VIEW EXPRESSED BY MR. JACOB SCHIFF.

Extract from a Report of a Speech by him, "American Jewish Chronicle," April 27, 1917.

I may say something which will surprise many of you elders. For the first time in the last three weeks the thought has come to me: " Why hasn't the Jew his own homeland?" I am not a believer in a Jewish nation built on " isms "—egotism first, atheism and agnosticism. I am a believer in the Jewish people, in the Jewish mission. I believe that somewhere there should be a great reservoir from which Jewish culture, unhampered by the materialism of the world, should spread its beautiful ideals to all parts of the world. This homeland, naturally, is Palestine.

THE JEWISH NATIONAL IDEA AND THE ZIONIST MOVEMENT AFTER THE RUSSIAN REVOLUTION.

Zionism in the Russian Provinces occupied by the Enemy.

It should be noted that 42 per cent. of the 6,000,000 of Russian Jews are not affected by the Russian Revolution. The ten governments of Poland (Warsaw, Petrokoff, Plozk, Kalisch, Lomza, Kielce, Radom, Lublin, Suvalki, Siedlce), with a population of about 1,800,000 Jews, are occupied by the enemy and have no connection with the recent events in Russia. The same applies to the Jews in the governments of Lithuania (Brest-Litovsk, Wilna, Grodno, Kovno, and a part of Minsk), with a population of at least 600,000 Jews. The remainder of the Jews who live in the few places of Volhynia occupied by the enemy are also unaffected by the Russian Revolution. In all the provinces, which are densely populated by Jews, and in the two most important Jewish communities of Russia (Warsaw and Wilna) the national idea and the Zionist movement have greatly developed during the last generation, and during the war have received an added impetus. The terrible hardships and sufferings which the Jewish population of these provinces have endured during the war have brought home to many of them the consciousness of their unity and the necessity of a refuge of their own.

E

Zionist Conference in Warsaw.

The popularity of the Zionist idea among the Polish Jews is demonstrated by the fact that, in spite of the appalling conditions under which they live under the oppressive German occupation, they convened in May last a Zionist Conference in Warsaw, which was attended by nearly 400 delegates, representing a great number of communities, synagogues, societies, and groups, consisting of all classes of the Jewish population. In July last a plebiscite was inaugurated among the Jews of Poland with a view to ascertaining their attitude towards Zionism. The plebiscite resulted in the acceptance of a resolution in favour of Zionist aims.

Attitude of Press.

The leading Jewish press in Poland is Zionist. It is noteworthy that the "Haint," which has the widest circulation of all the newspapers, Jewish and non-Jewish, has recently given its adherence to the Zionist programme.

Sacrifice for Jewish Colonists in Palestine.

Wilna has for several years been the centre of Russian Zionism. It was the seat of the Zionist Central Committee. Wilna, with its old Jewish traditions, as a centre of Jewish learning and as the cradle of the Neo-Hebraic literature, has always taken a leading part in the Jewish national movement. It is remarkable that in the darkest hour of their trial and struggle for existence, when they had to collect every penny to satisfy the most vital needs of thousands of their starving brethren, they devoted part of the funds which were sent to them for the relief of the Jewish colonists in Palestine and for the continuation of the educational work to prepare new settlers for the Palestinian colonies.

Bialystok has since the very outset of the national movement been a great centre for the organisation and preparation of groups of colonists for Palestine, a work which was initiated by the late Rabbi Mohilewer. During the last year new groups of pioneers for the colonisation of Palestine after the war have been organised in connection with the neighbouring Jewish Lithuanian communities of Zabludowo, Knishin, Wilkowishki, and Grayevo (in the Louza government).

All the reports published in the Jewish press and reports which have reached us in private letters are unanimous in the statement that the number of organised Zionists (Shekel-payers) has considerably increased and that the income of the Jewish National Fund has exceeded any amount ever reached before. The political standing and the influence of the Nationalist Jews in Poland and Lithuania is best shown by the fact that on the Town Councils of the capital of Poland, Wilna, and Bialystok and other places numerous Zionist representatives have been elected by the Jewish masses.

As already stated, these activities only concern the two and a half millions of Russian Jews who are living under the German occupation and who have not been influenced by the Russian Revolution.

Zionism in post-Revolutionary Russia.

The beginning of a modern constitutional régime heralded by the Revolution for all the inhabitants of Russia, the liberation of all oppressed nationalities, creeds and classes, have opened out an era which the Russian Jews have welcomed with enthusiasm.

Having now attained the status of full citizenship and equal rights, it is urged in some quarters that this change would weaken or even destroy the national solidarity. But such is not the case, as the history of the first revolutionary movement in 1905-6 demonstrates. The idea of liberty in Russia, far from weakening Jewish nationalism, did but intensify and deepen the national aspirations.

Immediately after the first Revolution a Zionist Conference was held in Helsingfors, at which they defined their attitude of solidarity with the international Zionist movement.

Amongst the Jewish masses nationalism made great progress all over Russia. The nationalist Yiddish press of Warsaw, which has since played such a considerable part in forming Jewish public opinion, is a product of that epoch. A great number of cultural nationalist Jewish societies (Hazamir and others) were established in that period (1906).

In regard to the present Revolution, so far as we can judge from the facts at our disposal, the national movement among the Russian Jews has made great headway.

APPENDIX B

The Zionist Organisation in Russia utilised the first few weeks of Russian liberty to combine its scattered forces and to develop propaganda upon a large scale.

New Moscow Zionist Committee.

In Moscow a Zionist District Committee was formed, comprising twenty-four provinces: Astrakhan, Vladimir, Vologda, Voronezh, Kazan, Kaluga, Kostroma, Kursk, Moscow, Nijni-Novgorod, Simbirsk, Smolensk, Tambov, Tula, Ufa, Jaroslav, and the Don district.

Zionist Demonstrations.

Almost in all towns splendid meetings have taken place, marked by extraordinary spontaneity and vigour. Particular mention may be made of the Zionist meeting at Odessa. Entire battalions of Zionist soldiers bore through the town blue and white banners with the motto: "Liberty in Russia, Land and Liberty in Palestine."

A hundred and fifty thousand men followed these banners, to which the Military Governor of Odessa insisted on showing honour publicly. We can likewise call attention to the Zionist meetings at Minsk, Saratov, Juriev, Kharkov, Theodosia, Nijni-Novgorod, Ekaterinburg, Homel, Proskurov, Baku, Dubrovno, Riazan, Kazan, Ekaterinoslav, Moscow, &c. The meeting organised at Kieff has likewise been very magnificent. When the procession approached the town hall the Zionist flag was hoisted on the balcony to the strains of "Hatikvah" (the Zionist anthem) played by the municipal orchestra.

At Berdischeff 15,000 Jews marched through the principal streets carrying Zionist banners. The municipality, the administration executive of the town, and the chiefs of the Ukraine National Organisations greeted the Zionist demonstrators.

According to advices from distant Turkestan and Bokhara, the Zionist movement has made remarkable progress there. The entire Sephardic element has adhered to the movement. The Ashkenazim and Sephardim, as is not often the case in Asiatic Russia, peacefully worked together at the great Asiatic Zionist Conference which was held at Samarcand. A meeting of five thousand Jews also held there adopted a resolution in favour of a Jewish Palestine.

In Moscow a Jewish mass meeting took place in the great hall of that town. The meeting was convened by a committee of the united Jewish organisations. Dr. Echiel Tchlenow, who was elected president, called to mind, in his speech, the victims of the old rule and greeted the liberty of all "political offenders," the Duma, the Russian proletariat, the army. Then the representatives of the different Jewish organisations delivered speeches. A series of claims were advocated; in one claim all agreed *to claim national rights for Russian Jewry*.

Resolution of Moscow Mass Meeting.

The meeting adopted the following resolution:—

"The Jewish mass meeting in Moscow salutes with great joy the freedom. We are firmly convinced that the Constituent Assembly, which is to be elected by universal suffrage, shall establish in Russia a thoroughly democratic administration, and that not only civil rights, but also national rights, national autonomy, and a free national evolution shall be secured to the Jewish as well as to all other peoples of Russia. The meeting resolves to convoke a general Jewish congress in Russia."

It is very characteristic of the present trend of mind of Russian Jewry that in Moscow Dr. Jechiel Tchlenow, the famous Zionist leader, has been elected head of the Moscow Jewish community, to-day the richest and most influential Jewish community in Russia. The three well-known Zionist leaders in Petrograd, Katzenelson, Rosoff, and Grunbaum, have been appointed members of the National Defence Commission created by the new Government. In Kieff, Bichowsky, the well-known Zionist, has been elected head of a new central communal organisation that comprises all local Jewish societies.

Attitude of Press.

It is also interesting to learn that, in spite of the activities and tremendous propaganda of the "Bund" (a Jewish Socialist organisation in Russia), *it is the nationalist element that is supreme in the Russian Jewish press*. The proportion between nationalist and Zionist papers as against non-nationalist is about ten to one. Even the non-nationalist papers no longer actively oppose Jewish Nationalism. They simply lay their chief stress on class interest.

All-Russian Zionist Conference, Petrograd.

The outstanding feature of recent Zionist developments in Russia has been the holding of the All-Russian Zionist Conference, which opened in Petrograd on May 24, 1917.

The Conference received official recognition. The Minister for Foreign Affairs, M. Terestchenka, wished the Conference success.[*]

Representatives of Jewish democracy assured the Conference that the masses would respond in a Zionist spirit to the question of a Jewish centre in Palestine.

The Conference was attended by 552 delegates from 680 towns. The most remotely situated districts were represented. There were delegates from Turkestan, Bokhara, and the Crimea. The Jewish soldiers at the front sent 24 representatives.[†]

In addition to the delegates there were 500 visitors from provincial towns, and over 1,100 from Petrograd. The proceedings were attended by 87 newspaper correspondents.

At the Conference speeches expressing welcome and good wishes were delivered by M. Warshavsky, President of the Petrograd Jewish Community, who had hitherto opposed Zionism, and by M. H. Sliosberg, the well-known politician and lawyer, who previously had also not been favourable to the movement. The latter declared that the Zionist idea was dear to him, and he uttered the wish that the aim of the Conference should be attained in the near future. Zionism had kept the flag of Judaism aloft, he said, and the whole future of Jewry now depended upon the future of Zionism.

The delegate from Samarcand (Turkestan) said: " In our city there are 12,000 Jews, and we are all Zionists. In the whole of Turkestan there are no Jews who are not Zionists. We are all with you. We bring you our means and our souls."

Delegation of Soldiers to Conference.

There was also a delegation of soldiers from the front, which announced *that practically all the soldiers at the front were Zionists*, and that as soon as the war was over they would be ready to go to Palestine at the bidding of the Zionist leaders and play their part in building up the new national life.

The Resolutions of Conference.

The Conference carried the following resolution on Palestine unanimously:—

" Considering first that the Jewish people, in view of its disposition and dispersion all over the world, can recreate for itself conditions for normal development of its national, cultural, and economic life only through the restoration of a national autonomous centre in its historic home, Palestine.

" Secondly, that the Jewish nation has never severed its ties with its ancient home, and has always longed for it, and that its moral and historic right to Palestine is incontestable and irremovable.

" Thirdly, that the aspirations of the Jewish nation so manifested fully coincide with the great principle of self-definition, of freedom and independence for the development of all nations proclaimed by the democracies and governments of all countries.

" The seventh Zionist Conference in Russia unanimously expresses its firm belief that when establishing the basis of the future national and political life the nations will recognise and count with the clearly stated will of the Jewish nation for the re-settlement and re-birth of Palestine as its national centre, and will consequently create conditions guaranteeing the free and successful development of the concentration of Jewish forces and of the restoration of Palestine.

" To ensure the concrete and full manifestation of the will of the Jewish nation the Conference considers it necessary first to organise among the Jews

---

[*] For attitude of the Russian Government see Appendix IV.
[†] See special Military Order of General Alexieff, Appendix V.

a referendum on the question, secondly to lay before the All-Russian Jewish Congress the question of Jewish claims in Palestine, and thirdly to claim the admission of a representative of the Jewish nation at the future peace conference to be held upon the closing of hostilities for the expression of the wishes of the Jewish nation and for the defence of its historic and national rights and interests."

Practical Zionism.

Passing to the practical side of the Zionist movement, we desire to mention the following facts:—

In Moscow the "Haboneh," a company with a subscribed capital of 5,000,000 roubles, has been formed for the purpose of building houses in Palestine on the cessation of hostilities.

The considerable monthly returns of the Jewish National Fund are due particularly to receipts from Russia. This willingness to make sacrifices evinced by the Russian Jews (280,000 roubles during the first month of their deliverance) opens up very favourable prospects for the development of the Jewish National Fund in the future.

THE GROWTH OF ZIONISM IN AMERICA DURING THE WAR.

On the outbreak of the war American Zionists promptly set up in New York a provisional Executive Committee for Zionist affairs, which became, for certain purposes, a real International Zionist Executive. The head of this organisation was Mr. Brandeis, now Mr. Justice Brandeis, of the Supreme Court. It made its chief task the maintenance of the Jewish settlements and educational and other institutions in Palestine. For this purpose it raised vast sums of money, and the persistence of Jewish work in Palestine through three years of war is due primarily to American Zionists. In three years over 360,000*l.* passed through its hands, independently of the ordinary Zionist collections such as Shekel and National Funds. The Provisional Executive, at the same time, established intimate relations with the political factors in the United States and laboured to assist in the development of Zionism throughout the American Continent, notably in Canada and the Argentine. The recent Zionist Convention in Canada was the most impressive in the history of the movement in the Dominion.

The United States.

What may be called local Zionist affairs are under the control of the American Zionist Federation and affiliated bodies. These have grown greatly in strength during the war. At the Baltimore Conference on the 24th June last, it was reported that there were 170 societies attached to the Federation, 41 to the Hadassah or Women's Union, 98 to the Zionist Union of the Western States, 450 to the Young Judah Association, 87 to the Order Sons of Zion, 190 to the Misraché or strictly orthodox Association, 95 to the Poalé-Zion or Zionist Labour Party. To these should now be added the Order Brith Shalom with 50,000 members. At the time of the Baltimore Convention it was announced that there were 50 new Zionist Societies in process of formation. The number of shekel payers had risen in 1917 to 320,000, which is more than 120,000 increase over the preceding year. Every shekel payer formally accepts the Zionist programme and subscribes to the Zionist funds.

Some idea of the financial power of Zionism in the United States may be gained from a few illustrations. At mass meetings held in conjunction with the Baltimore Convention it was announced that 60,000*l.* was raised for Jewish relief in Palestine and the other war zones. The National Fund, which exists for the purchase of land in Palestine to be held by the organised Jewish people, obtained over 12,000*l.* during the year in voluntary gifts. In May the various Achuzah and other American societies for the co-operative purchase of land and foundation of colonies in Palestine were formed into a union, which has an actual capital of 30,000*l.*, and within five or six years will have an income of 200,000*l.* It is worth observing that this union will make special provision for the settlement in Palestine of Jewish ex-soldiers.

18

Resolution of Jewish Ministers' Association of New York.

The Agudath Horabbonim Hamatifim, the Jewish Ministers' Association of New York, has adopted the following resolution:—

"Resolved that all Jewish rabbis of America, the true representatives of the Jewish faith, be called in conference to petition the President of our God-blessed country, the Senate and the House of Representatives, as well as the other Powers, favourably to consider the restoration of Palestine to the Jewish people."

Convention of Jewish National, Socialist, Workmen's Committee.

The first convention of the *Jewish National, Socialist, Workmen's Committee*, called together in the last days of March to discuss the vital questions which will have to be taken up by the American Jewish Congress, adopted various resolutions, the final clause of which stated:—

"The convention hereby declares that it is the historic and sacred duty of American Jewry to demand in concert with all other parts of the Jewish people full national liberation and the possibility of an independent development of the Jewish people in an assured home in Palestine."

Dr. Chaim Zhitlowsky, one of the leaders of the Jewish Socialists in the United States of America, has adopted Zionism and enrolled himself as a member of the Poalei Zion of America. Together with him, two other noted Jewish labour leaders, Dr. Elsberg and Mr. Rothenbaum, have joined the Poalei Zion.

o

BIBLIOGRAPHY

Primary Sources

Unpublished

National Archives, Kew, UK, formerly Public Record Office, Kew
Colonial Office, Foreign Office, Parliamentary Command Papers, Cabinet Office, Air Ministry.
The Middle East Centre, St. Antony's College, Oxford.
The Papers of Sir Herbert Samuel
National Archives. Washington. Records of the Department of State Relating to Internal Affairs of Turkey, 1910-1929.

Published

Aaronsohn, Aaron, 'Forgotten Man of History? Cecil Bloom', *Jewish Historical Studies*, Vol. 40 (2005), pp. 177-96.

Abransky, Chamen, 'Weizmann: a new type of leadership in the Zionist movement,' address to the Jewish Historical Society on the Centenary of Weizmann's birth; paper delivered to the Jewish Historical Society of England, 9 April 1975, Transactions, session 1973-75, Vol. XXV and miscellanies part X, 1977, pp. 137-49.

Abu Lughod, Ibrahim (ed.) with a foreword by Arnold Toynbee, *The Transformation of Palestine: Essays on the Origin and Development of the Arab-Israeli Conflict*, Northwestern University Press, Evanston, 1971.

Adelson, Roger, *Mark Sykes: Portrait of an Amateur*, London, 1975.

Amery, Leopold, *My Political Life, War and Peace 1914-1929*, Vol. 2, London, 1953.

Anderson, M.S, *The Great Powers and the Near East 1774-1923*, London, 1970.

Anon, 'Chaim Weizmann's Scientific Work: 1915-1919', *Arabic and Islamic Garland*, London, 1977.

Antonius, George, *The Arab Awakening*, Beirut, 1969.

Atran, Scott, 'The Surrogate Colonization of Palestine, 1917-1939', *American Ethnologist*, Vol. 16, no. 4 (November 1989), pp. 719-44.

Barbour, Nevill, *Nisi Dominus: A Survey of the Palestine Controversy*, London, 1946.

Barr, James, *A Line in the Sand: Britain, France and the Struggle that Shaped the Middle East*, Simon and Schuster, London and New York, 2011.

Berkowitz, Michael, *Western Jewry and the Zionist Project, 1914-1933*, Cambridge University Press, 1997.

Berlin, Isaiah, *Chaim Weizmann*, Farrar, Straus & Cudahy, New York, 1958.

Bermant, Haim, *The Cousinhood*, New York, 1971.

Bloom, Cecil, 'T E Lawrence and Zionism', *Jewish Historical Studies*, Vol. 38 (2002), pp. 125-45.

Bowle, John, *Viscount Samuel, a Biography*, London, 1957.

Brecher, F.W, 'French Policy Toward the Levant 1914-18', *Middle East Studies*, Vol. 29, no. 4 (October 1993), pp. 641-663.

Cocker, Mark, *Richard Meinertzhagen: Soldier, Scientist and Spy*, London, 1989.

Cornelius, John, 'The Balfour Declaration and the Zimmermann Note', *The Washington Report on Middle East Affairs*, Vol. XVI, no. 2 August/September 1997, pp. 18-20.

Cronin, David, *Balfour's Shadow: A Century of British support for Zionism and Israel*, Pluto Press, London, 2017.

Crossman, Richard, *A Nation Reborn, The Israel of Weizmann, Bevin and Ben-Gurion*, London, 1960.

Davis, John H, *The Evasive Peace: A Study of the Zionist-Arab Problem*, London, 1968.

Dugdale, Blanche, T*he Balfour Declaration: Origins and Background*, London, 1940.

Elie Kedourie, Sir Mark Sykes and Palestine 1915-16, *Middle Eastern Studies*, Vol. 6, 1970.

Ellenbergen, Nancy W, *Balfour's World Aristocracy and Political Culture at the Fin de Siècle*, Boydell Press, Woodbridge, 2015.

Elon, Amos, *Israelis, Founders and Sons*, London, 1971.

Fraser, T.G, Andrew Mango and Robert McNamara, *The Makers of the Modern Middle East*, Haus Books, London, 2011.

Fromkin, David, *A Peace to End All Peace, Creating the Modern Middle East 1914-1922*, London, 1989.

Gerwarth, Robert, *The Vanquished: Why the First World War Failed to End*, London, 2016.

Gilbert, Martin, *Exile and Return: The Emergence of Jewish Statehood*, London, 1978.

Gillon, D.Z, 'The Antecedents of the Balfour Declaration', *Journal of Middle Eastern Studies*, Vol. 5, 1969.

Gilmour, David, 'The Unregarded Prophet: Lord Curzon and the Palestine Question', *Journal of Palestine Studies*, Vol. XXV, no. 3, Spring 1996, pp. 60-68.

Gilmour, David, *Curzon*, London, 1994.

Goldstone, Patricia, *Aaronsohn's Maps: The Man Who Might Have Created Peace in the Middle East*, Berkley CA: Counterpoint, 2007.

Hadawi, Sami, *Bitter Harvest: Palestine Between 1914-1967*, New York, 1967.

Herrman, I.M, Anglo-Zionist Relations from Herzl to the Balfour Declaration 1902-1917. D.Phil. Thesis, Oxford University, 1971.

Herrmann, Klaus J, 'Political Response to the Balfour Declaration in Imperial Germany: German Judaism', *Middle East Journal*, Vol. 19, 1965.

Howard, H.N, *An American Inquiry in the Middle East: The King-Crane Commission*, Beirut, 1963.

Hughes, M, *Allenby and the British Strategy in the Middle East, 1917-1919*, London, 1999.

Huneidi, Sahar, *A Broken Trust: Herbert Samuel, Zionism and the Palestinians*. IBTauris, London, 2001.

Huneidi, Sahar, 'Was Balfour Policy Reversible? The Colonial Office and Palestine 1921-23', *Journal of Palestine Studies*, 106 Vol. XXVII no.2, (Winter 1998).

Hussein Agha and Robert Malley, 'Camp David: The Tragedy of Errors', *New York Review of Books*, 9 August 2001.

Hyamson, A.M, *Palestine Under the Mandate 1920-48*, London, 1950.

Ingrams, Doreen, *Palestine Papers, 1917-1922, Seeds of Conflict*, London, 1972.

Interview: Hussein Agha, *Middle East Policy*, Vol. XVII, no. 2, Summer 2010.

Jeffries, JMN, *The Palestine Deception 1915-1923. The McMahon-Hussein Correspondence, the Balfour Declaration and the Jewish National Home*, ed. with introduction by William M Mathew, Institute for Palestinian Studies, Washington DC, 2014.

John, Robert, *Behind the Balfour Declaration: Hidden Origins of Today's Mid-east Crisis*, Institute for Historical Review, August 1988.

Jones, Philip, *Britain and Palestine 1914-1948: Archival Sources for the History of the British Mandate*, Oxford University Press, London, 1979.

Kadegan, Allan Laine, *Soviet Zion: The Quest for a Russian Homeland*, Macmillan, London, 1994.

Kaufman, Edy, 'French pro-Zionist Declarations of 1917-18', *Middle Eastern Studies*, Vol. 5, 1979.

Khalidi, Rashid, *British Policy Towards Syria and Palestine 1906-14: a study of the antecedents of the Hussein-McMahon correspondence, the Sykes-Picot Agreement and the Balfour Declaration*, Oxford, 1980.

Khalidi, Walid (ed.), *From Haven to Conquest: Readings in Zionism and the Palestine Problem until 1948*, Institute for Palestine Studies, Beirut, 1971.

Khalidi, Walid, *Palestine Reborn*, London, 1992.

Khedourie, Elie, *In the Anglo-Arab Labyrinth. The McMahon-Husayn Correspondence and its Interpretations 1914-1939*, Cambridge University Press, 1976.

Khedourie, Elie, and Jon Kimche, *The Unromantics, The Great Powers and the Balfour Declaration*, Weidenfeld and Nicolson, London, 1968.

Klug, Brian, 'The Other Arthur Balfour, Protector of the Jews', 8 July 2013, http://www.balfourproject.org/the-other-arthur-balfour-protector-of-the-jews/. Accessed 19/07/17.

Knox, D. Edward, *The Making of a New Eastern Question: British Palestine Policy and the Origins of Israel 1917-1925*, The Catholic University of America Press, Washington, DC, 1981.

Knox, Dennis, 'The Development of British Policy in Palestine 1917-1925: Sir Gilbert Clayton and the "New Eastern Question"', Ph.D. Thesis, Michigan State University, 1971.

Krogh Peter F. and Mary C. McDavid (eds.), 'Palestinians under Occupation. Prospects for the Future', Georgetown University, *Symposia in Honour of Zafer Al-Masri*, 1989, Washington. D.C.

Landman, Samuel, *Great Britain, the Jews and Palestine*, London 1936.

Leon, Dan. *Chaim Weizmann, Statesman of the Jewish Renaissance, The Chaim Weizmann Centenary* 1874-1974, The Zionist Library, Jerusalem, 1974.

Lesch, Ann Mosely, *Arab Politics in Palestine 1917-1939: The Frustration of a Nationalist Movement*, Ithaca, Cornell Univ. Press, 1979.

Levene, Mark, 'The Balfour Declaration: A Case of Mistaken Identity', *English Historical Review*, Vol. 107, no. 422 (January 1992), pp. 54-77.

Lewis, Geoffrey, *Balfour and Weizmann: The Zionist, the Zealot and the Emergence of Israel*, Bloomsbury, London, 2009.

Lilienthal, Alfred, *The Zionist Connection: What Price Peace?*, Dodd Mead, New York, 1978.

Louis, Wm. Roger, *In the Name of God, Go! Leo Amery and the British Empire in the Age of Churchill*, W.W. Norton & Company. New York, London, 1992.

Ludendorff, General, *My War Memories, 1914-18*, (trans.) London, no date.

Makovsky, Michael, *Churchill's Promised Land: Zionism and Statecraft*, Yale University Press, 2008.

Mallison, W.T, *The Balfour Declaration: An Appraisal in International Law*, Northwestern University Press, 1971.

Mandel, Neville, *The Arabs and Zionism Before World War I*, Berkeley, Univ. of California Press, 1976.

Manuel, Frank E, 'The Palestine Question in Italian Diplomacy 1917-1920', *Journal of Modern History*, Vol. 27, 1955.

Marlowe, John, *The Seat of Pilate: An Account of the Palestine Mandate*, London, 1959.

Masalha, Nur, *Expulsion of the Palestinians: The Concept of "Transfer" in Zionist Political Thought*, 1882-1948, Institute for Palestine Studies, 1992.

Massey, W.T, *Allenby's Final Triumph*, London, 1920.

Massey, W.T, *How Jerusalem Was Won: Being the Record of Allenby's Campaign in Palestine*, London, 1919.

Massiri, A.Wahhab, *The Encyclopedia of Zionist Concepts and Terminology* (Arabic), Cairo, 1974.

McMeekin, *The Berlin-Baghdad Express: The Ottoman Empire and Germany's Bid for World Power*, 1898-1918, Penguin, London, 2011.

Merkley, Paul, *The Politics of Christian Zionism 1891-1948*, Routledge, London, 1998.

Monroe, Elizabeth, *Britain's Moment in the Middle East*, London, 1963.

Moore, John Norton (ed.), 'The Palestine Question', *Seminar of Arab Jurists on Palestine*, Algiers, July 22-27, 1967. Part One. *'Historical "Rights"'*, Princeton, New Jersey, 1974.

Musa Mazzawi, 'The Balfour Declaration. What Did Britain Promise In Palestine?', *The Council For the Advancement of Arab-British Understanding*, 1968, London.

Ormsby-Gore, William, 'Great Britain, Palestine and the Jews', *The XIXth Century and After*, Vol. 88, July-Dec 1920.

Palestine. A Study of Jewish Arab And British Policies, Published for the ESCO Foundation for Palestine, Inc. Yale University Press. 1947.

Penslar, Derek, *Zionism and Technocracy: The Engineering of Jewish Settlement in Palestine 1870-1918*, London, 1991.

Presland, John, *Deedes Bey*, London, 1942.

Quigley, Carol, 'Lord Balfour's Personal Position on the Balfour Declaration', *The Middle East Journal*. documents, comment, Vol. 22, 1968.

Reinharz, Jehuda and Anita Shapira (eds.), *Essential Papers on Zionism*, New York University Press, 1996.

Robert, John and Sami Hadawi, *The Palestine Diary 1914-45*, Vol.1, Beirut, 1970.

Robinson, Shira, *Citizen Strangers, Palestinians and the Birth of Israel's Liberal Settler State*, Stanford University Press, 2013.

Rogan, Eugene, *The Arabs, A History*, Allen Lane, London, 2009.

Rokach, Livia, *The Catholic Church and the Question of Palestine*, Saqi Books, London, 1987.

Rose, Norman (ed.), *From Palmerston to Balfour. Collected Essays of Mayir Vereté*, With an Introduction by Albert Hourani, Frank Cass, London, 1992.

Rosen, Jacob, 'Captain Reginald Hall and the Balfour Declaration', *Middle Eastern Studies*, Vol. 24, 1988.

Roskill, Stephen, *Hankey, Man of Secrets, 1919-31*, London, 1972.

Roth, Cecil, *A History of the Jews*, New York, 1961.

BIBLIOGRAPHY

Said, Edward, *The Question of Palestine*, New York, 1979.

Sanders, Ronald, *The High Walls of Jerusalem. A History of the Balfour Declaration and the Birth of the British Mandate for Palestine*, New York, 1983.

Schölch, Alexander, *Palestine in Transformation, 1856-1882: Studies in Social Economic and Political Development*, Institute for Palestine Studies, Washington DC, 1993.

Segev, Tom, *One Palestine Complete: Jews and Arabs Under the British Mandate*, New York, 2001.

Seikaly, Samir, 'Unequal Fortunes: The Arabs of Palestine and the Jews During World War I', *Studia Arabica & Islamica: Festschrift For Ihasan Abbas*, Wadad al-Qadi (ed.), American University of Beirut, 1981.

Shane, Leslie, *Mark Sykes: His Life and Letters*, with an introduction by the Rt Hon Winston Churchill, with portrait and thirty cartoons by Mark Sykes, Cassell and Co. Ltd, New York, London and Melbourne, 1923.

Sharif, Regina, 'Christians for Zion, 1600-1919', *Journal of Palestinian Studies*, Vol. 5, no. 3/4 (Spring-Summer, 1976), pp. 123-141.

Sharif, Regina, *Non-Jewish Zionism: Its Roots in Western Diplomacy*, London, 1983.

Shorrock, William, *French Imperialism in the Middle East: The Failure of French Policy in Syria and Lebanon 1900-1914*, Univ. of Wisconsin Press, 1976.

Sokolow, Nahum, *History of Zionism 1600-1918*, with an introduction by A Balfour, Longmans, Green and Co., London, 1919.

Stein, Leonard (ed.), *The Letters and Papers of Chaim Weizmann, August 1914-Nov. 1917*, Vol. 7, Oxford Universty Press, London, 1975.

Stein, Leonard, *The Balfour Declaration*, London, 1961.

Stevens, Richard P, *Zionism and Palestine Before the Mandate: A Phase of Western Imperialism*, The Institute for Palestine Studies, Beirut, 1972.

Stevens, Richard P., 'Smuts and Weizmann', *Journal of Palestine Studies*, Vol. 3 No. 1, Autumn 1973, pp. 35-59.

Storrs, Ronald, *Orientations*, London, 1937.

Sykes, Christopher, *Crossroads to Israel 1917-1948*, Indiana University Press, 1973.

Taylor, A.J.P, *The First World War*, London, 1966.

Taylor, Alan R, *Prelude to Israel: An Analysis of Zionist Diplomacy*, London, 1959.

Teveth, Shabtai, 'Kitchener, Grey and the Question of Palestine', in *From Palmerston to Balfour, Collected Essays of Mayir Vereré*, ed. Norman Rose, London, 1992.

Teveth, Shabtai, *Ben-Gurion: The Burning Ground, 1886-1948*, Boston, 1987.

Tibawi, A.L, *Anglo-Arab Relations and the Question of Palestine 1914-1921*, London, 1978.

Vereté, Mayir, 'The Balfour Declaration and Its Makers', *Middle Eastern Studies*, Vol. 6, 1970.

Vereté, Mayir, 'Why was a British Consulate established in Jerusalem?', *The English Historical Review*, Vol. LXXXV, 1970.

Vereté, Meyir, *From Palmerston to Balfour*, Frank Cass, London, 1992.

Vital, David, *Zionism: The Crucial Phase*, London, 1992.

Wasserstein, Bernard, *Herbert Samuel. A Political Life*, London, 1992.

Wavell, Colonel A.P, *The Palestine Campaigns*, London, 1928.

Wavell, Sir Archibald, *Allenby*, London, 1940.

Weisgal, Meyer, General Editor, *The Letters and Papers of Chaim Weizmann*, Oxford University Press, London, Israel Universities Press, Jerusalem.

Weisgal, W. Meyer and Joel M Carmichael (eds), *Chaim Weizmann, A Biography By Several Hands*, London, 1962.

Weizman, Eyal, *The Politics of Verticality*, https://www.opendemocracy.net/, accessed 19/07/17.

Weizmann, Chaim, *Trial and Error. The Autobiography of Chaim Weizmann*, London, Fourth Impression, 1950.

Weizmann, Vera, *The Impossible takes Longer: Memoirs by the wife of Israel's first President as told by David Tutaev*, London, 1967.

Westrate, Bruce, *The Arab Bureau: British Policy in the Middle East 1916-1920*, The Pennsylvania State University Press, 1992.

Wilson, Jeremy, *Lawrence of Arabia, The Authorised Biography of T.E. Lawrence*, London, 1989.

Yapp, M.E, *The Near East Since the First World War*, Longman, London and New York, 1991.

Zeine, Zeine, *The Struggle for Arab Independence. Western Diplomacy and the Rise and Fall of Feisal's Kingdom in Syria*, 2nd. ed., New York, 1977.

ENDNOTES

Introduction

1. Richard P. Stevens, 'Smuts and Weizmann', *Journal of Palestine Studies* 3 (1973): 56. Quoting *South African Zionist Record*, 25 November 1949. See also Jehuda Reinharz, "The Balfour Declaration and Its Maker: A Reassessment," *The Journal of Modern History* 64 (1992): 469. Isaiah Berlin and Lewis Namier—'both extremely good judges of people', according to one scholar—saw Weizmann as a 'Jewish Exilarch', ... 'leading his people back to their ancient land', and when negotiating with governments, Berlin wrote, Weizmann was 'the prime minister of a government in exile. He was not a suppliant but an equal, a voice speaking for a great historical nation, a figure of formidable powers whose proposals were not to be ignored'. Quoted in Chimen Abramsky, "Weizmann: A New Type of Leadership in the Zionist Movement," *The Jewish Historical Society of England*, XXV (1977): 148. It was also Isaiah Berlin who stated that it was certainly true that Weizmann's presence in Britain as 'an irresistible political seducer', was 'a characteristic case of the influence of accident in history' (William Matthew, "War-Time Contingency and the Balfour Declaration of 1917: An Improbable Regression," *Journal of Palestine Studies* (40): 2011, 38, quoting Isaiah Berlin, *Chaim Weizmann* [NY: Farrar, Strauss & Cudahy, 1958]). Moreover, Weizmann's skill to quickly connect with Britain's social and political elites and establishment was 'remarkable for a foreigner'. He cultivated contacts with influential Jewish families in Britain, such as the Rothschilds, as well as senior journalists from important papers such as the *Manchester Guardian*, and even met with David Lloyd George and Herbert Asquith at the height of

their power. See Robert Gerwarth, *The Vanquished: Why the First World War Failed to End* (London: Penguin/Random House, 2016), 183-84.

2. Quoted in Ronald Sanders, *The High Walls of Jerusalem: A History of the Balfour Declaration and the Birth of the British Mandate for Palestine* (NY: Holt Rinehart & Winston, 1984): 573. See also Reinharz, "The Balfour Declaration and Its Maker," 469. This was in the context when Weizmann threatened to resign and then retracted his threat the next day, avowing that he would remain in office until the government would make the pro-Zionist declaration.

3. Walid Khalidi, (ed.), *From Haven to Conquest: Readings in Zionism and the Palestinian Problem Until 1948.* (Washington DC: The Institute for Palestine Studies, 1971), xxii.

4. Ian Black, *The Independent*, 30 December 2015.

5. H. G Wells; George Bernard Shaw; Rudyard Kipling; and John Buchan.

6. Nancy W. Ellenberger, *Balfour's World: Aristocracy and Political Culture at the Fin de Siècle* (Woodbridge, Suffolk: The Boydell Press, 2015), 3.

7. Khalidi, *From Haven*, xxii.

8. Theodor Herzl's *Judenstaat (The State of the Jews)* having appeared in 1896.

9. Khalidi, *From Haven*, xxvii. Another far-reaching consequence of the Basel Programme is that, since 1897, although many Jews were anti-Zionist, it was the Zionists who claimed the leadership of 'World Jewry'. See Khalidi, *From Haven*, lix and also Appendix I of this volume, 841.

10. Khalidi, *From Haven*, xxvii.

11. The first clashes between Palestinian farmers and Jewish settlers were recorded as early as the 1880s with the arrival of the proto Zionists of the *Hovevei Zion* movement, and still occur today between the Jewish settlers and Palestinians in the West Bank.

12. Khalidi, *From Haven*, lxxvii.

13. For a comprehensive analysis on the deliberations preceding the Balfour Declaration from July to November 1917, see Reinharz, "The Balfour

Declaration and Its Maker," according to which: As late as September 19, Rothschild informed Weizmann that cabinet had discussed the matter and concluded that the moment was 'not opportune' for a declaration (477.) After another meeting on 4 October, possibly after Montagu and Curzon had made their case against the Balfour Declaration, the decision was again postponed (480). And even as late as 23 October, one week before the Declaration was announced, a decision in favour was postponed yet again, which drove Weizmann to his wits' end, and he wrote to Ahad Ha'am: 'I shall never in my life forget that day' (486).

14. See Joseph Mary Nagel Jeffries, "Analysis of the Balfour Declaration," as reprinted from JMN Jeffries, *Palestine: The Reality* (London: Longmans, Green and Co, 1939) in Khalidi, *From Haven,* 173-4.

15. Evelyn Shuckburgh, the British Under-Secretary for Middle East Affairs in the Foreign Office during the 1950s, wrote in his diary: 'How the Arabs hate us really . . . They will never forgive us [for] Israel'. Azriel Bermant, "How the Balfour Declaration Continues to Haunt Britain," *Haaretz,* 29 July 2016. Accessed 2 January 2017. Karma Nabulsi wrote in *The Guardian* wrote on 28 January, 2017, "This is a year of fateful anniversaries for the Palestinian people: the centenary of the Balfour Declaration . . . , 70 years since the *Nakba* ('disaster' in Arabic) began in December 1947 . . . .". Karma Nabulsi, "A Struggle with History", *The Guardian,* 28 January 2017. https://www.theguardian.com/books/2017/jan/28/a-struggle-with-history. Accessed May 7, 2017. And Robert Fisk wrote in *The Independent* in 2017 that Boris Johnson, 'Balfour's lamentable successor' at the Foreign Office, wrote two years prior that the Balfour Declaration was a 'bizarre . . . tragicomically incoherent document' and 'an exquisite piece of Foreign Office fudgerama'. Fisk added: 'Although the declaration itself has been parsed, de-semanticised, romanticized, decrypted, decried, cursed and adored for 100 years, its fraud is easy to detect'. Robert Fisk, "Theresa May wants British people to feel 'pride' in the Balfour Declaration. What exactly is there to be proud of?" *The Independent,* 2 March 2017. Available at: http://www.independent.co.uk/voices/

balfour-declaration-israel-palestine-theresa-may-government-centenary-arabs-jewish-settlements-a7607491.html. Accessed 10 June 2017.
16. Gerwarth, *The Vanquished*.
17. Gerwarth, *The Vanquished*, 8-9.
18. Robert Fisk, "Refugee crisis: Thank god for Germany taking responsibility – the rest of Europe seems to have forgotten the age-old lessons of history." *The Independent*, 9 September 2015. Available at: http://www.independent.co.uk/news/world/europe/refugee-crisis-thank-god-for-germany-taking-responsibility-the-rest-of-europe-appears-to-have-10493715.html. For more on the dire and tragic situation of Palestinian refugees in Lebanon, see "Where We Work – Lebanon, UNRWA web site, available at https://www.unrwa.org/where-we-work/lebanon, accessed on 25 June 2017, and Richard Cook, Policy and Governance in Palestinian Refugee Camps (Beirut, Lebanon: Issam Fares Institute, American University of Beirut, October 2008), available at: https://www.aub.edu.lb/ifi/public_policy/pal_camps/Documents/memos/ifi_pc_memo02_cook_english.pdf. Accessed on 25 June 2017.
19. *The Independent* reported on 15 October 2016 that director of the Israeli human rights organization B'Tselem, Hagai El-Ad, said that Israel has controlled Palestinian lives in Gaza, the West Bank and East Jerusalem for the past 49 years and counting. With the fiftieth anniversary of the 1967 war approaching in June 2017, B'Tselem and Peace Now issued a statement that: "The occupation is a threat to Israel's security and to Israel's very existence." Edith Lederer, "Israeli Human Rights Group Urges UN to Take Action to End Country's 'Brutal Occupation of Palestine", *The Independent*, 15 October 2016. Available at http://www.independent.co.uk/news/world/middle-east/israel-palestine-un-human-rights-occupation-a7362786.html Accessed 7 May 2017.
20. Sahar Huneidi, *A Broken Trust: Herbert Samuel, Zionism, and the Palestinians*. (London: I.B. Tauris & Co., 1999).
21. Maryanne Rhett, *The Global History of the Balfour Declaration: Declared Nation*. (New York: Routledge, Taylor, & Francis Group, 2016).

ENDNOTES

22. Sic. As shown in the War Cabinet Secret Memorandum of 1917 reproduced in Appendix B, present work, there were seven drafts, not ten.
23. Rhett, *The Global History*, 53.
24. Rhett, *The Global History*, 519.
25. Rhett, *The Global History*, 44.
26. The work was published as Sahar Huneidi, *The Balfour Declaration in British Archives, 1922-1923: New Insights into Old Controversies*, Volume XIX, Monograph *139, Annals of the Faculty of Arts* issued by the Academic Publication Council of Kuwait University, 1998-1999.
27. Interestingly, Harry Sacher, the British solicitor and Zionist leader who contributed early drafts of the Balfour Declaration, wrote immediately after the declaration was announced that ' . . . All the archives were contained in a box which Mr. Sokolow kept under his bed in his small room at the [hotel] . . . It was a long process which led to the Balfour Declaration . . . ' Quoted in Reinharz, "The Balfour Declaration and Its Maker," 455.

A General Historic Background

1. William Shorrok, *French Imperialism in the Middle East. The Failure of French Policy in Syria and Lebanon, 1900-1914*, Madison WI: Univ. of Wisconsin Press, 1976, 17.
2. Abdul Latif Tibawi, *Anglo-Arab Relations and The Question of Palestine 1914-1921*, London: Luzac & Co. Ltd, 1978, 13-14.
3. These included, among others Jesuits, Franciscans, and Lazarists, etc.
4. Shorrok, *French Imperialism*, 16-17.
5. Shorrok, *French Imperialism*, 79.
6. Shorrok, *French Imperialism*, 66. On German influence in the Ottoman Empire, see Sean McMeekin, *The Berlin-Baghdad Express: The Ottoman Empire and Germany's Bid for World Power 1898-1918* (London: Penguin Books Ltd, 2010).
7. Tibawi, *Anglo-Arab Relations*, 27.
8. Shorrok, *French Imperialism*, 97.

9. Tibawi, *Anglo-Arab Relations,* 26.
10. Oriental scholar, archaeologist, and government official. Member of the Arab Bureau, Cairo 1915 and Oriental Secretary to the High Commissioner, Iraq, 1917-20.
11. Shorrok, *French Imperialism,* 100.
12. Alexander Schölch, *Palestine in Transformation 1856-1882: Studies in Social, Economic and Political Development.* (Washington DC: Institute for Palestine Studies, 1993), 61-62. And for an elaboration on this point see Regina Sharif, *Non-Jewish Zionism: Its Roots in Western History* (London: Zed Books), 1983. Also see Mayir Vereté, "The Restoration of the Jews in English Protestant Thought 1790-1840", *Middle Eastern Studies,* 8 (1972): 3-50.
13. Desmond Stewart, *Herzl* (London: Hamish Hamilton Ltd., 1974): 209.
14. Advocates included Lord Shafstbury, Lord Palmerston, Benjamin Disraeli, and the novelist George Eliot's *Daniel Deronda* and others.
15. Schölch, *Palestine in Transformation,* 65.
16. In November 1914, after Britain declared war on Turkey, and again in January 1915, Herbert Samuel, then a cabinet minister, submitted a memorandum to Prime Minister Herbert Asquith advocating the establishment of a Jewish state in Palestine under British protection on grounds of its strategic importance to Britain and urged large-scale Jewish immigration there. See Huneidi, *A Broken Trust,* 5, 10, 82-84, and 230.
17. This was a turning point in British policy towards the Ottoman Empire. What was known as the Eastern Question had been governed by the need to safeguard the routes to India keeping the Ottoman Empire intact. This policy meant that Britain could not afford to lose the Arab provinces of the Ottoman Empire. See Dennis Edward Knox, "The Development of British Policy in Palestine, 1917-1925: Sir Gilbert Clayton and the 'New Eastern Question'" (PhD diss., Michigan State University, 1971): 26.
18. Robert John and Sami Hadawi, *The Palestine Diary 1914-45, Vol. I,* (Beirut: New World Press, 1970): 60. See also Knox, "The Development of British Policy in Palestine," 40.

ENDNOTES

19. Sir Herbert Samuel, "Great Britain and Palestine" (The Second Lucien Wolf Memorial Lecture delivered at The Jewish Historical Society at University College, London, 25 November 1935): 11.
20. Samuel, "Great Britain and Palestine," 12-13.
21. John and Hadawi, *The Palestine Diary,* 60-61.
22. Kitchener of Khartoum.
23. Oriental Secretary, British Agency in Egypt, 1909-17. Military Governor of Jerusalem, 1917-20. Civil Governor Jerusalem and Judea, 1920-26.
24. David Fromkin, *A Peace To End All Peace, Creating the Modern Middle East, 1914-1922* (NY: Henry Holt & Co, 1989): 143, quoting the Kitchener Papers PRO 30/57 45 Document 0073. The author does not give the exact date of this document.
25. Huneidi, *A Broken Trust,* 82.
26. Reinharz, "The Balfour Declaration and Its Maker," 465.
27. David Vital, *Zionism: The Crucial Phase* (Oxford: Clarendon Press, 1987): 95.
28. Fromkin, *A Peace to End All Peace*, 142-3.
29. By the end of the Nineteenth Century, Jews in Poland held key positions in foreign trade, timber, grain, and metal trades and in all branches of finance, industry, and free professions. A distinct anti-semitism prevailed, and Polish anti-semites launched a campaign against the Jews. Geoffrey Wigoder (ed.), *The New Standard Jewish Encyclopedia*, 7th edition (New York: Facts on File, 1992, 760. Added to that, when World War I started, Russian commanders pointed to the alleged disloyalty of Russia's population and its complicity with the enemy (Germany) and involvement with espionage. As a direct result of the January 1915 declaration of charges against Jews, the Russian command made several attempts to carry out mass deportations from the front lines (particularly Poland). This then degenerated into violence and looting against the Jews during the 'Great Retreat' of the Russian army in the summer/ autumn of 1915. International Encyclopedia of the First World War online: 1914-1918. Available at http://www.1914-1918-online.net/. Accessed 16 April 2017. See also Mark Levene, "The Balfour Declaration: A Case of Mistaken Identity," *The English Historical Review* 107 (1992): 54-77.

In 1916, three-quarters of a million people were brutally expelled from the Pale of Settlement. Levene, "The Balfour Declaration," 60.

30. For more details about the wave of anti-semitism sweeping Eastern Europe, see Irwin M. Herrman, "Anglo-Zionist Relations from Herzl to the Balfour Declaration 1902-1917" (PhD diss, University of Oxford, 1971): 93, 95.

31. Leopold Amery, *My Political Life. Vol. II: War and Peace. 1914-1929* (London: Hutchinson, 1953): 114.

32. Born in Motel near Pinsk in 1874, Weizmann was a chemist by profession, and in 1904 was appointed lecturer in biological chemistry at Manchester University. In 1916, he became director of the British Admiralty Chemical Laboratories. One theory, promoted by none other than Lloyd George himself, has it that Weizmann's discovery of the use of acetone in explosives was an important element in the war effort and helped secure the Balfour Declaration for the Zionists. However, this theory has been challenged. See, for instance, Ronald Sanders, *The High Walls of Jerusalem: A History of the Balfour Declaration and the Birth of the British Mandate for Palestine* (NY: Holt, Rinehart, & Winston, 1984): 285-86 & 423-24, and Levene, "The Balfour Declaration," 71. See also Christopher Simon Sykes, *The Man Who Created the Middle East: A Story of Empire, Conflict, and the Sykes-Picot Agreement* (William Collins, London, 2016), 27.

33. AR Taylor, *Prelude to Israel: An Analysis of Zionist Diplomacy, 1897-1947* (NY: Philosophical Library, 1959): 14-15.

34. Herrman, "Anglo Zionist Relations," 95. See also Taylor, *Prelude to Israel*, 13.

35. PRO. Cabinet [CAB] 37/126. Secret Cabinet memo entitled *Palestine*, March 1915.

36. PRO. Cabinet [CAB] 37/126. Secret Cabinet memo entitled *Palestine*, March 1915.

37. PRO. Cabinet [CAB] 37/126. Secret Cabinet memo entitled *Palestine*, March 1915.

38. i.e., wild; extravagant.

39. John and Hadawi, *The Palestine Diary*, 62.

ENDNOTES

40. Fromkin, *A Peace to End All Peace*, 270.
41. Fromkin, *A Peace to End All Peace*, 146. de Bunsen was a British diplomat who served as ambassador to Spain from 1906 to 1913 and to Austria from 1913 to 1914. At the outbreak of the war in 1915, he was recalled to London to head a committee to determine British wartime policy towards the Ottoman Empire.
42. Herrman, "Anglo Zionist Relations," 56-57.
43. At the beginning of the war, Kitchener had intended Britain should not be drawn into any involvement in the East. His main view was to disregard the East while focusing on the Western front, on the ground that Turkey did not pose a serious threat. This situation, however, changed later (see Fromkin, *A Peace to End All Peace*, 119).
44. Fromkin, *A Peace to End All Peace*, 146.
45. Fromkin, A Peace to End All Peace, 62.
46. Fromkin, *A Peace to End All Peace*, 73.
47. CO 733/58 CP149 (23), 13 March 1923.
48. CO 733/58 CP149 (23), 13 March 1923.
49. CAB 63/9 CID, Secret 24 August 1915, CE Heathcote-Smith to [Hankey?], (CAB 63 being Lord Hankey's Papers at the Public Records Office – Kew).
50. John and Hadawi, *The Palestine Diary,* 30.
51. Levene, "The Balfour Declaration," 62.
52. Taylor, *Prelude to Israel,* 14-15. Another author challenges Weizmann's patent for the production of acetone (which was an essential ingredient in the production of shells) on the grounds that Weizmann was accused of having 'lifted' the secrets of the Synthetic Products Company, and that the voluminous official History of the Ministry of Munitions makes no mention of Weizmann's work. For a more detailed analysis, see: Zaid. "Chaim Weizmann's Scientific Work 1915-1918", *Arabic and Islamic Garland: Historical, Educational and Literary Papers Presented to Abdul Latif Tibawi*

    by Colleagues, Friends, and Students (London: The Islamic Cultural Centre, 1977): 228-239.

53. Vereté, "The Balfour Declaration and Its Makers," 56.
54. Taylor, *Prelude to Israel*, 17-18.
55. The other position was filled by Leopold Amery, a parliamentary Under-Secretary in Lloyd George's government.
56. Taylor, *Prelude to Israel*, 15.
57. Shane Leslie. *Mark Sykes: His Life and Letters. With an Introduction by Winston Churchill* (London: Cassell and Company Ltd., 1923), 269.
58. Patricia Goldstone, *Aaronsohn's Maps: The Man Who Might Have Created Peace in the Middle East* (Berkley CA: Counterpoint, 2007), 138.
59. Zeine Zeine, *The Struggle for Arab Independence: Western Diplomacy and the Rise and Fall of Faisal's Kingdom in Syria*, 2nd Ed. (NY: Caravan Books, 1977). The British were not only driven by military or strategic considerations. Since Britain was at war with Turkey, this meant that blockading the port of Jeddah would have placed the Holy cities of Islam into the possession of an alien power. With the bulk of the British armed forces in India and Egypt being Muslim, this situation was seen by Lord Kitchener, Hardinge, and Wingate as a dangerous one. Zeine, *The Struggle for Arab Independence*, 5-6.
60. Zeine, *The Struggle for Arab Independence*, 122.
61. Zeine, *The Struggle for Arab Independence*, 7-9. Subsequently, in 1939, the British government published part of the correspondence in Cmd. 5957 (five out of the ten letters). However, the parts that were published were not the original English texts, but English translations of the Arabic version.
62. PRO, CAB 24 (1). Memo entitled: *The War—After the Dardanelles—The next steps—Notes by the Secretary*. Secret G10 dated 1 March 1915.
63. Norman Rose (ed.), *From Palmerston to Balfour. Collected Essays of Mayir Vereté*. (London: Frank Kass, 1992), 27.
64. Jeremy Wilson, *Lawrence of Arabia - The Authorised Biography of T.E. Lawrence* (London: Heinemann, 1989), 5-6.

ENDNOTES

65. Wilson, *Lawrence of Arabia,* 227-28. See also Fromkin, *A Peace to End All Peace,* 173, 176. Al-Faruki was killed in a road accident to Iraq in 1920, and quickly disappeared from the history books.
66. Cecil Bloom, "Sir Mark Sykes: British Diplomat and a Convert to Zionism," *Jewish Historical Studies* 43 (2011): 145-6.
67. Leslie, *Mark Sykes: His Life and Letters,* vi.
68. Leslie, *Mark Sykes: His Life and Letters,* vii.
69. PRO. CAB 24 (1). *Report of an Inter-Departmental Committee on the Strategical Situation in Mesopotamia.* 16 October, 1915.
70. Rose, *From Palmerston to Balfour,* 5.
71. Wilson, *Lawrence of Arabia,* 217, 234.
72. Wilson, *Lawrence of Arabia,* 237, 246.
73. Wilson, *Lawrence of Arabia,* 238-9. And for more interesting details, see 244-48.
74. Bloom, "Sir Mark Sykes," 146.
75. Nahum Sokolow was one of the leading Zionists of his time. Together with Weizmann, he worked towards securing the Balfour Declaration. His book *History of the Jews 1600-1918* was published in 1919, a few months after Sykes' death, and in it, he devoted 20 pages to Sykes' role in advancing the Zionist cause.
76. Rose, *From Palmerston to Balfour,* 18-19.
77. Bloom, "Sir Mark Sykes," 146.
78. Wilson, *Lawrence of Arabia,* 76-78.
79. Bloom, "Sir Mark Sykes," 147.
80. Wilson, *Lawrence of Arabia,* 431.
81. Wilson, *Lawrence of Arabia,* 403-404.
82. Wilson, *Lawrence of Arabia,* 431.
83. Wilson, *Lawrence of Arabia,* 403-5; 431.
84. Wilson, *Lawrence of Arabia,* 229-30; 405. Wilson also points out that comments in Foreign Office files show that Sykes' activities were regarded with apprehension. See, for instance, 247.

85. Wilson, *Lawrence of Arabia*, 405.
86. Leslie, *Mark Sykes: His Life and Letters*, 252.
87. John and Hadawi, *The Palestine Diary*, 67. James Malcolm was a British Armenian pro-Zionist. The papers concerning his evidence to the Peel Commission on the origins of the Balfour Declaration are available at the PRO. Another considerable collection exists in the Weizmann archives. See Arthur Phillip Jones (compiled for the Anglo-Palestinian Archives Committee), *Britain and Palestine 1914-1948: Archival Sources for the History of the British Mandate* (Oxford: Oxford University Press for the British Academy, 1979), 85. For the role played by James Malcolm and the Zionists in bringing America into the war on the side of the Allies, see also Samuel Landman, *Great Britain, The Jews and Palestine* (London: New Zionist Press, 1936). Landman was a well-known English Zionist and from 1917-1922 was Solicitor and Secretary to the Zionist Organisation, and later legal advisor.
88. Taylor, *Prelude to Israel*, 17, see also John and Hadawi, *The Palestine Diary*, 69.
89. Taylor, *Prelude to Israel*, 17.
90. Vera Weizmann, *The Impossible Takes Longer: Memoirs of Vera Weizmann, the Wife of Israel's First President*, as Told to David Tutaev (NY: Harper & Row, 1967), 66.
91. Chaim Weizmann, *Trial and Error: The Autobiography of Chaim Weizmann*, Fourth Impression, (London: Hamish Hamilton, 1950), 235, 237.
92. Weizmann, *Trial and Error*, 235.
93. Vera Weizmann, *The Impossible Takes Longer*, 66.
94. Within the Ottoman Empire, a *millet* was an autonomous self-governing religious [non-Muslim – typically Christian or Jewish] community, each organized under its own laws and headed by a religious leader, who was responsible to the central government for the fulfilment of millet responsibilities and duties, particularly those of paying taxes and maintaining internal security. "Millet Religious Group," Encyclopedia

Britannica web site, available at https://www.britannica.com/topic/millet-religious-group. Accessed 14 May 2017.
95. Leonard Stein, *The Balfour Declaration* (Jerusalem and London: Magnes Press, 1961), 623.
96. Sir Archibald Wavell, *Allenby: A Study in Greatness* (London: Oxford University Press, 1941), 236.
97. Wilson, *Lawrence of Arabia,* 441-2, 445. Lloyd George wrote decades later that Sykes 'was always ashamed' of the Sykes-Picot Agreement, and defended his action by explaining that he was acting under Foreign Office instructions. See Fromkin, *A Peace to End All Peace*, 344.
98. Wilson, *Lawrence of Arabia,* 464.
99. Knox, "The Development of British Policy in Palestine," 178-9.
100. Vera Weizmann, *The Impossible Takes Longer,* 68, 70.
101. Interesting that the FO refers to it as ' Arrangement' and not 'Agreement' as is commonly held.
102. Leslie Shane, *Mark Sykes: His Life and Letters*, 250-260, 271.
103. CAB 63/ 19 1917. Memo written by AG Anderson and Devonport, 3 February 1917.
104. Amery, *My Political Life,* 119.
105. Amery, *My Political Life,* 119.
106. Fromkin, *A Peace to End All Peace*, 288-291.
107. Herrman, "Anglo Zionist Relations," 195.
108. PRO. War Cabinet GT 363 Secret Cabinet memo 63/20 18 April 1917.
109. Herrman, "Anglo Zionist Relations," 201.
110. Vera Weizmann, *The Impossible Takes Longer,* 70.
111. Meyer W. Weisgal and Joel Carmichael, eds. *Chaim Weizmann: A Biography, by Several Hands.* (London: Weidenfeld and Nicholson, 1962), 149.
112. Vera Weizmann, *The Impossible Takes Longer,* 70.
113. An *intermezzo* is a short comic entertainment inserted between the acts of more serious elements.
114. Vera Weizmann, *The Impossible Takes Longer,* 71.

115. In Rose, *From Palmerston to Balfour: Collected Essays of Mayir Vereté*, 25. Vereté adds that Reginald Hall and possibly also Fitzmaurice and Hugh O'Beirne of the Foreign Office contributed more suggestions. O'Beirne was British Chargé D'affaires in Petrograd until 1915 and apparently was consulting with Fitzmaurice and Sykes on Zionism at this early stage. See Levene, "The Balfour Declaration," 66. O'Beirne drowned with Kitchener on the ill-fated HMS Hamspshire in June 1916, and Levene contends (p. 68) that with their deaths, two of the initial key players in the Zionist story were lost.

116. Jan Smuts was an Afrikaner South African who served in the Boer War, was instrumental in drawing up the Constitution for the Union of South Africa in 1909, and held three ministries in its first government. In World War I, he commanded South African troops in several campaigns in Africa. Early in 1917, he was invited to join the War Cabinet by Lloyd George, after he declined to assume the post of Commander of the Middle East (Allenby was appointed instead). He was a key negotiator at the Paris Peace Conference, and later served as Prime Minister of South Africa.

117. There is an interesting South African connection in the advocacy of a British pro-Zionist policy in Palestine. General Smuts was one of the strongest advocates of the Balfour Declaration, arguing from an imperial point of view that a Jewish Palestine under British protection was desirable as a way of linking the British Empires in Africa and Asia. In January 1917, Smuts was invited to represent the Union at the Imperial Conference and in the Imperial War Cabinet. Lloyd George thereafter invited him to join the British War Cabinet, which Smuts did in the unpaid capacity as a minister without portfolio. At the same time, he remained a member of the South African cabinet and parliament. During 1917, Smuts emerged as a world figure, and was offered the Palestine command, which he refused. He subsequently got involved with the problems of peace, and proposed the Mandate system in a paper he published in December 1918 entitled *The League of Nations: A Practical Suggestion*, which helped shape President Wilson's ideas on the subject. See LGW Legg and ET Williams, eds.

Dictionary of National Biography, 1941-1950 (Oxford, 1959). Moreover, it is interesting to point out that as Britain found it exceedingly difficult to honour the Balfour Declaration without jeopardizing other imperial interests, Smuts responded to Weizmann's appeals for assistance again and again. Whether it was the White Paper of 1922, the Passfield White Paper of 1930, the Royal Commission Report of 1937, or the White Paper of 1939, Smuts intervened to demand the fulfilment of the Balfour promise. And in late 1923, while attending the Imperial Conference, Smuts was in close contact with Weizmann, who informed him of the difficulties, and Smuts once again convinced the British government to adhere to its national home policy. Stevens, "Smuts and Weizmann," 40- 41.

118. Fromkin, *A Peace to End All Peace*, 193-4.
119. Sacher's formula read: "The British Government declares that one of its essential war aims is the reconstitution of Palestine as a Jewish State and as the National Home of the Jewish People."Sacher was adamant despite Sokolow's warning that "If we want too much we shall get nothing", and his second draft was even more forceful. During all this time as the Zionists drafted and redrafted their formula, contact with Mark Sykes was maintained by Sokolow. Reinharz, "The Balfour Declaration and Its Maker," 461.
120. Col. House resisted the pro-Zionist declaration and advocated a policy of leaving Asiatic Turkey intact and of a separate peace with Turkey (Reinharz, "The Balfour Declaration and Its Maker," 483). This ran counter to Zionist aims, and alarmed Weizmann. It was at this point that Weizmann sought Justice Brandeis' intervention to influence President Wilson.
121. Reinharz, "The Balfour Declaration and Its Maker," 470-71. For a comprehensive account, see 461-488.
122. Reinharz, "The Balfour Declaration and Its Maker," 494.
123. Reinharz, "The Balfour Declaration and Its Maker," 469.
124. Reinharz, "The Balfour Declaration and Its Maker," 476.
125. Naomi B. Levine, *Politics, Religion and Love: The Story of the Love Affair That Changed the Face of Politics in the British Empire* (NY and London: New York University Press, 1991), 422.

126. Reinharz, "The Balfour Declaration and Its Maker," 477.
127. Reinharz, "The Balfour Declaration and Its Maker," 465, 471.
128. Reinharz, "The Balfour Declaration and Its Maker," 455-6.
129. Reinharz, "The Balfour Declaration and Its Maker," see 462, 486, 496.
130. Interestingly, when the War Cabinet hesitated again on 6 October and decided to solicit the views of representative Zionist and non-Zionist Jews (see Appendix B), Edwin Montagu wrote to Lloyd George shortly after the 4 October Cabinet meeting, referring to Weizmann: "It is a matter of deep regret to me . . . that you are being . . . misled by a foreigner, a dreamer, an idealist . . . who . . . sweeps aside all practical difficulties with a view to enlisting your sympathy on behalf of his cause . . . I believe firmly that if you make a statement about Palestine as a national home for Jews, every anti-Semitic organization and newspaper will ask what right a Jewish Englishman, with a status at best of a naturalised foreigner, has to take a foremost part in the Government of the British Empire: The country for which I have worked ever since I left the university—England—the country for which my family have fought, tells me that my national home, if I desire to go there, there my natural home, is Palestine. How can I maintain my position?" Quoted in Reinharz, "The Balfour Declaration and its Maker," 480-81.
131. Reinharz, "The Balfour Declaration and Its Maker," 488.
132. PRO. CO 733/16.14 December 1921.
133. Chaim Bermant, *The Cousinhood: The Anglo-Jewish Gentry* (London: Eyre and Spottiswoode, 1971), 134.
134. Leonard Stein, ed., *The Letters and Papers of Chaim Weizmann*. Vol. VII, Aug. 1914-Nov. 1917 (London: Oxford University Press, 1975).
135. JMN Jeffries, "Analysis of the Balfour Declaration." In Khalidi, *From Haven*, 175.
136. John and Hadawi, *The Palestine Diary,* 90, quoting Cmd 5479—Palestine Royal Commission Report (Peel Report) 1937. It is also important to note that in 1917, it was Germany, and not Russia, that controlled about 6 million Jews following German conquests in Eastern Europe. See for

instance, Abdul Latif Tibawi, *Anglo-Arab Relations and The Question of Palestine 1914-1921* (London: Luzac & Co., 1978), 213.

137. John Presland, *Deedes Bey: A Study of Sir Wyndham Deedes, 1883-1923* (London: Macmillan & Co., 1942) 322.

138. The First Battle of Gaza, fought on 26 March 1917, was the first attempt by the Egyptian Expeditionary Force to invade Southern Palestine, and it ended in defeat. It was followed by a subsequent defeat at the Second Battle of Gaza in April 1917. The Third Battle of Gaza was fought 1-2 November 1917, and this was finally successful in breaking the Gaza to Beersheba Line that had been held by the Ottomans up to that point. The Ottoman Army was forced to evacuate Gaza on 6-7 November.

139. Wavell, *Allenby,* 236-37.

140. Fromkin, *A Peace to End All Peace,* 317.

141. JMN Jeffries, "The Palestine Deception—'Tricks of the Balfour Declaration,'" *Daily Mail,* 10 January 1923. CO 733/54.

142. Oskar K. Rabinowicz, "The Aliens Bill and Jewish Immigration to Britain, 1902-1903," in Khalidi, *From Haven,* 98.

143. One hundred and seventy-five witnesses gave evidence to the Commission, among them Theodor Herzl, the founder and president of the World Zionist Organization, who was invited to testify. In his testimony to the Commission, he stated that 'Nothing will meet the problem the Commission is called upon to investigate and advise upon, except a diverting of the stream of migration that is bound to go on with increasing force from Eastern Europe. The Jews of Eastern Europe cannot stay where they are—where are they to go? If you find they are not wanted here, then some place must be found to which they can migrate without that migration raising the problems that confront them here. Those problems will not arise if a home be found for them which will be legally recognised as Jewish'. See Rabinowicz, "The Aliens Bill," 98.

144. Rabinowicz, "The Aliens Bill," 99-100.

145. They argued that the Bill could be taken as a justification 'for every Jew hater and Jew persecutor' who might point to this Act and say 'if England had to

legislate against the Jew, is it not proof that he is right in other circumstances to exercise towards him more violent methods?' See Rabinowicz, "The Aliens Bill," 109.

146. Rabinowicz, "The Aliens Bill," 108.
147. Rabinowicz, "The Aliens Bill," 112.
148. Rose, *From Palmerston to Balfour,* 177.
149. Fromkin, *A Peace to End All Peace,* 323-24.
150. Shane, *Mark Sykes: His Life and Letters,* 288.
151. Wilson, *Lawrence of Arabia,* 518-19; 532-33.
152. Doreen Ingrams, *Palestine Papers 1917-1922: Seeds of Conflict* (London: John Murray, 1972), 42.
153. Ingrams, *Palestine Papers,* 43.
154. Francis Aidan Gasquet. English Benedictine monk and historical scholar. Vatican Librarian and Archivist of the Holy Roman Church, created Cardinal in 1914. In 1917, he was appointed Archivist of the Vatican Secret Archives.
155. Shane, *Mark Sykes: His Life and Letters,* 284.
156. Wilson, *Lawrence of Arabia,* 609.
157. Gerwarth, *The Vanquished,* 185-86.
158. Huneidi, *A Broken Trust,* 15-18.
159. Khalidi, *From Haven,* 216.
160. Khalidi, *From Haven,* 213-218.
161. Huneidi, *A Broken Trust,* 18.
162. Memorandum by Balfour, August 11, 1919. See Khalidi, *From Haven,* 201-211.
163. Memorandum by Mr. Balfour (Paris) Respecting Syria, Palestine, and Mesopotamia. 1919. See Khalidi, *From Haven,* 201-13. See Introduction, xxi-lxxxiii, and also 207-8.
164. Khalidi, *From Haven,* xxxiii.
165. For full memo see "Memorandum by Mr. Balfour (Paris) Respecting Syria, Palestine and Mesopotamia, 1919," in Khalidi, *From Haven,* Chapter 19, 201-211.
166. Khalidi, *From Haven,* xxxiv-xxxv; lxii.

167. Rose, *From Palmerston to Balfour,* 185; 188-9.
168. Elie Kedourie, "Sir Herbert Samuel and the Government of Palestine," *Middle Eastern Studies* 5 (1969): 44.
169. Quoted in Yehoshua Porath, *The Emergence of the Palestinian Arab National Movement 1918-1929* (London: Frank Cass, 1974), 137-8. Conversation between Milner and a delegation of the Muslim-Christian Society of Haifa.
170. Huneidi, *A Broken Trust,* 46.
171. Cited in Huneidi, *A Broken Trust,* 38.
172. When Samuel asked, 'For what?' Bols replied, 'For Palestine'. As Samuel recorded in his memoirs, he objected, 'But I can't do that. You don't mean it seriously'. To which Bols replied: 'Certainly I do, I have got it typed out here'. After this, Bols produced a slip of paper that read: *'Received from Major General Sir Louis Bols, K.C.B. — One Palestine, complete',* with the date and a space for Samuel's signature. Samuel again objected, but Bols insisted, so Samuel signed and added: *'E&O.E'* (Errors and Omissions Excepted).
173. PRO. Foreign Office [FO] 371/5034 Samuel to Curzon 27 March 1920.
174. Rose, *From Palmerston to Balfour,* 185; 188-9.
175. Huneidi, *A Broken Trust,* 18, 27.
176. See Huneidi, *A Broken Trust,* 25, 43-44. The name of Lord Meston (James Scorgie, an India civil servant) was considered.
177. Stein, *The Balfour Declaration,* 555.
178. Cited in Huneidi, *A Broken Trust,* 19.
179. PRO. Foreign Office [FO] 371/5034 Samuel to Curzon 27 March 1920.
180. Huneidi, *A Broken Trust,* 245, footnote no. 55.
181. FO 371/ 5246. 14 Oct 1920. Telegram from Sir E Geddes fro Washington.
182. FO 371/ 5245.
183. Permanent Under-Secretary Foreign Office, 1916-1920.
184. FO 371/5245.
185. Cited in Huneidi, *A Broken Trust,* 61.
186. Wilson, *Lawrence of Arabia,* 227.
187. Shane, *Mark Sykes: His Life and Letters,* 271.
188. Fromkin, *A Peace To End All Peace,* 495-96. See also 170-71.

189. Churchill (as War Secretary) and Curzon had been engaged since mid-1920 in a struggle for control of Britain's Middle East policy. Churchill wanted a Middle East department within the Colonial Office, while Curzon favored either a separate department with its own Secretary of State or, failing that, Foreign Office responsibility for the Middle East. Curzon later called the Balfour Declaration a "striking contradiction of our publicly declared principles." David Gilmour, *Curzon* (London: John Murray, 1994), 522-25. On Curzon's anti-Zionist views, see also Ingrams, *Palestine Papers*.

190. In addition to Samuel as High Commissioner, Norman Bentwich was attorney general and Wyndham Deedes (a Gentile Zionist) was Chief Secretary.

191. For the formation of the department, see Hubert Young, *The Independent Arab* (London: John Murray, 1933), 23, 325; Wilson, *Lawrence of Arabia*, 632-34, 643-45. See also John McTague, "British Policy in Palestine" (PhD diss., New York University, 1974), 235.

192. "Enquiry into Rioting in Jerusalem in April 1920" (Palin Report), submitted Port Said, August 1920, Public Record Office [PRO] Foreign Office [FO] 371/5121 E9373, 44-46.

193. Quoted in John and Hadawi, *The Palestine Diary*, 174.

194. Quoted in Ingrams, *Palestine Papers*, 139.

195. Memo by Shuckburgh, 7 November 1921, PRO CO 733/15.

196. In the summer of 1921, the Arab Executive Committee, leading the Arab nationalist movement in Palestine, decided to send a delegation to London to seek to convince the British government to abandon the Balfour Declaration. Having spent a year in London, they nevertheless returned empty-handed due to the pro-Zionist policy adopted by the Colonial Secretary, Churchill, as well as the staff of the Middle East Department of the Colonial Office under whose authority Palestine was placed.

197. Fromkin, *A Peace to End All Peace*, 524.

198. Fromkin, *A Peace to End All Peace*, 525.

199. Huneidi, *A Broken Trust*, 5, 11, 25.

200. Huneidi, *A Broken Trust*, 159–161.

ENDNOTES

201. Christopher Sykes, *Crossroads to Israel: Palestine from Balfour to Bevin* (London: Collins, 1965), 24.
202. Sykes, *Crossroads to Israel*, 25.
203. Fromkin, *A Peace to End All Peace*, 525-526.
204. CO 733/58 - Secret Cabinet Memo 17 February 1923, C.P. 106 (23).

Official British Account of Events Leading Up to the Balfour Declaration as Rendered in the 1922-1923 Inquiries

1. Throughout this section, I use the terms "minute" and "memorandum" to reflect different types of correspondence as found in the original archives. A "minute" is generally a handwritten note, sometimes in a margin, while a "memorandum" is a more official, generally typewritten statement of policy.
2. CO 733/35 - Memo from Shuckburgh, 21 December 1922.
3. For a detailed and comprehensive account of the story of the Balfour Declaration in those months, Reinharz's "The Balfour Declaration and Its Maker," quoted above, is an indispensable source.
4. CO 733/58 C.P. 60 (23), *History of the Negotiations Leading up to the Balfour Declaration*, December 1922.
5. It may be of interest, in this regard, to mention that Mrs. Weizmann, in her diary entry for November 6, 1930, the day Weizmann met Ramsay MacDonald, quotes the Prime Minister as saying: 'Balfour was always ambiguous in his statements, the Colonial Office always speaks of some secret documents in its possession about the Declaration'. See Vera Weizmann, *The Impossible Takes Longer*, 116.
6. C0733/58, *History of the Negotiations Leading up to the Balfour Declaration*, December 1922.
7. CO 733/58. Minute, Shuckburgh to Ormsby-Gore; 10 January 1923.
8. CO 733/58. Minute, Shuckburgh to Ormsby-Gore; 10 January 1923.

9. The War Cabinet Paper referred to is in PRO, G 164, Oct. 17th 1917, Cab 24/4 and also 63/23. Secret Memo. Written by Hankey, entitled 'The Zionist Movement'. It consists of 18 pages and is a highly significant document. It is reproduced in full in Appendix B.
10. CO 733/58. Minute, Shuckburgh to Ormsby-Gore; 10 January 1923.
11. CO 733/28. The last paragraph of Ormsby-Gore's handwritten minute was omitted from the printed version of the abovementioned Cabinet Paper. Ormsby-Gore's minute will be analysed in detail later. (See page vii of this volume for original handwritten minute C0733/35). When Ormsby-Gore wrote this minute, he had just been appointed Under-Secretary of State for the Colonies. It may be of interest to note that a writer in the Hebrew newspaper *Doar Hayom* wrote on 3 November 1922 expressing the view that he was optimistic about the future now that Ormsby-Gore was appointed Under-Secretary of State for the Colonies, and that this was a very important gain for the Zionist cause.
12. CO 733/ 58. Secret Cabinet Memo. C.P. 60 (23), *Palestine and the Balfour Declaration,* 10 January 1923.
13. Abraham Goldberg. Journalist and Zionist leader. Co-founder of *Poali Zion* movement (Labour Movement), and one of the leaders of the Hebrew-speaking movement in America.
14. Ronald Graham was Assistant Under-Secretary, Foreign Office from 1916 to 1919. He was in the confidence of Mark Sykes, and during the time he spent in the FO, he was indispensable to Zionists. One author (Fromkin, *A Peace to End All Peace*, 291) suggests that Graham was probably more responsible than anyone else in the government for embodying the commitment to Zionism in an official document (i.e., the Balfour Declaration).
15. It is indeed curious that negotiations of such magnitude were conducted on a personal level with no official record.
16. CO 733/58. Secret Cabinet Memo. C.P. 60 (23) *Palestine and the Balfour Declaration,* 10 January 1923.
17. Ahmed Jemal Pasha, or Djemal Pasha, was one of the leading members of the Young Turk administration prior to and during World War I. He

held numerous wartime posts, including Fourth Army Commander on the Palestine Front and military governor of Ottoman Syria. He was one of the Three Pashas who ruled the Ottoman Empire as a triumvirate in World War I and were the main perpetrators of the Armenian genocide, the Greek genocide, and the Assyrian genocide. His public hanging of Syrian nationalists in 1916 was one of the triggers of the great Arab revolt of Sharif Hussein in Mecca. He was assassinated in 1922 in retribution for his role in the Armenian genocide.

18. According to Leonard Stein, there were signs of interest in Zionism on the German side as early as November 1914, when the Counselor at the German Embassy in Constantinople, von Kuhlmann, told Richard Lichtheim, representative of the Zionist Organization in Geneva, that he would like to see the Zionists concentrating all their activities in Germany, hinting clearly as Lichteim says, that he looked forward to the Zionist movement being within the German sphere of influence. Stein, *The Balfour Declaration*, 211.
19. Secretary of State for India, 1917-22. Anglo-Jewish anti-Zionist.
20. Ten representative Jews were chosen for that purpose, including E. Montagu, with the result that six favoured the declaration and the rest did not. Their views are printed in full in Hankey's above-mentioned War Cabinet Memo of 17 October, 1917. (For full document, see Appendix B).
21. CO 733/58 Secret Cabinet Memo CP 60 (23) *Palestine and the Balfour Declaration,* 10 January 1923.
22. CO 733/58 Secret Cabinet Memo CP 60 (23) *Palestine and the Balfour Declaration,* 10 January 1923.
23. C0733/58 Secret Cabinet memo CP 106 (23). 17 February, 1923.
24. Evelyn Baring, First Earl of Cromer. Encyclopedia Britannica. https://www.britannica.com/biography/Evelyn-Baring-1st-Earl-of-Cromer.
25. See Appendix B for full text.
26. CAB 24/4 Secret Cabinet memo G-164.
27. CAB 24/4 Secret Cabinet memo G-164.
28. CAB 24/4 Secret Cabinet memo G-164.

29. By August 1917, Milner took it upon himself to draft a text of the pro-Zionist declaration. He objected, according to Reinharz, to the term 'reconstituted', and 'secure' and suggested a fundamental change: Instead of the original formulation "***the*** National Home ***of*** the Jewish people', he proposed '***a*** home ***for*** the Jewish People'. Reinharz, 'The Balfour Declaration and Its Maker', 264. And although Milner's draft had in mind anti-Zionist Jews in Britain, this formula still did not allay the fears of Edwin Montagu, the fiercest critic of the government's Zionist policy, who had recently been appointed Secretary of State for India. Reinharz, 'The Balfour Declaration and Its Maker', 465.
30. CO 733/39 Shuckburgh to Samuel. 7 November 1922. Private.
31. CO 733/65 Report on the Political Situation for the Month of January 1924. Samuel to JH Thomas (Colonial Secretary). Thomas served as Secretary of State for the Colonies from 22 January 1924 – 3 November 1924.
32. CO 733/58 Memorandum by Secretary of State for the Colonies, C.P. 121 (24) Secret, entitled *Palestine*, 19 February 1924.
33. CO 733/83. C.P. 121(24), 19 February 1924.
34. CO O 733/58 Memorandum by Secretary of State for the Colonies, C.P. 121 (24) Secret, entitled *Palestine*, 19 February 1924. For a detailed analysis of the deliberations of the Middle East Department of McMahon's pledge to Sharif Hussein during 1923-24, see Sahar Huneidi, "Sir Herbert Samuel, Zionism and the Palestine Arabs, 1920-25" (PhD diss, University of Manchester, 1995), 427-440.
35. CO 733/78 Memo by the Middle East Department 12 February 1924 Printed for the Cabinet.
36. See Huneidi, *A Broken Trust*, 48-78.
37. Sir Alfred Charles William Harmsworth. (1865-1922), Newspaper proprietor. Founder of *Answers, Daily Mail* etc. Proprietor of *The Times*. Director of Propaganda in Enemy Countries, 1918. Anti-Zionist. Through *The Times* and *The Daily Mail*, Northcliffe was said to have controlled the 'classes' and the 'masses'.
38. Vital, *Zionism*, 209, 211.

39. Amery, *My Political Life,* Vol.2, 107.
40. Amery, *My Political Life,* 93; and for more details, see 94-96.
41. Amery *My Political Life,* 93. Christopher Sykes also reveals that in 1917, L.S. Amery and Sir Mark Sykes, though both known as 'Assistant Secretary to the War Cabinet', in fact had the authority of junior Ministers and were sometimes empowered, as in the Sykes-Picot Agreement, to act as plenipotentiaries for the Government, and that Amery once explained to the author that they adopted the inferior title 'Assistant Secretary' as this enabled them to sit in the House of Commons 'as private members without having to answer questions there'. Sykes, *Crossroads to Israel,* 129 n. 2.
42. Amery, *My Political Life,* 92.
43. Stephen Roskill, *Hankey: Man of Secrets: 1919-1931, Volume II* (London: Collins, 1972) 422-23.
44. See Jones, *Britain and Palestine*, 162. See also Fromkin, *A Peace to End All Peace*, 232, 234, and 280 and Knox, "The Development of British Policy in Palestine," 40.
45. Vital, *Zionism,* 95.
46. Fromkin, *A Peace to End All Peace*, 232-36; 270-71.
47. Vital, *Zionism,* 209-210.
48. Knox, "The Development of British Policy in Palestine," 39.
49. The still-secret Sykes-Picot Agreement had in fact partitioned the Ottoman Empire in such a way as there would be nothing left of it. Russia was to get Constantinople and the Straits, in addition to northeast Anatolia, and the Black Sea coast. Italy was to get the southwestern coast of Anatolia from Smyrna to Adalia; France was to get most of eastern Anatolia, including Mersin, Adana, and Cilicia, in addition to Kurdistan, Alexandretta, Syria, and Northern Mesopotamia, as well as Mosul. Britain was to get the Levant from Gaza south to the Red Sea, Transjordan, most of the Syrian Desert, all of Mesopotamia south of Kirkuk, including Baghdad and Basra, and most of the Persian Gulf coast of Arabia. It was also proposed that western Anatolia around Smyrna would go to Greece. The Holy Land was to be internationalized. Little was left to the Turks from the Ottoman Empire

except about 250 miles around Ankara. See Carroll Quigley, *Tragedy and Hope: A History of the World in Our Time*. First Printing (New Millenium Edition, 1966), 178.

50. Fromkin, *A Peace to End All Peace*, 234-35.
51. Fromkin, *A Peace to End All Peace*, 273-74.
52. Roger Adelson, *Mark Sykes: Portrait of an Amateur* (London: Jonathan Cape, 1975), 224-25.
53. Georges Clemenceau, French statesman, radical politician, and journalist. As a persistent opponent of the government during the early years of World War I, he became premier in 1917 and saw France through to victory in 1918.
54. Roskill, *Hankey*, 29.
55. Roskill, *Hankey*, 201.
56. Quigley, *Tragedy and Hope*, 179.
57. Leopold Greenberg, one of Weizmann's long-term political opponents, wrote to him on 2 November 1917: 'I am sure I did not say half or even much less of what I felt in regard to your wonderful success when I had the pleasure of seeing you this evening. You have performed miracles, especially having in mind surrounding circumstances . . . .' Quoted in Reinharz, "The Balfour Declaration and Its Maker," 490-91.
58. Reinharz asserts that later historians, mostly those friendly to the Zionist cause, have in hindsight questioned the importance of Weizmann's role in obtaining the Balfour Declaration; however, he points out that in the immediate aftermath of the Cabinet's decision, 'there was little doubt in the minds of those who had observed the entire political process at close range about who deserved the lion's share of the credit'. Reinharz, "The Balfour Declaration and Its Maker," 490.
59. Reinharz, "The Balfour Declaration and Its Maker," 491.
60. Reinharz, "The Balfour Declaration and Its Maker," 489.

61. Churchill's White Paper of 1922 was the first official interpretation of that declaration.
62. CO 733/58. C.P. 106 (23).
63. CO 733/58 Minute, Shuckburgh to Marsh. 22 January 1923.
64. CO 733/58 Minute, Shuckburgh to Marsh. 22 January 1923.
65. Sir Edward Howard Marsh. Private Secretary to W Churchill, 1917-22 and 1924-29; to the Duke of Devonshire 1922-24; and to J H Thomas, 1924.
66. CO 733/58 Minute. Shuckburgh to Marsh 22 January, 1923.
67. Stein's hypothesis was later challenged by two important works: DZ Gillon's "The Antecedents of the Balfour Declaration," *Journal of Middle Eastern Studies* 5 (1969): 131-150; and Mayir Vereté, "The Balfour Declaration and its Makers," *Middle Eastern Studies* 6 (1970): 48-76. Vereté's work continues to be of vital importance to the subject, although he takes his hypothesis too far by discounting any influence by Weizmann and other Zionist leaders on British statesmen, asserting that it was British interests alone that led the British government to support a pro-Zionist policy.
68. WT Mattison, *The Balfour Declaration: An Appraisal in International Law* (Evanston IL: Northwestern University Press, 1971), 64.
69. Stein, *The Balfour Declaration*, 196. And for a diametrically opposed view, see Landman, *Great Britain, The Jews and Palestine*, London, 1936.
70. Chaim Weizmann, *Trial and Error,* 224.
71. See, for instance, CO 733/83 24 February 1924.
72. Ormsby-Gore's minute has been referred to by Ingrams in *Palestine Papers,* 7. However, Ingrams mistakenly quotes another minute by Shuckburgh printed in the same Cabinet Paper instead of that of Ormsby-Gore. It would also appear that Vital has seen a printed India Office copy of the Cabinet Paper, rather than the original hand-written minute by Ormsby-Gore, which is quoted above (Vital, *Zionism,* 370). Moreover, Vital mentioned the minute *en passant,* without drawing any particular attention to it.
73. Roskill, *Hankey,* 450.
74. Roskill, *Hankey,* Vol. 1, 270.

75. Fromkin, *A Peace to End All Peace*, 86, 88; 147-49; See also C. Sykes, *The Man Who Created the Middle East*.
76. Fromkin, *A Peace to End All Peace*, 149. See also Mayir Vereté, "Kitchener, Grey and the Question of Palestine." In Rose, *From Palmerston to Balfour*. 41. Vereté, however, does not mention any part played by Fitzgerald.
77. Vereté, "Kitchener," 41. Quoting PRO. 30/57/91: Sykes to George Arthur, 12 September 1916.
78. Weizmann, *Trial and Error,* 229.
79. Weizmann, *Trial and Error,* 229-30.
80. i.e., the Allied Powers (France, Britain, Russia, Italy, Japan), as distinct from the Central Powers (Germany, Austria-Hungary, the Ottoman Empire, and Bulgaria) that they fought against during World War I.
81. Weizmann, *Trial and Error,* 238-40.
82. Shane, *Mark Sykes: His Life and Letters,* 284.
83. Shane, *Mark Sykes: His Life and Letters,* 286.
84. Shane, *Mark Sykes: His Life and Letters,* 287-8.
85. Aaron Aaronsohn (1876-1919) worked in the Edmond de Rothschild settlements. His parents were among those who founded the colony of Zichron Ya'acov, in the north of Palestine. In 1906, Aaronsohn discovered the wild *Emmer* wheat in Palestine, and in 1911, he founded an agricultural experimental station in Atlit. During World War I, he was the chief agricultural adviser to Jemal Pasha (in connection with the locust invasion), but at the same time he organised the underground espionage intelligence network *Nili* on behalf of the Allies to realize Jewish aspirations in Palestine. He thus served as a staff officer of the British Army Headquarters in Cairo to advise General Allenby in his advance in Gaza, and was sent on several missions. In 1919 he advanced Zionist interests at the Paris Peace Conference. He died in an airplane crash over the English Channel in 1919 in ambiguous circumstances. See also Shmuel Katz, *The Aaronsohn Saga* (Jerusalem: Gefen Publishing House, 2007). Patricia Goldstone, *Aaronsohn's Maps: The Untold Story of the Man Who Might Have Created Peace in the Middle East* (Orlando, NY, London: Harcourt Inc., 2007).

ENDNOTES

86. For more interesting details see: Stein, ed, *The Letters and Papers of Chaim Weizmann*, Vol. 7, 523.
87. Goldstone, *Aaronsohn's Maps,* 141-42.
88. Fromkin, *A Peace to End All Peace,* 278.
89. Col. Richard Meinertzhagen. Pro-Zionist, Chief Political Officer, Palestine and Syria 1919-1924. Military Adviser, Middle East Department, Colonial Office, 1921-24.
90. Fromkin, *A Peace to End All Peace,* 308.
91. Stein, ed., *The Letters and Papers of Chaim Weizmann*, Vol. 7, 421.
92. Vital, *Zionism,* 369.
93. Fromkin, *A Peace to End All Peace,* 255. Also Sami Hadawi, *Bitter Harvest. Palestine between 1914-1967* (New York, 1967), 18. See also John Cornelius, "The Balfour Declaration and the Zimmerman Note," *Washington Report On Middle Eastern Affairs* XVI (1997): 18-20.
94. David George Hogarth. Traveller and Keeper of the Ashmolean Museum, Oxford. Director of Arab Bureau, Cairo 1916-1918.
95. Vital, *Zionism,* 192, 214.
96. Vital, *Zionism,* 260.
97. See Levene, "The Balfour Declaration," 70 and 71-72 for more interesting details.
98. Levene, "The Balfour Declaration," 73-4.
99. Vital, *Zionism*, 260-261. Quoting FO 371/2996.
100. Vital, *Zionism*, 259-262; 288.
101. Albert Montefiore Hyamson, *Palestine Under the Mandate 1920-48* (London: Methuen & co., 1950), 34.
102. Martin Gilbert, *Exile and Return: The Emergence of Jewish Statehood* (London: Weidenfeld & Nicolson, 1978), 105.
103. John and Hadawi, *The Palestine Diary,* 90-91.
104. Fromkin, *A Peace to End All Peace,* 295.
105. Klaus J. Herrmann, "Political Response to the Balfour Declaration in Imperial Germany: German Judaism," *Middle East Journal* 19 (1965): 303-304.

106. Derek J Penslar, *Zionism and Technocracy: The Engineering of Jewish Settlement in Palestine 1870-1918* (Bloomington: Indiana University Press, 1991), 150.
107. John and Hadawi, *The Palestine Diary*, 59.
108. Fromkin, *A Peace to End All Peace*, 296.
109. National Archives, Washington. Microfilm Roll no. 79-130 G 141. Samuel Edelman to Hugh Wilson. Bern, 1 December 1917. Near Eastern Intelligence Section.
110. National Archives, Washington. Microfilm Roll no. 79-130 G 141. Samuel Edelman to Hugh Wilson. Bern, 1 December 1917. Near Eastern Intelligence Section.
111. Ronald Graham to Balfour, 25 October 1917. See Reinharz, "The Balfour Declaration and Its Maker," 486.
112. Fitzmaurice was official interpreter and First Dragoman to the British ambassador in Constantinople, Sir Gerard Lowther, on whom he had a great influence. According to Fromkin, Fitzmaurice's interpretation of events in 1908 was misleading to the British government. It was he who thought that the Jews in the Ottoman Empire and in the world wielded political power, and their support had to be bought by promising them the establishment of a national home in Palestine, a reasoning that helped persuade the Foreign Office that it ought to support the Zionists—which eventually it did in 1917. (Fromkin, *A Peace to End All Peace*, 41-44). By 1914, Wingate and Clayton at the Arab Bureau in Cairo fell into believing Fitzmaurice's mistaken views that the Ottoman government was under the influence of a group of pro-German Jews (Fromkin, *A Peace to End All Peace*, 92), and that the Young Turks were tools in Jewish hands, which historians now know to be false (Fromkin, *A Peace to End All Peace*, 466). Fitzmaurice was also an old public school friend of Mark Sykes, and they both shared the same prejudices. For example, Fromkin maintains that Fitzmaurice was the main force behind the fallacy that the Sublime Porte had fallen under Jewish influence. (Fromkin, *A Peace to End All Peace*, 198).
113. Fromkin, *A Peace to End All Peace*, 291.

ENDNOTES

114. Russian-born Zionist leader (1880-1940). During World War I, he advocated the recruiting of Jewish regiments to fight on the Palestine front. This led to the establishment of the Zion Mule Corps in 1915. In 1917, the British government formed the Jewish battalions. In 1925, Jabotinsky formed the World Union of Zionist Revisionists in opposition to official Zionism.
115. Fromkin, *A Peace to End All Peace*, 291.
116. Fromkin, *A Peace to End All Peace*, 255. Also Hadawi, *Bitter Harvest,* 18. See also Cornelius, "The Balfour Declaration and the Zimmerman Note," 18-20.
117. Fromkin, *A Peace to End All Peace*, 295.
118. Fromkin, *A Peace to End All Peace*, 299-300.
119. Reinharz. "The Balfour Declaration and Its Maker," 485.
120. John and Hadawi, *The Palestine Diary,* 63. See also Geoffrey Wigoder (ed.), *The New Standard Jewish Encyclopedia*, 836. For more details, see Vital, *Zionism,* 115.
121. John and Hadawi, *The Palestine Diary,* 72, quoting the review *World Jewry* 1 March 1935 described by Samuel Landman, Secretary of the World Zionist Organization 1917-22.
122. Stein, *The Balfour Declaration,* 196-97.
123. See Jones, *Britain and Palestine*, 96.
124. See for instance, Fromkin, *A Peace to End All Peace,* 233.
125. Taylor, *The First World War,* 224.
126. Vital, *Zionism,* 298. Quoting a minute by Ronald Graham. F.O.371/ 3083, 3 November 1917.
127. Roskill, *Hankey*, Vol. I, 304.
128. Roskill, *Hankey,* Vol. X, 390-91.
129. Taylor, *The First World War,* 211.
130. It is interesting to note that, at least until 1920, *The Times* continued to be an enthusiastic supporter of the Balfour Declaration, calling it the 'only sound policy' the Allies could have adopted towards the Jewish people. But as time passed, and difficulties multiplied in Palestine, this enthusiasm faded, and we begin to read reports in *The Times* from its correspondents on the spot severely criticising the government's pro-Zionist policy.

131. Alan Palmer, Penguin Dictionary of Twentieth Century History (London: Allen Lane, 1979), 188.
132. Fromkin, *A Peace to End All Peace*, 255.
133. General Eric Ludendorff, *My War Memories 1914-18*, (2 vols). English Trans. (London: Hutchinson & Co., 1919), Vol. 2, 458.
134. Ludendorff, *My War Memories*, Vol. 2, 458.
135. Ludendorff, *My War Memories*, Vol. 2, 470. See also 458.
136. Ludendorff, *My War Memories*, Vol. 2, 471-72.
137. Ludendorff, *My War Memories*, Vol. 1, 204.
138. War Cabinet Paper, G-164, 17 October 1917, 14. (See Appendix B).
139. CO 733/ 58. C.P. 60 (23).
140. Stein, ed., *The Letters and Papers of Chaim Weizmann*, Vol. 7, 431.
141. Stein, ed., *The Letters and Papers of Chaim Weizmann*, Vol. 7, 431.
142. Stein, ed., *The Letters and Papers of Chaim Weizmann*, Vol. 7, 438.
143. McMeekin, *The Berlin Baghdad Express*, 353.
144. Taylor, AJP, *The First World War*, 206. And for a more detailed analysis of the German aspect of the Zionist question in general, see in Stein, *The Balfour Declaration* Chapter 36, 533-542, which deals with German Zionist leaders and the German government during World War I. Also see Klaus J Herrmann, "Political Response to the Balfour Declaration in Imperial Germany: German Judaism," *Middle East Journal* (19): 1965.
145. Vital, *Zionism*, 231-32.
146. Stein, *The Balfour Declaration*, 489-90; 493.
147. Zionist leader, formerly Shimshelevitz (1884-1963). Second president of Israel. Born to the Ukraine, he joined the Zionist movement in his youth. He organized the Poalei Zion party in Palestine and was prominent in the Jewish underground military movement during the early 1920s.
148. For more details see Vital, *Zionism*, 228-232.
149. Abdel Wahab El-Messiri. *The Encyclopedia of Zionist Concepts and Terminology*, (Ar.) (Cairo, 1974), 286; see also Shabtai Teveth, *Ben-Gurion: The Burning Ground, 1886-1948* (Boston: Houghton Mifflin, 1987), 768.

150. Cecil Roth, *A History of the Jews* (New York, Schocken Books, 1961), 362-3. The Pale of Settlement consisted of 25 provinces in Czarist Russia (in Poland, Lithuania, White Russia, Ukraine, Bessarabia and Crimea) where Jews were permitted permanent residence. Permission to live outside its confines was only granted to certain groups. The Pale was abolished in 1915 in effect and legally in 1917. See Wigoder, ed, *The New Standard Jewish Encyclopedia*, 731.
151. Teveth, *Ben-Gurion*, 125.
152. The Histadrut was founded in 1920 as a Jewish labor federation to represent the interests of Jewish workers. It pushed for separation between Arab and Jewish workers and did its best to undermine any possible cooperation. Arab workers were only allowed to join the Histadrut as full members much later, in 1966, after nearly two decades of living under Israeli military government rule. Odeh Bisharat, "Class Warfare: How 'Hebrew Labor' destroyed Arab-Jewish Solidarity," *Haaretz*, March 7, 2015. Available at: http://www.haaretz.com/jewish/books/.premium-1.645483. Accessed February 28, 2017.
153. Amos Elon, *The Israelis: Founders and Sons* (New York: Holt, Rinehart & Winston, 1971), 133; see also Teveth, *Ben-Gurion,*124.
154. Elon, *The Israelis: Founders and Sons*, 133.
155. Elon, *The Israelis: Founders and Sons*, 126.
156. Elon, *The Israelis: Founders and Sons*, 132.
157. Stein, *The Balfour Declaration*, 587. For more details see Rose, *From Palmerston to Balfour*, 26.
158. Frank E. Manuel, "Judge Brandeis and the Framing of the Balfour Declaration," in *From Haven to Conquest*, ed. Walid Khalidi, 168-69.
159. Manuel, "Judge Brandeis and the Framing of the Balfour Declaration," in *From Haven to Conquest*, ed., Khalidi, 171.
160. Manuel, "Judge Brandeis and the Framing of the Balfour Declaration," in *From Haven to Conquest*, ed., Khalidi, 165-172.
161. The Jewish Agency for Palestine. *Documents Relating to the Palestine Problem* (London: the Jewish Agency for Palestine, 1945).
162. C0733/ 58 C.P. 60 (23). 10 January 1923.

163. Edy Kaufman, "French pro-Zionist Declarations of 1917-18," *Middle Eastern Studies* (15): 1979, 377.
164. Director-General of the French Foreign Ministry.
165. Kaufman, "French pro-Zionist Declarations,"374, 384-5.
166. Kaufman, "French pro-Zionist Declarations," 384-5, 396.
167. Stein, *The Balfour Declaration,* 588.
168. Stein, *The Balfour Declaration,* 590.
169. Stein, *The Balfour Declaration,* 590-91.
170. Kaufman, "French pro-Zionist Declarations," 390.
171. JMN Jeffries, *The Balfour Declaration* (Beirut, Lebanon: The Institute of Palestine Studies, Monograph Series No. 7, Beirut, 1967), 19. Compare Jeffries' translation to that of Leonard Stein, *The Balfour Declaration,* 592. The two translations have the same spirit; with only two words differing. Whereas Stein used the more accurate 'Hebrew national centre' [*ebraico* in the original], Jeffries translated it as 'Jewish national centre'. The other difference is the use of the word 'legal,' which Stein translated as 'juridical'.
172. Stein, *The Balfour Declaration,* 593 (Footnote 17).
173. For an in-depth analysis of Italian diplomacy regarding Palestine, see Frank E. Manuel, "The Palestine Question in Italian Diplomacy, 1917-1920," *Journal of Modern History* (27): 1955, 263-280.
174. Jeffries, *The Balfour Declaration,* 19.
175. For more details see Bernard Wasserstein, *Herbert Samuel—A Political Life* (New York: Oxford University Press, 1992), 254.
176. CO 733/54. JMN Jeffries, "The Palestine Deception," *The Daily Mail,* 24 January 1923.
177. Stein, *The Balfour Declaration*, 471-72. Also compare this to Weizmann's description of the sequence of the same events from a letter that he wrote to Gaston Wormster in Paris on 16 October 1917, in Stein, ed., *The Letters and Papers of Chaim Weizmann,* Vol. 7, 535.
178. Stein, *The Balfour Declaration,* 472. In this respect, Stein asserts that Harold Nicolson and Ormsby-Gore are the two authorities on the Balfour Declaration. (Not to be confused with Sir Arthur Nicolson, Permanent

ENDNOTES

      Under-Secretary at the Foreign Office, 1916, who corresponded with Mark Sykes. See, for instance, Levene, "The Balfour Declaration," 64).
179. See, for instance, Fromkin, *A Peace to End All Peace,* 189-90.
180. Bloom, "Sir Mark Sykes," 143.
181. Chaim Weizmann, *Trial and Error: The Autobiography of Chaim Weizmann,* (London: Hamish Hamilton, 1950), 262.
182. The Spectator, 3 January 1947.
183. FO 371/3083, 2 November 1917.
184. Ormsby-Gore later became Secretary of State for the Colonies, 1936-38. It is not without significance that the partition of Palestine was first mooted in 1937, while he was Colonial Secretary.
185. Goldstone, *Aaronsohn's Maps,* 141.
186. William Ormsby-Gore, "Great Britain, Palestine and the Jews," in *The Nineteenth Century and After* (88): 1920, 621-631.
187. See Knox, "The Development of British Policy in Palestine," 180. Quoting *Report on the Existing Political Situation in Palestine and Contiguous Areas by the Political Officer in charge of the Zionist Commission.* FO 371/ 3395 and 3389 August 1918.
188. Levene, for example, discusses the 'Zionist Lobby in the Foreign Office and War Secretariat' during 1917. Levene, "The Balfour Declaration," 72.

Summary and Conclusion

1. Sykes, *Crossroads to Israel,* 16.
2. Rose, *From Palmerston to Balfour,* 204.
3. See WT Mallison, *The Balfour Declaration: An Appraisal in International Law* (Evanston, Ill: McGraw-Hill, 1971), 85-86.
4. Mallison, *The Balfour Declaration,* 605.
5. Mallison, *The Balfour Declaration,* 618-619.
6. Stein, *The Balfour Declaration,* 552.
7. Stein, *The Balfour Declaration,* 555.
8. For more details see Huneidi, *A Broken Trust,* 390-441.

9. David Vital quotes the authors of one of the volumes of the official history of the great war as saying: 'The development of the war, which was ever engaging more nations and affecting more interests, the imperative pressure of Allied needs, and the international power of the Jewish race, had made desirable the recognition of Jewish aspirations for a "National Home" in Palestine.' (See Lt. Gen. Sir George Macmunn and Capt. Cyril Falls. *Military Operations: Egypt and Palestine August 1914-June 1917*, London, 1928, p. 219. Vital states that as such, the Balfour Declaration 'was an act designed primarily to achieve advantages in the short term. That for the Zionists it represented a promise of great things to come was incidental to its main and immediate purpose . . . ' (Vital, *Zionism*, 297).
10. Vital, *Zionism*, 297-98.
11. C0733/58. 2 July 1923.
12. Sir Eric Geddes.
13. Elizabeth Monroe, *Britain's Moment in the Middle East: 1914-1971* (Washington, DC: Johns Hopkins University Press, 1981), 43.
14. Stein, *The Balfour Declaration*, 619.
15. CO 733/ 58. Secret Cabinet Report CP 351 (23), 27 July 1923.
16. Arnold Toynbee, Foreword to *The Palestine Diary 1914-1945*. Robert John and Sami Hadawi, Beirut 1970. Pp. xiii, xiv-xv.

INDEX

Aaronsohn, Aaron 119–20, 158, 187, 222
Aliens Act 51–52
Aliens Bill 51, 211–12
Allenby, Edmund 48, 52, 81, 119–20, 144, 222
Amery, Leopold 20, 43–44, 83, 88, 99–101, 108–9, 116, 119, 126, 154–55, 157, 187, 191, 202, 204, 207, 219
Arab Bureau 30, 53, 117, 120, 122, 158, 194, 200, 223–24
Asquith, Herbert 15, 19, 21–23, 27, 98, 102, 104, 135–36, 195, 200

Baghdad 31, 33, 35, 104, 219
Balfour, Arthur James 2–3, 48, 52, 70, 190
Baring, Evelyn 89, 217
Beirut 53, 188–89, 190, 198, 200, 228, 230
Bell, Gertrude 13
Ben-Gurion, David 142–44
Bentwich, Herbert 116
Bentwich, Norman 38, 214

Ben-Zvi, Itzhak 142–3
Berlin 86, 127–28
Berthelot, Philippe 105
Bols, Louis 49, 213
Brandeis, Louis 37, 131
British Mandate 13, 63, 73, 97, 190, 193, 196, 202, 206
British Policy 27–8, 67, 75, 112, 123, 127, 135, 190, 194, 200, 207, 214, 219, 229
Buchanan, Edward 20
Bunsen, Maurice de 23

Cabinet Paper 24, 81–83, 108–9, 112, 154, 216, 221, 226
Caldwell, Charles 23
Cambon, Jules 148–49
Cavendish, William 108
Cecil, Robert 45, 116
Chamberlain, Joseph 103–4
Churchill, Winston 30, 51, 68, 70, 165, 193, 204
Churchill's White Paper 72, 221
Clayton, Gilbert 30, 50, 118, 190, 200

Clemenceau, Georges 105, 220
Cohen, LL 91–92
Cowen, Joseph 116
Crane, Charles 56
Curtis, Lionel 101

Declaration Cambon 148–49
Dobeler, Gustav von 139

Edelman, Samuel 128–29, 224
Egypt 14, 23, 28, 44, 53, 67–68, 84, 89, 120–21, 126, 128, 131, 140, 201, 204, 211, 230
Elon, Amos 143, 227

Fisk, Robert 6, 197–98
Fitzmaurice, Gerald 130, 208, 224
France 11–13, 21, 31–35, 37, 41–42, 57, 59–60, 144, 148–50, 188, 219–20, 222

Gaza 6, 43, 50, 119, 198, 211, 219, 222
George, Lloyd 10, 15, 18–23, 27, 36, 40, 43, 45, 53, 55, 61, 63, 68, 70, 99, 102–6, 126, 131, 156, 161, 195, 202, 204, 207–8, 210
Germany 85, 121, 123, 125–7, 129, 133, 136–38, 140–41, 189, 198, 199, 201, 210, 217, 222–23, 226
Graham, Ronald 10, 45, 82, 84, 120, 123–25, 129, 133, 139–40, 163, 216, 224–25
Grey, Edward 16–17, 19–20

Ha'am, Ahad 38, 47, 197
Haldane, Richard 19
Hall, Reginald 121, 192, 208
Hankey, Maurice 10, 43–44, 70, 82–83, 91, 98–100, 112, 122, 133–34
Hardinge, Charles 66
Henderson, Arthur 99
Herzl, Theodor 103, 196, 211
Hindenburg, Paul von 137
Hogarth, DG 30, 117, 223
House, Edward 131
Hussein-McMahon correspondence 2, 28, 75, 92, 95, 190
Hyamson, Albert 120, 125

Ibn Saud 96
India 19, 24, 45–48, 103, 131, 140, 200, 204, 213, 217–18

Jabotinsky, Vladimir 47, 130, 142
James, Williams 122
Jeffries, JMN 4, 50, 153, 197, 210–11, 228

Kerr, Philip 45, 86, 101
Khalidi, Rashid 2
Khalidi, Walid 1, 3, 196, 227
King-Crane Commission 56–59
King Hussein 93, 96
King, Henry Churchill 56
Kitchener, Herbert 18, 23
Kuhlmann, Richard von 86

INDEX

Landman, Samuel 120, 206, 225
Law, Bonar 99
Lawrence, TE 30, 33, 35–36, 69, 188, 194, 204
League of Nations 13, 56–57, 69, 73, 98, 208
Lebanon 11, 13, 35, 42, 198, 199, 228
Lichtheim, Richard 140, 217
Ludendorff, Erich, 136–139, 191, 226

MacDonogh, George 10, 81, 114, 118–120
Magnus, Philip 91–92
Malcolm, James 37, 110, 131, 133, 206
Manuel, Frank E. 146, 191, 227–28
Marsh, EH 109, 221
McMahon, Arthur Henry 28, 31, 92–93, 190, 218
Meinertzhagen, Richard 69, 120, 188, 223
Milner, Alfred 10, 44–46, 61–62, 91–92, 99–102, 120
Milner-Amery draft 154
Monroe, Elizabeth 165, 192, 230
Montagu, Edwin 19, 45–48, 87, 91–92, 197, 210, 217, 218

Nicolson, Harold 155–56, 228

Occupied Enemy Territory Administration (OETA) 49, 52, 63
Ormsby-Gore, William 9–10, 45, 53–54, 64, 79–81, 83, 108–9, 112–14, 116, 118–21, 123–24, 130–31, 134–37, 141, 144, 146, 150, 152–54, 157–61, 163, 192, 215, 216, 221, 228, 229

Pasha, Jemal 86, 142, 216–217, 222
Peel Commission 5, 212
Pichon, Stephen 149–150
Picot, Georges 31–36, 39, 54–55, 121, 148

Reinharz, Jehuda 47, 195
Robinson, Geoffrey 101
Rosen, Jacob 122, 192
Roth, Cecil 143, 192, 227
Rothschild, Walter 4
Russell, Edward 70
Russian Revolution 42–43, 123

Sacher, Harry 32, 38, 45, 116, 120, 199, 209
Samuel, Herbert 7, 16–23, 32, 44, 61–63, 70, 72, 82, 91–93, 96–97, 113, 115–16, 152–53, 187, 189, 194, 198, 200–201, 206, 213, 218, 228
Schiff, Jacob 133
Scott, CP 20, 104, 107
Shane, Leslie 27, 30, 37, 41, 55, 117, 193, 204, 207, 212, 213, 222
Sharif Hussein 28, 31, 35, 61, 78, 95, 97, 217, 218
Shuckburgh, John Evelyn 9, 69, 80, 108

Simon, Leon 74, 120
Smuts, Jan 1, 10, 45, 111, 208–9
Sokolow, Nahum 32, 91, 116, 147, 151, 205
Sonnino, Sidney 151
Stein, Leonard, 109, 134, 149, 151, 155, 161–62, 207, 210, 217, 228
Storrs, Ronald 18, 116
Suez Canal 24, 29, 128
Sykes, Christopher, 74, 161, 215, 219
Sykes, Mark 10, 23–24, 27–28, 35, 37–38, 41, 53, 74, 79, 82–85, 98–100, 113, 116–18, 130–31, 144, 147–48, 156, 187–88, 193, 204–7, 209, 212–13, 216, 219–20, 222, 224, 229
Sykes-Picot Agreement 2, 31, 34, 36, 40–41, 43–44, 54, 60, 62, 65, 121, 148, 190, 202, 207, 219
Syria 11–13, 23, 31–33, 35–36, 41–42, 53–56, 58–62, 102, 190, 193–94, 199, 204, 212, 217, 219, 223

Taylor, AJP 136, 193, 226
Thomas, James Henry 94, 218, 221
Toynbee, Arnold 54, 166, 187, 230

Vereté, Mayir 45, 161, 192, 194, 200, 204, 208, 221, 222

Wavell, Archibald 39, 194, 207
Webster, Charles 107
Weizmann, Chaim 1, 17, 32, 41, 53, 61, 70, 104, 117, 133, 142, 188, 191, 193–95, 206, 207, 210, 221, 223, 226, 228–29
Wilson, Hugh 129, 224
Wilson, Jeremy 33, 35–36, 204
Wilson, Woodrow 37, 39
Wingate, Reginald 53

Young, Hubert 69, 214

Zimmerman, Arthur, 121

ABOUT THE AUTHOR

Sahar Huneidi has a B.A. in Political Science from the American University of Beirut, and a Ph.D. from the University of Manchester, where her thesis formed the basis of her subsequent published work on Herbert Samuel. She has contributed numerous articles to academic journals and has edited studies on Israel/Palestine. She has also received diploma certificates in art history from Christie's Education. She is the director of East & West Publishing and lives mainly in London.

www.ingramcontent.com/pod-product-compliance
Lightning Source LLC
Chambersburg PA
CBHW020904080526
44589CB00011B/435